MAVERICK MARKETING

TRAILRIDE INTO THE WILD WEST
OF
NEW MARKETING

TOM HAYES

ISBN: 1-4392-0415-2
ISBN-13: 9781439204153

Library of Congress Control Number: 2008906728
Visit www.booksurge.com to order additional copies.

ACKNOWLEDGEMENTS

Our Clients, coveted by other marketing firms, must absolutely be acknowledged in the development of *Maverick Marketing*. After all, Clients provide not only the funding but also the trust to enable us to ride across The Great Plains and plan a truly different marketing idea. It takes a courageous (comes from the Western "cougar") Corporate Client to listen to an outside person's, from say... Bain, McKinsey, or the New England Consulting Group... present a truly edgy idea. By nature, "maverick" marketing has a higher risk factor than more traditional approaches and can potentially subject a company or individual to the cruel court of public ridicule. Brave-hearted Clients (Note: At the New England Consulting Group, we always capitalize "Client") who understand and are willing to take such risks are to be applauded and cherished. Many are "mavericks" themselves and encourage our stimulating and challenging recommendations with comments like:

- "You want me to make ketchup what color?"

- "Let me get this straight: We should use Kirstie Alley as a spokesperson because she is 100 pounds overweight and is starring in a show called *Fat Actress*?"

- "Your position is that we should terminate your current assignment immediately and cut it short by three months because you already have the answer?"

- "You're really recommending we run an ad for our airline that proclaims ourselves 'Guilty' of price fixing?"

- "Despite our prior world's largest consultant's recommendation, NECG is pressing for an immediate Rx-to-OTC switch as the most profitable option."

- "You want us to pay how much for the Burt's Bees Company?"

One of the most enjoyable and stimulating aspects of being a consultant is the ability to enter the world of different corporate cultures and learn, first hand, from numerous top managers. However, bravery and appropriate and productive risk-taking are often qualities in short supply in corporations around the globe.

So we tip our Stetsons to those Clients and Marketers who are willing to independently "zig" where their peers tend to "zag."

Second, I would like to thank my colleagues and fellow Partners at the New England Consulting Group (www.necg.net), focusing on Marketing and Management Strategy. Celebrating over twenty-five years, a lifetime in the Client counsel business, the New England Consulting Group is based on our "Principal Principle," utilizing only consultants who have had successful line management experience in the "C" suite. Each Principal is "experience-advantaged," with twenty plus years in the marketing and management business. The concept of the "Principal Principle" is that if you have faced the same or very similar "gun fight" (marketing issue) ten different times and across multiple categories, you should be able to arrive at a successful solution much more rapidly and with superlative results.

For the purpose of clarity and the more public availability of information and case studies *Maverick Marketing* focuses mainly on Consumer products and services. However, we have experienced the same basic phenomenon with our many business-to-business Clients.

My Partners have been quite generous in sharing their experience and valuable insight in this book. Their extensive, longitudinal experience has been invaluable.

Maverick Marketing is dedicated to Walt Turner, a senior sales executive at the Campbell Soup Company and my mentor for many, many years.

Throughout this book, "we" refers to the New England Consulting Group. Travis Boyer, Project Manager, contributed significantly to the writing and development of this book. In addition, other contributors include, Salandra Grace, Melis Abacioglu, Lisa Baer, Anthony Bonitatibus, Alexander Cucharale, Kathy Lavery, Connell McGill, Emily Nichols, Lauren Pade, Noah Rosenberg, Michael Stenman, and Debbie Wirkus. Thank you.

Maverick Publishing

Given the subject matter, it seemed totally inappropriate to go to a traditional, white-gloved publishing house for *Maverick Marketing*. The old concept of printing, warehousing, shipping boxes of books, management of the inventory, and even take-backs is just too antiquated... and counterintuitive to the philosophy of this book.

After considerable research, I was able to find a "maverick" publisher in BookSurge, a publishing arm of Amazon that, in my opinion, represents the future rather than the past of book publishing.

BookSurge utilizes futuristic technology to print-on-demand (POD) which eliminates many of the problems and complexities of the traditional book industry business model. As a result of printing only on the demand of a single order, each copy, potentially, can have different, updated information. With BookSurge, *Maverick Marketing* becomes a living organism that is interactive with the reader and adaptive to new information and insights.

CONTENTS

CHAPTER ONE

THE GREAT PLAINS

Are you and your organization ready for the Wild West of New Marketing?

Tom Hayes

As we gaze at the ambiguous horizon simmering in the heat across the undulating Great Plains of Marketing, ideas "are a changin'" at an exponential pace. Marketing has always been a living organism function... bubbling and evolving in response to the cultural and demographic environment. The difference today is that we are approaching a "border stampede" across the entire cowboy's marketing landscape. Marketing has become increasingly difficult, as if a combined art-and-science function were not already unfathomable. Still, every manager and common law mother-in-law believes they are an expert.

The Thundering Herd

No "horse apples," you say.

Absolutely. According to the venerable executive recruiting firm, Spencer Stuart, the average tenure of a Chief Marketing Officer is now less than two years and declining. You can hardly bring a yearling or a new product to market in less than two years. Many advertising campaigns take that long to strategize, validate, and execute. The acquisition of a strategically vital brand and its subsequent integration into the corporate organization and culture takes two full years. And remember, two years is the AVERAGE. Many CMOs have even a shorter window in which to successfully brand the Company with their own initials and initiatives.

As more and more corporate Boards emerge from their shell, they are becoming increasingly more independent and critical of the Management Team. The Board is building a roaring campfire under the Chief Executive Officers. Over 1,300 Chief Executive Officers were changed in the past year, doubling the rate in prior years. In turn, the CEO shares the heat with their Chief Marketing Officers. Perhaps more so than with other Company disciplines, 70%, of CMOs aspire to be in their boss's position. This creates a dynamic situation with competitive alpha wolves loose on the corporate prairie.

I remember fondly one of my Clients, Chesebrough-Pond's, which was organizationally ADD/HD. They recruited heavily for marketing skills and action-orientation... and only for those pre-qualified as a potential, future CEO. The final result was an active volcano or crucible of egos, spewing ideas and action steps. I persevered through six presidential changes in just one Division. At each juncture, the entire organizational structure, objectives, and strategies had to be rebooted. Only the iron hand of Ralph Ward at the top and very strong brands like Vaseline Intensive Care, Pond's, and Elizabeth Taylor's Passion prevented anarchy, while capturing the productive energy of a controlled explosion. Many of these "maverick" Chesebrough alum have gone on to "C" level positions at L'Oréal, Church & Dwight, Duracell, Unilever, Bristol-Myers, and even a Partner at the New England Consulting Group.

Quarter Horse Speed

Two years is a very short period in which to impact any business organization. Just consider some of the environmental changes to which marketers must respond. We recommend that one productive and efficient means to execute Strategic Planning is to "rehearse the future" and review the past. The following are just a few of the dramatic issues a short-term CMO could have been forced to address in their brief two-year or less tenure.

Changes in a Two-Year Period

Number of Wal-Marts	+848
Wal-Mart Revenue	+22%
Prime Interest Rates	+100%
Price of Gas	+69%
Newspaper Circulations	-2%
Number of Banks	-25%
U.S. Birthrate	+38%
Sales of Organics	+45%
$ in Pharmaceutical Advertising	+53%
Number of iPods	+13 million
New Home Sales	-9%

Marketing organizations have become frenetic both in terms of responding to the changing environment and the realization of the reduced half-life of their career. Short term CMOs become a self-fulfilling phenomenon as these pressured executives rush to claim their territory. Knowing of their likely short tenure, today's CMOs manage much differently and with greatly reduced time horizons.

And the pressures from Wall Street for stellar quarter-to-quarter results fuel the "need for quarter-horse speed." This is further compounded by the earlier and broader access by financial analysts to marketing and sales data. During the launch of a major new pharmaceutical, the Street looks to the number of IMS prescriptions written in the very first week as a key indicator or measure against their expectations! Those early results on a single new drug form the basis of their "buy" or "sell" recommendations for the entire pharmaceutical corporation, endangering the CMO and forcing her or him to front-load the marketing expenses in order to be labeled as a "quarter horse" by Wall Street.

In consumer package goods, one of the most dangerous new innovations is the Wal-Mart Team, which most often has access to daily sales across this dominant account. A large storm over the Southeast during a launch week could depress store traffic and unjustifiably cause serious concerns about the viability of a new product.

The interest and investment of time and money by marketers in "maverick" activities has exploded exponentially. In years past, only the smaller scrappy organizations "dropped their long johns" clawing for recognition and awareness. Now, even the global galactic marketers are heavily engaged in marketing programs that would have in the past been considered "cute," "not strategic," "destructive," or even... "beneath the Brand."

We attribute this dramatic shift in attitude toward "maverick" marketing to three very dominant environmental factors:

Ⓜ Consumer Empowerment

Ⓜ The Media "Big Bang"

Ⓜ Digital Leverage

Ⓜ Consumer Empowerment

In the "Bonanza" days of the sixties and seventies, the marketing engine was driven by Marketers and Manufacturers. They dominated the equation with size, massive advertising, "must have" new products, and a domination of the data. Marketers were the marriage broker between the Consumer and the Retailers. The approach was middle-of-the-road and required "mass" execution. The preferred media was network television, with an emphasis on daytime and primetime reflecting the "nuclear family" composition. The Procters, Nabiscos, AT&Ts, GEs, and United Airlines' of the World ruled The Great Plains of Marketing. The main threat was not the Consumer or the corporations of the Retailer channel, but rather the competitors in their category corral.

Fer Us ... or Agin' Us

In the Wild West, all issues were very much "black or white" and people quickly divided into clearly distinguished camps of "friends" or "foes."

The prevailing winds of marketing are towards maximizing every potential opportunity for exposure to the Consumer... being at every point of contact or communication opportunity. The press is on for distribution in 100% of All Commodity Volume. Marketers are snarling like wounded mountain lions over every scrap of distribution. The channels of distributing products and services are blurred. Drug outlets now sell huge volumes of food... supermarkets are offering banking and financial services... and Target and Costco sell virtually any product or service a Consumer needs or wants.

Like a herd in breeding season, the landscape of Retailing in the eighties and nineties began to change rapidly in order to dominate many marketing considerations.

Go West Young Man!

It dawned on me that many of the dominating Marketers of the sixties and seventies were headquartered east of the Mississippi River and north of the Mason Dixon Line, including Cincinnati. Like the population, the marketing power has shifted south and west. And then there was this Retailing "maverick" in the lonely western outpost of Bentonville, Arkansas. Virtually all Retailers "zagged" as a monolithic herd with selective and promoted pricing. The Walton "mavericks" zigged and created a dramatic departure from the placid grazing herd of other Retailers. While the Retail herd based pricing on "cost plus," Wal-Mart took a totally different trail to water with an Everyday Low Pricing strategy based on supply chain management.

Its entire organization, marketing, vendor relationship, logistics, DCs, sourcing, labor cost and policies were centered on delivering the lowest possible price... and the price at which the Consumer would buy, everyday. This "maverick" marketer's focal point was entirely divergent from their competitive Retailers and forever changed The Great Plains landscape... not unlike the wagon trains. The emergence of Wal-Mart from a regional discounter to the largest non-oil corporation in the World has changed Procter & Gamble more than its major competitor, Unilever... altered Sears more than home real estate prices... had more impact on forcing the consolidation of the supermarket industry than astronomical fuel prices... and caused the sourcing and the manufacture of apparel and Consumer electronics in China more than any diplomatic treaty or "wan" exchange rate.

A recent study calculated that the savings accrued to Consumers as a result of Wal-Mart exceeds $287 billion annually. Just ask the AFL-CIO! All by being a very successful "maverick"! But Wal-Mart is merely emblematic of other successful box-stores and category-killers, who bucked the prevailing breeze.

And suddenly a town in Arkansas, where even the wagon train didn't pass through, has become the epicenter of retailing. A posse of Customer teams from virtually every major manufacturer has converged on Bentonville to address the needs of Wal-Mart. The Wal-Mart teams may even dwarf the marketing teams at headquarters in terms of both numbers and IQ. You'd better send the "A" team to Fort Bentonville in order to get your product into every single Division of Wal-Mart. It is a store-by-store battle for every single point of distribution.

Whoa Nellie, Back Up!

Wal-Mart will even consult with, or make strong recommendation to a manufacturer at what target price point the retailer will offer one of their items. If Wal-Mart designates $4.99 as the targeted retail price, the manufacturer has two choices... compromise their own profit margins or cut cost by re-engineering the product and packaging. We call this "price point marketing," which is the enabling mechanism of Wal-Mart's EDLP strategy.

The Wal-Mart business model provides one of the most successful and dominant pricing strategies ever. The price point at which the Consumer will buy drives the traditional marketing process... in reverse.

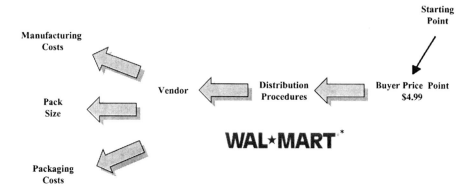

Wal-Mart strongly encourages vendors to manufacture and market to specific price points.

Outside of CPG, the world of Retailing was also changing dramatically. Immigrating or rather charging across The Great Plains of Marketing were new-wave Retailers such as Amazon, Expedia, e-Bay, drugstore.com, and of course, Dell. It is debatable if Dell is a Manufacturer or a Retailer... but certainly an industry "maverick" cowboy.

For a decade or two, the Retailer has been the dominant player and stud stallion. The Marketer's primary concern became the acceptance by the appropriate Retail channel rather than the Consumer. For Marketers, the "Big Box" dilemma is having so much of your business concentrated in one retailer and subject to a single 25 year-old buyer, whose decisions can destroy an entire brand or business sector. The fact is that these category-killers are growing much faster than other CPG, apparel, home furnishing, and Consumer electronics retailers.

The concentration of business in Wal-Mart or any other big Retailer is so material to the financial health and wellbeing of a Company that this information is disclosed in virtually every CPG Company's Annual Report. What could be more material than the concentration of annual revenue subject to the whims or priorities of a single

Customer like Wal-Mart! The following concentrations are clearly "good news" and "bad news."

Percent of Dollar Sales Through Wal-Mart

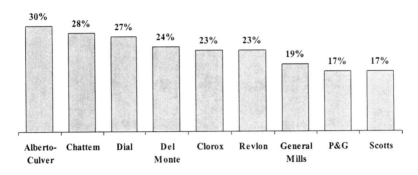

The incredible growth of Target, Wal-Mart, and others elicited a further compression of the supermarket channel. Between 2003 and 2005, the number of independent supermarkets declined by 31% with the business absorbed by the holding companies. Manufacturers have been forced to deal with fewer and more powerful and demanding Retailers. Down the Chisholm Trail came the "Big Box" chains and category-killers. The exponential growth of Home Depot, Staples, Sports Authority, Circuit City, and many more compounded the carnage among marketers.

Wal-Mart's U.S. sales are over $239 billion dollars and continue to grow. The New England Consulting Group has done numerous analyses on Wal-Mart pricing and that of other domestic and global retailers as well. We estimate that an average Consumer saves slightly in excess of 10% on a comparable shopping basket of goods when purchased from Wal-Mart versus a competitor in the same geographic market. Therefore, U.S. shoppers at Wal-Mart save in excess of $21 billion dollars a year just because of the lower prices they get at Wal-Mart.

But, that's just the first $21 billion dollars. Our analyses have shown that Wal-Mart competitors reduce their prices by an amount approaching 5% when Wal-Mart enters their marketplace. That number varies dramatically over time, around the world, and from category to category, but it approaches 5-6% on average. If you apply that 5% price reduction to the $1.9 trillion dollars of retail sales in stores competing with Wal-Mart on like merchandise, you get over $95 billion dollars of savings that Consumers achieve as a result of competitors reducing their prices to be more competitive with Wal-Mart. "In total, U.S. Consumers alone save over $116 billion dollars a year because of Wal-Mart," indicates my partner, Gary Stibel.

Suddenly, the Sales function within many Manufacturers has been equalized in importance to Marketing. The risky business of not properly aligning with the more important Retail conglomerates wield tremendous power over Manufacturer... demanding slotting allowances, insisting on promotional allowances, focusing on SKUs exclusive only to one Retailer, and originating Retailer specific New Product strategies.

The Pendulum Swings Like The Pendulum Do

Or at least, that is the philosophy expressed by the lyrics of a popular Country Western song.

By the end of the nineties, Retailers found themselves in a "war of real estate" with their business model and Wall Street demanding an ever-expanding geographical footprint. Every chain must expand, even at increasing costs and reduced new store sales rates. Retail has followed the "buffalo" dinosaurs of steel and airlines to overbuild and increase capacity well beyond the demand curves. Retail, in virtually all categories, over-services its Customer base. Even Wal-Mart has been forced to re-evaluate their strategy and to slow the growth of domestic stores.

At the same time, the Corporate Management gurus have begun to subtly rebel against the Retail dominance. The new mantra has become to outgrow their sales in the big retail chains. Countless CEOs have asked us to assist them in holding on to their business development in the Big Boxes while accelerating the growth of their other Customers at a rate exceeding new store count.

While the Marketers and Retailers were focused on each other in a marketing duel at High Noon, the new Centennial continues to belong to the Consumer. The cumulative impact of the Big Box factor, cheap China sourcing, over anxious Retailers beginning Christmas sales before Thanksgiving, rewards programs, and special discounts all combine to empower the Consumer. The Retailer, in "cahoots," that's a cowboy word, with Marketers, has trained the Consumer to look and wait for the best price. By the time Kohl's offers me a 10% discount with their credit card, a 20% discount on a given day, and an early bird special, I can purchase a branded shirt for about what it costs to have it cleaned. At least in apparel, we are nearing the cost crossover for disposable or "one-two occasion wear" clothes.

An excellent example is the advancement or expansion of the Christmas season by Retailers... not the Consumer. The expanded season provides a longer period of discounted sales. Most recently the big boxes such as Wal-Mart, Best Buy, and Lowe's have begun to ring the Holiday bell even before Halloween, almost a month prior to Black Friday.

New Trail Boss

A brand new Toro mower made offshore costs only a slight premium over having a mower repaired, if I wait for the Home Depot sale. They have trained and empowered me, as a Consumer, very well. But it is not the traditional mass, brand-driven marketing model of previous decades. As the sun settles in the Western sky, silhouetted across The Great Plains, the new trail boss has emerged... the Consumer.

Just listen to Maurice Levy, Chief Executive Officer of Publicis Group, the third leading global communication Company. In his dramatic presentation at Cannes, he reflects, "The way the Consumer is changing is something that has never been seen before. It's not just a change in media but also a change in society. Power has shifted to Consumers in a way that has never happened."

The Consumer has truly grabbed the reins of control and is dictating the game of Marketing for virtually all goods and services. At an early age, Consumers are educated by both Marketers and Retailers to be "smart shoppers."... at an earlier and earlier age. The "Age of Necessities" has morphed into the "Age of Wants" for the great bulk of America's buying public. The purchasing of "wants" versus "needs" is postponable and therefore can be timed to the advantage of the buyer... not the Retailer or the Marketer.

A powerful example is the tidal wave of stored-value gift cards. The value of gift cards has exploded up to $100 million last year and has been the number one gift for the past four years. That's equal to the GNP of Turkey! The impact has been of such magnitude that the December sales of key Retailers are no longer indicative of the true Holiday sales picture. We estimate gift cards have shifted $50 billion in retail sales, from December to January and February. Even a C-Freshman in high school comprehends that his December gift card is worth about double in January.

More and more Consumers are becoming hardened against many of the classical mass marketing techniques. An attitude of proactive defensiveness against being "marketed to" is prevalent among Consumers. Consumers react with skepticism and visceral distrust to couponing, complicated discounts, rebates, and certainly advertising. Across the entire age spectrum from pre-teens to World War II veterans, today's Consumers are "shoppers," ... not "responders." The latter have seen more than forty iterations of "newly improved" Tide. Try convincing them that #49 is truly a breakthrough product, meriting retrial. Regardless of the chronological age, Consumers today see legal mice-type disclaimers in every marketing approach. "What's the catch?" they ponder.

We have worked closely with a number of marketing companies in studying this issue. We attribute the environmental changes leading to the growth in Consumer power and new leadership to four key sources:

- Control of the marketing interaction or equation

- More available channels (multi-levels, direct, "around")

- Availability of "near perfect" information... particularly pricing

- Collectivism, whereby Consumers have been linked together (Marketers enjoyed a "one-on-one" game for many years but now must play against "zone defense.")

The Consumer is empowered and flexing muscle. As a result, Marketers are themselves being forced to become more innovative and more "maverick-like" in their marketing. This is a tactic, which they hope does not alert or inflame the Consumer's allergic reaction to and deliberate rejection of the commercial messaging.

ᙏ The Media "Big Bang"

Like our exploding universe, the World of Media has not only exploded but also fragmented into nano-sized particles. David Ogilvy's adage that advertising's chief obstacle was to breakthrough the competitive clutter of 1,500 other ads or commercials seen by the Consumer everyday seems antiquated and quaint. *Just* 1,500 commercial messages per day? It is difficult to imagine Ogilvy, the epitome of Hollywood casting of an ad man, plugging away on his Mac. Various experts have concluded that the average daily advertising onslaught is now at least double the old guidelines. Television is no longer confined to the home but appears at retailers, gas stations, airports, bars, elevators, and public transportation. U.S. Airway, prompted by its double-digit million-dollar revenue from advertising on napkins and tray tables, is adding "barf bags" to the ad venues.

According to the Cinema Advertising Council, advertising in movies is almost a half a billion-dollar venue. And coming soon is yet another "cannot miss" venue with ads on food-court tables, ads adjacent to stop lights, third-party advertising on your bill or invoice, tiles in the floor of sports arenas, and posters in the physician's office.

Everywhere the retina scans, it is met by a marketing message... from urinals to blimps... from pop-ups to branded menus... from stadium names to classroom TVs... and this includes hereto, sacrosanct, PBS, doctor offices, hit songs, and even church bulletins.

Forgive Me, Laura Ingalls

And what would our favorite *Little House on the Prairie* family say about advertising in their church bulletins? It is true... I can make a highly effective 2 million circulation buy in church bulletins that cuts through the clutter of traditional media... and likely invokes a brand endorsement from the pulpit.

Chrysler is smartly harnessing this unique religious venue with a strategic alliance with African-American mega-churches. The Company is holding physical test-drives in conjunction with gospel tours by Patti LaBelle. The Consumer receives free tickets to the concert and participating churches garner financial support for designated charities, plus additional financial incentives.

The crescendo of Media grows louder and pounds at the Consumer's psyche more relentlessly everyday. Pure Media is expanding exponentially faster than a wildfire dancing across The Great Plains

There is growing evidence and certainly an alarming level of concern among Marketers that Consumers are becoming more difficult to reach and to engage through Media... traditional or bizarre. The Consumer may very well be desensitized or their circuit board simply overloaded with messaging. In the mind's classical response to stimuli, Consumers process only what is most interesting or appealing.

The good news for Marketers is that the growth of Media volume has been constant over time. Today's Consumers have been trained to accept and process a greater load factor of Media impressions than before.

Custer's Last Stand

We regard Yankelovich as one of the foremost longitudinal culture researchers. They provide a sobering perspective into "adversion" with more than 60% of adults saying they:

- A are interested in skipping or blocking ads.

- A are advocating more restrictions on advertising.

- A feel overwhelmed by commercial messaging.

- A are concerned about the deceptive practices of marketers.

- A feel the volume of marketing is simply "out of reasonable control."

- A have a more negative attitude about marketing.

It is no wonder that the Marketers relying on more traditional marketing approaches are panicked. This growing "adversion" provides an opportunity for "mavericks" who can and must address this key issue of communication.

There are a substantial number of major advertisers who have researched and sense a growing barrier between themselves as a marketing entity and the Consumer. A recent study by the Association of National Advertisers indicates that three-fourths of these powerful Marketers believe their television advertising is less effective than just two years ago.

However, the major advertising copy testing services are not observing a deterioration trend or declining effectiveness score. On the other hand, most of these copy-testing methodologies are based on "forced or invited" exposure and may not reflect the fragmented realities of the current viewing environment.

Listening to the recent pundits one can only conclude that Media and particularly, television, is taking on the role of General George Custer of the Little Big Horn, a glorified as a past hero... but under attack.

A confessional and surprisingly repentant book, *What Sticks: Why Most Advertising Fails And How to Guarantee Success,* is based on extended research from 30 major Marketers and will certainly raise eyebrows. The authors, Rex Briggs and Greg Stuart, conclude that much of advertising is wasted. Whoa! Call the Pony Express! That's *news?*

Their estimate, based on both anecdotal and quantitative research, is that one-third of advertising is not effective or rather, not as effective as it could be. If even true, such a dismal assessment of advertising value would probably come as a great relief to much of Madison Avenue, certainly between 5th and 6th Street in Cincinnati or La Brea Street and the Renaissance Center in Detroit.

Load The Rifles!

An issued report from McKinsey & Co., which addresses the impact of Media proliferation and technology, is even more alarming. This report focused on television media and projects forward based on an extrapolation of historical trends.

The statistical data points in this report are truly scary… 37% decline in messaging impact due to advertising overload, 23% decrease in viewing due to being TiVoed, and a 15% increase in cost, per thousand viewers. The overall McKinsey conclusion is that with 1990 as the "base period," traditional television advertising will be only two-thirds as effective by 2010.

This estimate of decline in advertising effectiveness is noteworthy and certainly adds credence to "maverick" marketers searching for new-to-the-world approaches.

Full Disclosure

As the Western dance hall girls used to say, "This is full disclosure."

In the spirit of full disclosure, I should disclose that we, at the New England Consulting Group, often compete with McKinsey in the marketing and management strategy space. We receive many of the same Requests-for-Proposals on marketing and top line revenue-related issues. And it is not unusual that we are called in by Clients, as a follow-up or "second opinion" to a project… or even "side by side," with NECG concentrating on Marketing and McKinsey focusing on Operations and Supply Chain issues. We are a Special Forces Team. Sometimes a Client needs a SWAT Team… and, in another situation, a more traditional structure "occupying army."

Gold Mine

That said the McKinsey New Media Proliferation Study is a "gold mine" for television advertisers. The true and very substantial value is as a negotiating tool in discussions with the representatives selling television airtime. How would you like to be the NBC salesperson trying to sell a schedule in the new Fall line of shows while a Ford media buyer continues to rail with this study in hand? What is going to be the impact on the final negotiated price?

The selection of 1990 as the base year for this study could have certainly exacerbated the television cost differential. Without the Olympics or a national election and compounded by the Gulf War, 1990 was certainly not a high point for television costs. The line-up of the most watched TV shows was very "traditional."

In 1990, Johnny Carson passed along *The Tonight Show* to Jay Leno and *Barbarians at the Gates* was published. The Dow hit a low 2,365 in the middle of the Fall introductory TV season, so using "pre-Net 1990" as the base exaggerates the increase in TV costs... and likely many of the other degradations of TV impact as outlined by this McKinsey report.

Bury Me Not on the Lone Prairie

...the cowboy's lament. In the thunderstorm of buzz regarding the Net and how traditional media is disappearing, we need to confuse ourselves with the actual facts concerning the demise of traditional television.

It is our ADD lifestyle that redefines the issue of multi-tasking with various media. It is normal at any age. How many of us can do only one activity at a time? Frankly, at the New England Consulting Group, we regard ADD as a competitive advantage. My sixteen year-old son agrees, as he listens to his iPod, keeping an eye on the computer screen for emails and translating Kanji for his Japanese homework.

The fragmentation of Media presents Marketers with a more difficult issue of how to manage the process in a cost efficient manner. In the good ole' days of *Butch Cassidy and the Sundance Kid* it was relatively easy to plan and execute Network TV, with high double digit ratings, and numerous high reach national magazines. Today, the world has been altered considerably. Going beyond merely "reaching" to actually "engaging" the Consumer is much more complex and difficult.

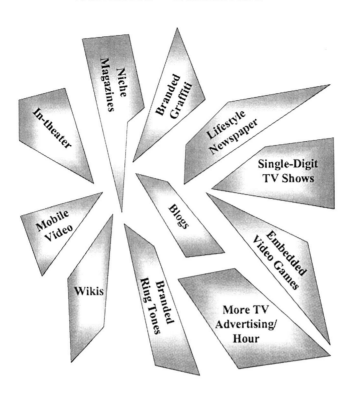

Responding to this fragmentation of more, but smaller, media vehicles, there has been a substantial "blurring" and melding of advertising and promotion which is a characteristic of "maverick" marketing. This splintering of media into smaller slivers and components has enhanced the promotional capabilities and opportunities available to marketers in penetrating the Consumer's protective shell.

As broadcast ratings and print circulation have declined, Marketers have assembled media plans with multiple, more complex and smaller components. Perversely, this has actually enhanced the value of the high reach media vehicles and "must see" destination programs such as the Super Bowl, final episodes, and the *American Idols* of TV land.

In herding cattle, cowboys found it is easier to lead and sing songs to the doggies rather than continuously driving to cattle with a whip.

Steve Farella, a grizzled media expert and CEO at TargetCast, makes this observation: "What is changing the media paradigm, from mass media companies 'pushing' content, to individual Consumers 'pulling' it themselves?

- Consumers are now empowered with digital media management tools.

- Consumers want control of their exposure. They want to:

    - Choose it: search, record, save and manage

    - Change it: cut, paste, delete and blend favorite bits

    - Create it: write, film, record, and build

    - Share it: send, post, collaborate

Burger King's powerful positioning line represents the theme for "new" Media's approach... "Have it your way!"

Nielsen Media Research recently reported that the number of television sets in the home now exceeds the total adult and kid population of the U.S. There are 2.6 people and 2.7 television sets in the average home. A TV set is blasting in the house over an hour more than ten years ago. Viewership is now up to 8 hours and 14 minutes per day.

The average person watches more than four hours every day... and the viewership of the Net Generation, 12 to 17 year-olds, rebounded upward this year. And *American Idol* continues to command $900,000 for a 30-second commercial or $30,000 per second... about the duration of an online "click."

It is much too early to bury ABC, CBS, or Fox out on The Great Prairie of Marketing.

𝕸 Digital Leverage

While Consumer empowerment and the Media "Big Bang" had been transpiring for some time, the important factor or inflection point in forcing "maverick" marketing has been the rapid emergence of the new digital world. This has been the final enabling factor in two important ways. First, the Digital Age created an entirely new and comprehensive delivery system of information and commercial messaging. Second, the Net has made it economically and speed-feasible for Marketers to actually execute "maverick" activities, which previously they could plan... but not executed efficiently.

Papa John's Pizza is generating over a billion dollars in sales via the Net and texting orders. And their digital-sourced business continues to accelerate, based on the convenience and real-time order status provided to consumers. In addition, telesales are now much more efficient for Papa John's.

Equalizer

The "e" in Net should stand for "equalizer." In the flash of a lightning strike on The Great Plains, the Consumer stands on an equal footing with Marketers and Retailers. Converting knowledge into purchasing power, the Consumer has outflanked both on The Great Plains. If I can sit anywhere in the world and find the schedules and costs of the buses from Sydney, Australia to the Thredlo Ski Area, which, by the way, is excellent skiing, why should I pay for a travel agent? If I can "shop" for every supermarket's weekly specials on the Net, how hard is it to selectively create two smaller but separate "shopping baskets" for Stop & Shop and Shaw's, based solely on "better" price? If I can buy the exact same exotic Italian couch for $4000 less, direct from Europe, why should I go to the local furniture store except to get the correct model number? Like prairie dogs, the Consumer has burrowed into every crevice of knowledge.

Six-Gun

The Six-Gun proved to be a great equalizer. Even the diminutive dentist, Doc Holliday was on an equal footing with the biggest, baddest cowboy... as long as he had his trusted six-shooter. Ditto, the Net, which has become the great Marketing equalizer.

In many cases, the "maverick" marketers have no choice but to depart from the standard operating marketing procedures of the "herd." The "scrappy number twos" and the distant competitors cannot match or afford to compete head-on with major rivals... or even their own major Customers.

Necessity is, in fact, the mother of invention for "mavericks." They must find or invest in a new means of marketing and promoting their brand. And once again, the Net has become a substantial enabler or equalizer by providing an entire landscape of new alternatives on which to wage the marketing battle... new media and new pathways to the Consumer and to the Customer.

Importantly, the Net offers "mavericks" the opportunity to build their business in smaller, more affordable increments not feasible in more traditional media. Traditional or mass media, particularly on a national basis, has an extremely high threshold of dollar investment. It is an expensive proposition to achieve the frequency of impressions necessary to move the Consumer or Customer to action.

Many marketing experts including ourselves, concur that a brand should not even contemplate national advertising without a $20 million war chest for television or $10 million in print. This creates an effective barrier to many marketers and start-ups. In contrast, with the Net, tiny niches and slivers of segments which can be reached in a more affordable manner for smaller "mavericks."

The Net has empowered "mavericks" to start small and to grow their business in manageable, incremental stages. The Net is essentially an electronic version of direct mail and is effective at low levels of absolute marketing investment... and, importantly, enhances step-up incrementally.

Netralization

At the New England Consulting Group, we originated a term to describe this phenomenon: "netral." "Netralization" is the neutralization or equalization of power due to the Internet. Traditional Marketers and Retailers have been "netralized," just like the Winchester repeating rifle neutralized the buffalo and the Indian tribes.

Now the foals utilizing "maverick" tactics can run a good race against the stallions. They are the primary beneficiaries of marketing "netralization." Search engines such as Google and Yahoo! have proven to be a great "netralizing" factor, empowering smaller "maverick" marketers to ride with their larger competitors. The Net provides a means for these entrepreneurs to reach highly defined niches in a very efficient manner. How does a ski area in Chile find U.S. skiers in the summer, when the traditional options of *SKI or SKIING* magazines are not even published?

Ever since the first small "tombstone" ad in newspapers, Manufacturers have unilaterally marketed to the "masses," as if they were unconnected individuals. Now at the OK Corral, the tables are turned. The Net has unified the "masses," making the Consumer much more of an equal the Marketer. When a GM car or Customer Service response disappoints a single Consumer, that information can and will ricochet around the world in a split second and be further magnified at each repetition. Through blogs, email, and chat rooms, Consumers now have the power and mechanisms to fire back at Marketers. The isolated, individual complaint letter from an irate Consumer of the past may now take the form of a destructive parody long-form commercial, which is reviewed by millions.

The Net has also created a persuasive attitude both online and in more traditional media of "opt-in" marketing. If the Consumer has some degree of interest, she can "opt-in" to the marketing activity. The Consumer now has the power and the inclination to decide if, when, and how they wish to engage with the Marketer. The "engager" role has been reversed by the Net. Marketers have responded with more "maverick" rather than mainstream approaches and ideas in order to gain that "opt-in" engagement. The focus has been on more provocative marketing programs, with narrower but potentially deeper engagement power.

The household penetration of TiVo and similar mechanisms is projected to be 12-24% by next year. Clearly, millions are opting out of traditional advertising. The sharp declines of newspaper readership are further evidence of deliberate avoidance. Of course, media investment via the Net is exploding in volume, as Marketers have had no choice but to follow media consumption patterns. The growth rate is such that several industry analysts are predicting a shortage of available space. There is just not enough "space" to accommodate Marketers, to fully harness this media... particularly with paid searches.

Just as digital media has empowered the Consumer, it has also enabled Marketers to actually execute "maverick" marketing with an efficiency and turnkey technology not possible before. Information is now a two-way trail on the Net. In contrast to traditional media where Marketers attempt to execute unusual marketing activities, digital communication is more easily customized to narrower and more self-classified target audiences.

The speed of the Internet has greatly enhanced the ability of Marketers to execute in a timely fashion. A Marketer can now seize and capitalize on highly topical subjects and issues and, in this manner, more readily engage the Consumer. to have them "opt-in."

Boot Hill

Bury 'em deep. Chapter 11.

The body of once flamboyant Tower Records is going to be laid to rest as a casualty of the digital war. Strangled between the mass retailers and digital technology, its *raison d'etre* has been eclipsed. Faced with the Wal-Marts and Targets of the world, Tower Records, like so many music retailers, has been fatally wounded by the technological "maverick," Apple. Making a quantum leap to convenience and involvement, iTunes has become a giant killer.

Ditto in the video arena. Just witness the excruciating financial difficulties of Blockbuster, who continuously seems to be in Chapter 10, 11, or 12. Even with a forty share of the video rental market and the resources of almost six thousand retail outlets, the Company, like a bull elephant, has been no match for a "mouse."

Back in 1985, when Blockbuster (What an appropriate name for a "maverick"!) burst onto The Great Plains of Marketing, it was a "maverick" with an entirely new business model and marketing power, wiping out legions of independents. Over time, Blockbuster built an empire based squarely on these brick-and-mortar outposts. It has transitioned from being a "pioneering" Company into a "settler," entrenched in its retail model which has both assets and liabilities. Like many "mavericks," the Blockbuster organization became too comfortable in its success and, in turn, opened themselves up attack by the next generation of "mavericks." In this case, the "mavericks" were based on technology. Blockbuster faced and continues to face an array of "Hobson's choices."

In contrast to the small independent mom-and-pops it conquered in the late 80's, the Company finds itself in a "shoot-out" with Wal-Mart, NetFlix, cable and satellite feeds, Disney, Pay-Per-View, supermarket chains and even McDonald's which is experimenting with video rental kiosks. Emerging technologies such as self-destructing or limited-access video DVDs and Internet VOD are additional arrows in the air. The latter is heavily backed by Blockbuster's absolutely vital supply chain partners... the Hollywood studios themselves.

Ambush

Having contributed greatly to the diminishment of Blockbuster, now Wal-Mart finds itself being threatened. This highly successful

Retailer accounts for 40–45% of the multi-billion dollar DVD market. Utilizing its revolutionary and successful model in music, iTunes is turning its attention to selling downloadable, digital movies. This would place a major arrow in Wal-Mart's profitable DVD business. The leverage of digital technology is quickly altering not only media availabilities but also the entire retail landscape. Even the Wal-Mart fortress is vulnerable to an aggressive "maverick."

Any "maverick" must always continue to innovate and evolve, even in the absence of immediate competition. Otherwise they face the dangers of the new gunslinger in town.

Campfire Coffee

Throughout this book, we will be utilizing the venerable Folgers Coffee brand as the basis of discussion and to test various hypotheses.

The Folgers brand was selected for a number of reasons. Coffee is an "old" and mundane center-of-store category. The demographic profile is older... and diametrically opposite of that assumed for most "new" media. This is a declining category, or at least in in-store sales, with incidence of use directly related to age.

Folgers' direct competition, other in-store coffee brands, may be less of an influence than the indirect competition of Starbucks, Dunkin Donuts, and carbonated soft drinks (CSD). A few years ago, the sales of CSD exceeded that of coffee in McDonald's... for breakfast!

Major marketing support and media of all varieties is placed behind the Folgers brand, including a $50 million advertising campaign. Its brand positioning, "The best part of wakin' up is Folgers in your cup," (Sing along)... has not changed in over 20 years. This is a highly successful billion-dollar brand.

Further, this is a long-term Procter & Gamble brand whose marketing acumen is the world-class standard, even for non-CPG categories. The Company's "marketing-by-the-numbers" approach is legendary. This is a Company quantitatively directed to an extreme. P&G

folklore regales us with the story that its engineers discovered that the Sixth Street headquarters' urinals on each end would wear out more often than the ones in the middle. That solution was easy... periodically shutdown the end urinals to even out the wear and required maintenance. I cannot verify this story, but have personally observed only the end urinals at Procter's HQ covered on numerous occasions.

If the Folgers brand and the Procter and Gamble Company can be "maverick" marketers, then there is hope for other traditional marketers and brands.

Just as we were going to press with Ⓜ*averick* Ⓜ*arketing*, the J.M. Smucker Company announced it was acquiring the Folgers brand from Procter for almost $3 billion. This is similar to Smucker's acquisition of the Jif and Crisco brand in a clever Reverse Morris Trust arrangement during the time in which the New England Consulting Group was consulting for Smucker's.

Trail Markers

 For virtually all corporate managers, long-term strategic planning adapt to the new realities of the Wild West Show of Marketing, with greater flexibility and agility infused into the process.

The quarter horse speed of change in new marketing demands a "maverick" philosophy and a readiness to change directions and tactics in a timely manner.

 Harness the phenomenon of Consumer empowerment to seize control of the marketing equation.

 Address the Wal-Mart dilemma on two fronts to increase your business with this key retailer that offers substantial operational advantages of scale, willingness to experiment, and no slotting fees… while creating equally differentiating programs with other key non-Bentonville Customers.

 Understand and manage, rather than merely accept the Consumers' aversion to marketing and fragmentation of media. Change the game from "one-to-many" to "one-on-one" in terms of offense… and play "zone" defense against the Net-connected Consumers.

 Do not fall for the Fool's Gold notion that the burning issue is the Net versus Network TV. The real issue is how to get these two horses to pull in the same direction.

 Act like the "maverick" Scrappy Number Two, even if you are the lead horse.

 Pay significant attention to the changing business model and the threat of evolving from a competitive "pioneer" to an antiquated, static fort.

CHAPTER TWO

THE MAVERICK

Maverick

Adj: independent in behavior or thought; [syn: irregular, unorthodox]

n:

1. someone who exhibits great independence in thought and action [syn: rebel]

2. an unbranded range animal straying away from the herd.

3. one that refuses to abide by the dictates of or resists adherence to a group; a dissenter.

"Hi ho, Silver." That was the Lone Ranger's trusty horse.

By nature, "maverick" marketing is somewhat ambiguous and difficult to corral neatly. "Maverick" marketing clearly involves taking an action, which is different or stands out from the programs of other Marketers, specifically any direct competition. It is often deliberately irreverent and rebellious, with a touch of human warmth. In many cases, "maverick" marketing has an objective to appeal to younger and narrower target audiences than the basic or traditional marketing programs. "Maverick" marketing is the gangling teenager psyche of marketing.

By our definition, it is more than advertising or just being creative. The ubiquitous advertising for Verizon is brilliantly creative and impressive but it is not "maverick" marketing. Bayer's use of retro advertising with the famous Alka-Seltzer line, "I can't believe I ate the whole thing," while casting the parents from *Everybody Loves Raymond* was highly successful. Jay Kolpon, Vice President of Marketing at Bayer Consumer HealthCare, attributed the 12% increase in usage to the retro campaign. Smart, effective... but not "maverick" marketing.

Unilever Australia's "Lynx Jet" advertising campaign for Lynx Body Spray featuring a sexy parody of an airline with aspirational "hot" hostess is creative and effective on its own. But it was only just great advertising until converted into a more powerful and comprehensive program of "maverick" marketing, winning two prestigious Gold Lions at Cannes. This strong creative television campaign was leveraged at the grassroots level with teams of the fake airline hostesses handing out samples on the street... a website with a fake airline check-in counter... and local newspapers further parodying the Lynx Airline... and a full scale plane painted as a Lynx Air aircraft. Immediately following, the Brand flew high and achieved a stratospheric 80% plus share of the male body spray market.

By our analyses, a "maverick" marketing program must include at least three of seven key components.... marketing Innovation, Consumer engagement, buzz or public relations, new media usage, a viral aspect, promotion, or opt-in marketing.

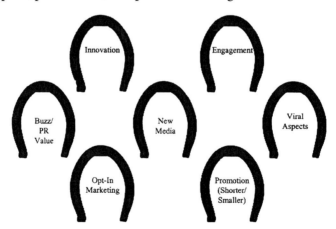

We reserve an entirely separate discussion of Innovation and New Product Development as an important characteristic of "mavericks" in Chapter VII.

It is difficult to consider the world's second largest revenue Company as a "maverick" marketer but Wal-Mart does fit the bill. Its everyday low pricing strategy better known as EDLP, was a revolutionary "zig" away from the retail herd.

Look how it mobilized on an absolute global basis to fully develop the marketing opportunity around the World Cup. The marketing adage, "Think Global, Act Local" applies to Wal-Mart as it bolted from centralized policies, permitting local stores to tailor their own promotions and product offerings. Early on in the planning stages, its global vendors were made an integral part of the Wal-Mart "World Cup."

Wal-Mart's Integrated "World Cup" Ball

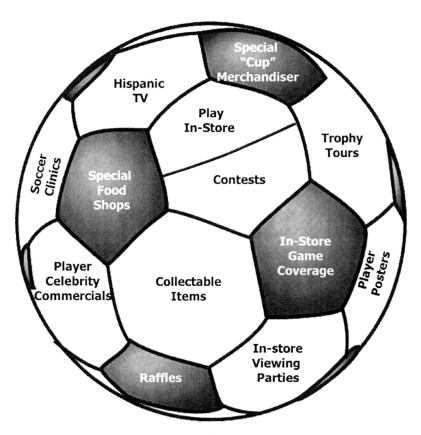

Wal-Mart was highly innovative and comprehensive in developing new-to-Wal-Mart marketing programs. As an example, in non-Hispanic countries, Wal-Mart set up in-store viewing events related to soccer for visiting Hispanic workers. The scope and breadth of global execution was unprecedented and impeccable.

You don't have to be small to be a "maverick." Wal-Mart de Mexico, Walmex, reported a 25% increase in net profits fueled by the buildup of sales related to the World Cup Soccer Championship.

⑩ Engagement

A key tenet or objective of "maverick" marketing is often to enhance the engagement or depth of relationship between the Brand or Company and a specific target audience. There is a genuine and growing acceptance that Consumers are creating a deeper canyon between themselves and Marketers, which must be overcome.

The Consumer's historical passive acceptance of marketing activities and, very specifically advertising, is now moving in the direction of proactive resistance. Under the increased onslaught of media and programming content, the Consumer is becoming vaccinated and immunized to traditional marketing approaches... more skeptical and less accepting.

Sunset Over The Sierras ... Anytime

Most disconcerting to many advertisers and traditional media companies is the conscious and proactive avoidance of commercial messaging.

Originally, digital video recorders like TiVo, now four million units strong, were meant as "time-shifters" for desirable programming in which the Consumer had a particular interest in viewing. In today's hectic environment, almost 10% of the adult population travels everyday. People are taking fewer vacations and the average person has less time, even for meals. Time-shifting of Media is merely a pragmatic reflection of this extremely busy and harried Consumer. The chaos of commercial messaging has made control a valuable element.

The household penetration of DVRs has an exponential growth curve. JP Morgan is projecting that, in 2008 fully, one-third of U.S. households will have such a device or service. However, the threat of DVRs to Marketing civilization as we know it today lies in the secondary function of commercial skipping. Once digital, the pixels of commercials are easily deleted and this ancillary functionality becomes as important as the primary.

Perversely and inversely to traditional marketing wisdom, the deletion of commercials from highly desirable programs may be more important now that the Consumer is so empowered. If you watch *Gilligan's Island* reruns or an ice fishing tournament, commercial interruption may not be such an inconvenience. On the other hand, if you took the time and effort to record for posterity the last seasonal episode of *24* or a particularly obnoxious *House*, commercials may be a greater annoyance... and worth more effort to avoid.

Thanks to the commercialization of technology, the Consumer can now see the Western sunset any time, day or night... or simply delete it.

Bank Robber

"Jesse James" would be too mild a label for TiVo, according to the managers of traditional television media. After all, TiVo didn't actually rob the bank; it just provided the appropriate gun.

Now, to add insult to injury, TiVo will add a measurement of just how many people it can "steal away" with their technology. TiVo is challenging the proverbial sheriff at the OK Corral, ACNielsen, on the measurement of advertising viewing through its DVR distribution network. It will begin to test, validate, and report on every national commercial. The basis is, as yet, an un-weighted subset of 20,000 households.

With an estimated current household penetration of 15%, DVRs represent a significant and growing potential for the Consumer to proactively opt out of commercial viewing. The precise degree to which people zap or skip specific commercials may allay the fears of advertisers terrifyingly confirm "The Great Train Robbery and the avoidance of the advertising which make programming possible."

Roper Market Research indicates based on a recent survey, that two-thirds of men with a DVR skip commercials and a little over half of women. As in the analysis of any research, knowing the actual question is vital. We should note these survey results do portend or give the impression that "all" commercials are skipped. .In fact, only a fraction are currently skipped. As with much of the research and commentary on the New Marketing, the bad news always makes for better headlines.

The "mavericks" are fighting back against the time-shifting, ad-skipping TiVo by capitalizing on its own technology. When reverting back to show content, the DVR essentially "rewinds" leaving an unblockable small window of time. Innovative mini-burst commercials placed at the end of the commercial pod are TiVo-proof.

"Maverick" marketing seeks to find new pathways to close the attitudinal gap with the Consumer. This avenue may have to be less direct and more on the Consumer's "terms of acceptance." Instead of the traditional head-on collision of mind and message, "maverick" marketing can be more oblique and indirect, rendering it more acceptable and less demanding. One could call this a gentle encounter.

A major component of engagement through "maverick" marketing is to make the Brand or Company more approachable to the Consumer. However, in today's environment, the "approacher" is the Consumer. Pioneers and mountain men found that there were two different methods to hunt: You could aggressively march through prime hunting grounds, hoping to flush a deer from the deep forest. This is akin to traditional marketing.

The Indians taught another way of hunting by intensely studying the feeding habits of the deer and their pathways through the terrain. They would bait a shooting area, wait stealthily, and let the deer approach. That is "maverick" marketing.

Pocket Watch

Advertisers were once confined to pre-set advertising times based on the broadcaster's need for equal time length commercial pods. Creative personnel were well trained to develop exclusively 60-second or 30-second commercials.

Empowered by technology, more and more "mavericks" are experimenting with varying lengths of messaging to addressing the Consumer's evolving attention span.

Now the message length varies by media, brand, and message. In order to preserve their business, the Media has become much more flexible and accommodating of non-standardized lengths.

Message Lengths (Seconds)

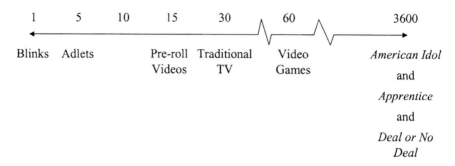

A number of Marketers under differing degrees of scrutiny are coming to the conclusion that the length of messaging, shorter or longer and tailored, can substantially impact the communications value in non-intuitive ways. For example, more than one Marketer has actually reduced the length of their "pre-rolls" or commercials from 30 down to 15 seconds for greater, not less, communication. Thirty seconds is viewed as being too long and interruptive when online while remaining acceptable in the broadcast medium.

Marketers and the Media are co-operating to adapt commercial messaging for specific situations. Based on numerous Marketing and Advertising Audit projects, we have come to the conclusion that the commercial messaging length is best utilized in an appropriate mix of lengths. This is a factor of the message itself, the creative execution, and the media vehicle of delivery. While under the same fundamental strategic banner, each individual messaging component must be tailored for the specific objective or task. Some messaging is tasked with building the imagery... some as "reminders" to strengthen brand awareness... and others to "ask for the order."

Them 'r Curse Words

In the ole West, even the most grizzled cowpoke would refrain from cursing in the presence of a woman.

However, in today's world of commercial messaging, Marketers will do anything to garner Consumer attention, including cursing. A number of major advertisers have resorted to including partial curse words, which are intentionally "bleeped" as a means of getting in synch with today's less respectful audiences.

On this issue, my teenager wants to take the powerful "tree in the forest" argument. If "frigging" is known as the stand-in for the real "f-word," is "frigging" a curse word? A similar parent-teenager debate rages between the FCC, network censors, and more provocative advertisers. Shock value is a proven technique to demand attention. An excellent example is the use of the code phrase "OMFG" to promote the new season of the highly successful *Gossip Girl* TV series.

Dodge City

Another informative data point of the shift of both dollars and interest among Marketers and advertising agencies is the change in submissions at the prestigious Cannes International Advertising festival. The number of entries per category, as reported in *Advertising Age*, is very telling. "Traditional" submissions are in decline, paired with a surge in of "maverick" categories like Innovation, New Media, and Utilization of Digital Capabilities.

Cannes Entries by Category

Radio	+1%	Innovation	+52%
Television Commercials	-3%	Media	+36%
Direct Mail	-7%	Digital	+32%
		PR	+10%

This reflects the growing presence of smaller and more "maverick" marketers. Cannes is now deriving many of its entries from the independent ad agencies, outside of the gravitational forces of the global conglomerates.

"Maverick" marketers are moving online in order to shrink the scope of their target audience and to appear "closer" to a narrowed attitudinal base. Ironically, the tendency is to utilize only the larger, heavily clicked sites, which is essentially the online equivalent of attracting the main audience in network television. Advertising planning on the smaller and more iconoclastic websites remains a very difficult task even for a "maverick" marketer.

Church Choir

Innovators and "mavericks" tend to look for leverage points on how to magnify their efforts. These "mustang" marketers often lack the resources of larger organizations and must be entrepreneurial in their activities.

They look outside their own organization and experience in order to tap into new stimuli and perspectives. The "catalyst of creativity" may very well lie with Consumers themselves, who have a point of view unavailable to someone inside the organization. Our internal marketing personnel can know entirely too much about the problem making it difficult to focus on the opportunities and answers.

One innovative Company that decided to listen to the "church choir" of Consumers is Netflix. It has one of the industry's best collaborative filtering systems, which predicts and promotes new film rentals for an individual based on past preferences. Even with a database of 100 million movie ratings and a highly sophisticated development team, it was nearing a very high percentile of achievement. Enhancing the predictability and profitability of the system was becoming increasingly difficult... when relying totally on internal resources.

Netflix has turned to the "church choir" of computer geeks around the world. It is offering a $1,000,000 prize to the person who develops a recommendation engine, which results in a 10% improvement in accuracy of prediction. This resulted in a worldwide competition and placed additional pressure on its internal cadre of computer scientists. What if a teenage math prodigy in the wilds of the Chilean Andes bests all the Cal Tech and MIT PhDs?

As a result, Netflix has generated considerable buzz and public relations coverage as well as further enhancement of its prediction model.

Ⓜ Buzz or Public Relations Value

In some cases, the most valuable and tangible outcome is that of the resulting public relations itself. A brilliant "maverick" marketing program should generate press coverage that extends and magnifies the impact of the Brand. Once again, this places a substantial burden on the "maverick" marketer to be sufficiently "different" or outrageous so that it garners the desired interest and coverage from the Press and bloggers.

In some cases, the press coverage is the real objective and becomes the actual media form for the program. This applies to Consumer, Retailer, and Trade press where a relatively small investment can produce substantial impressions. That said good press coverage is not as easy as it may seem and requires intricate pre-planning to generate maximum impact. The better "maverick" programs are designed in advance to generate press coverage with built-in sound bites and story lines much like a political campaign.

How do you "sample" a hotel before it is built? One "maverick" marketer, Peninsula Hotels, solved that issue by opening branded boutiques that carried "the Peninsula experience" in advance of the area hotel opening. These "branded shops" feature a mix of high-end luxury items as well as hotel-branded accoutrements. The buzz around these satellite gift shops built substantial awareness for the coming hotel.

Some "maverick" marketers never actually execute their activities but rather rely totally on the public relations value itself. Perception can easily exceed reality in strong "maverick" marketer's programs.

Tall Tales

In the Old West, a good storyteller always had a place at the campfire. He could turn the ordinary aspects of life into an interesting tall tale that would be repeated over and over again, from one wagon train to another.

To generate buzz or public relations coverage, in traditional media or on the Net, one must have or create a story of interest about your product or Company. Reaching out to accredited journalists or bloggers requires them to have something they think would interest readers. This can be news, humor, human interest, or even the bizarre.

The launch or, rather, the re-launch of Tickle Me Elmo is a great example. This outrageously successful and loveable toy was aging and needed a substantial update. For the tenth anniversary, Fisher-Price embarked on a major upgrade with the revamped T.M.X. Elmo.

With great and deliberate care, the Company shrouded the launch in "deep throat" procedures and made that secrecy the foundation of a considerable public relations campaign. Fisher-Price delayed the commercial shoot until the last possible instant for security reasons, lest a premature disclosure let the steam out of the story. Even major retailers were denied a product preview and were forced to place orders without complete knowledge of what they were buying. This was the same for most of the Company's sales personnel, who didn't have complete knowledge of their own new product.

The buzz, based on tantalizing secrecy, has been considerable. When people cannot get an item... they want it even more.

Draw!

Perhaps there is no area where the Internet has been more of an "equalizer" than in Public Relations.

The traditional, pre-Net activity of generating public relations was and continues to be a very difficult and involved process, particularly for a smaller Company or marketer. Much of the successes were hit or miss. Furthermore, the probability of achieving meaningful coverage was extremely small. Without a skilled, connected, and expensive public relations agency, generating any real Consumer coverage was a frustrating activity. Remember, we only hear about the relatively few which succeed.

To compound the issue public relations was essentially a passive endeavor. Companies merely sent out print or broadcast materials and waited for a nibble of interest.

In contrast, the new digital world has been a substantial enabler. Net-based public relations are more proactive and place much of the control in the hands of the Company or Brand. One can now virtually guarantee publication at some level. Suddenly, a small Company is on more equal footing with its larger competitors.

Not only are Consumers in general utilizing the Net for informational searches, so is the Media. The Net is more democratic and convenient than a truckload of hard copy press releases arriving at every editor or producer's inbox. It has a real-time impact and accelerates the pick up of information and marketing stories.

Pony Express

Today, much of the news is carried by blogs and one well worth reviewing by any "maverick" marketer is called blogmaverick.com, originated by Mark Cuban, the ostentatious and boisterous owner of the Mavericks.

Cuban (only partially tongue-in-cheek) said that marketers desiring "buzz" and media coverage should create an "apologement." As Mark explained, an "apologement" is designing an event which is deliberately so controversial or outrageous that you *know* you will have to apologize for it, sooner or later. Your brand generates media coverage not only from the original event but also from the pre-planned apology or aftermath story.

It is clear that all involved constituencies from the Consumer, to the media, and even the indignant reactors enjoy "apologements." They're fun. Everyone really loved the Janet Jackson Super Bowl wardrobe malfunction. The Media got a juicy story... ratings for the Super Bowl Halftime Show increased as ninety million people watch for a repeat... and the network got a bargain for its FCC fine which was eventually thrown out of Federal Court.

Water Divining

Like a "divining rod," a blog or weblog can greatly assist the "maverick" in finding a treasure trove. With in excess of 48 million blogs currently ricocheting around cyberspace, there are enumerable opportunities to catalyze coverage in Net blogs and in traditional media. But here again, you must be both a creative and tenacious storyteller to be found and heard in the galaxies of data. Like traditional media, online public relations or buzz online is becoming much more competitive. While not "free," the cost threshold on the Net to generate "press" coverage is considerably lower.

One means to achieve buzz is to become your own media or publisher on the Net. Buzz blogging is part art, part digital science. This is not a casual exercise that you can delegate to your teenage niece. A buzz strategy and a detailed budgeted plan with dedicated resources will greatly enhance the ultimate business contribution.

Ⓜ New Media

One of the most common and vital elements of "maverick" marketing is innovation in Media, meaning different utilization or just different media. It is sufficient to be a media pioneer in your category so that your Brand is differentiated from the competition. Our philosophy and recommendation to our Clients is to "copy and steal" from the best of marketers, beyond the smaller corral of your own Brand category. Time and time again, we have found that utilizing the appropriate analog pays powerful dividends.

A good example is Pfizer's use of behind-the-plate signage for Viagra in major league baseball parks. Of course, marketers have used this type of advertising ever since the origination of the sport. However, placing Direct-to-Consumer advertising for a sensitive, prescription product in such a social environment was the footprint of a "maverick" marketer. Viagra has been in your face as a way to reach its key demographic audience.

Pfizer was a "maverick" in that it captured a very appropriate medium for a pharmaceutical product, while "shutting out" competitors, Levitra and Cialis. A key component was the sheer shock value of promoting a sexual performance pharmaceutical where one would more likely see a beer or credit card advertisement. Clever marketing and message placement such as this enabled the Company to normalize this medical condition and make its treatment more socially acceptable.

For Marketers targeting men, especially, younger, beer drinking, auto-focused men, the difficulty is in reaching and engaging them. This lifestyle cohort is more diverted by gaming, multi-tasking, and less traditional media pursuits. And much of non-sports programming and commercials are targeted specifically to women.

It is just as difficult and perhaps just as mathematically impossible to forecast the weather, as it is to ascertain the true impact of the increased messaging clutter. The influence of accelerated messaging has reached cataclysmic proportions, with Consumers becoming more irritated to such a degree that they simply shutdown.

We can only anecdotally question the results of saturated messaging from the multitude of sources on the receptivity and value of marketing... traditional and non-traditional. However, there are some key reasonable measurements on the destructive power of clutter in a single medium. IAG Research, which has rapidly propelled itself onto the stage of measuring television programming and commercials, provides excellent insight and learnings. Harnessing a multi-million Consumer online panel, IAG provides several well-substantiated precepts:

- Higher levels of commercial test achievement correlate to low clutter.

- Advertising performance is very much enhanced by surrounding programming or editorial.

- Creative trumps clutter.

- Adjacent competitive messaging is particularly destructive to a Brand's communication.

Many astute media planning agencies prepare highly sophisticated analyses and detailed plans for their Client marketers. It is a mathematical and scientific process, equaling a space launch... but remains theoretical. A high percentage of media plans, even those involving billions of advertising dollars, fail in the real world of execution when these precepts are ignored.

Paint An Ad On My Outhouse?

Yep!

This is the "Burma Shave" advertising generation on steroids, with marketing messages assaulting our retina at every turn. Every venue or surface: flat, convex, concave; public or personal; static or mobile, has become a commercial messaging opportunity. Marketers place their message over urinals, on dogs' and peoples' foreheads, at diaper changing stations, in blood pressure kiosks, emblazoned on umbrellas, in menus, on gas nozzles and rickshaws, and even other products as an ingredient.

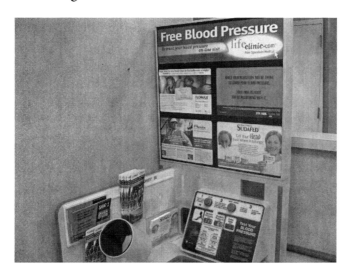

Retail Solutions

Even pharmacies have become a venue for intense advertising interaction. A very smart company called Retail Solutions places blood pressure monitoring stations in thousands of Wal-Marts and other retail pharmacies. More then 40 million people annually sit down, take their own blood pressure readings, and read the surrounding advertising and brochures from some of the nation's most astute marketers.

Some advertising is pure electronic manipulation. Ads and logos are shown within these venues that do not exist there in reality. Many of the ads in the form of televised stadium signage are "painted" in electronically. Such "stimuli saturation" has pushed the Consumer toward alienation and gaining more control and selectivity of the marketing message pinging on their synapses.

Ever since the Indians carved on rocks and the 49ers painted signs on their ramshackle stores, the outdoors has been a primal advertising medium. Tremendous innovation is taking place with 3-D applications, special electronics effects, the incorporation of text messaging, and linkage with mobile phones. These provide the Consumer with little respite or relief from commercial messaging assaulting the senses.

In terms of mobile venues, we have advertisements on golf carts, commercials on GPS screens, a shopping cart with digital ads, and television screens at the gas pumps. Is nothing sacred? Certainly not college text books, where numerous companies are taking advantage of the opportunity to reach students in a new manner. An innovative media company is offering over one hundred textbook titles to advertisers, who will enable the students to receive these books free of charge. This could result in savings of hundreds of dollars in college expenses better spent on beer.

Now available to "mavericks" is advertising on supermarket conveyor belts. What had been one of the few blank screens starring in the face of every grocery shopper is now filled with colorful advertising. Talk about "in your face." Who can miss seeing this venue?

In this evolving media environment, "intensity" and "focus" are replacing the traditional "reach" and "frequency" as media planning criterion. Once you, at last, have the Consumer's attention the advertising impressions must be molded to the needs and attitudes of the individual Consumer... who has achieved the rank of the Trail Boss on The Great Plains of Marketing.

This desire for "intensity" of messaging has translated into a resurgence of sponsored programming or editorial content. Being a random advertiser among many different shows provides no accretive value. On the other hand, "sponsored by" and "brought to you by" has increasing relevance and currency. Presumably, a program specifically selected for viewing by the targeted audience has some particular interest in connection with the Consumer. The Marketer's association with and sponsorship of certain programs assist in garnering Consumer interest.

Marketers highly value such sponsorships, particularly if their corporate name can be associated with the show or event. Some electronic programming and print media are beginning to look like a NASCAR driver, emblazoned with company logos. The resulting program titles become quite a mouthful for the announcer. Consider one stock-car race entitled, "ITT Industries, Systems Division and Goulds Pumps 'Salute to the Troops' 250 presented by Dodge."

Over the years, advertising agencies (and to a lesser extent Marketers) have been "created" and catapulted upward after seizing upon the emergence of a new advertising medium... both creatively and in media planning and buying. This has been consistent in creating a substantial competitive advantage and a surge of business into the agency. "Back in the day," Colgate-Palmolive was regarded as a "maverick" marketer as it and its partner ad agency, the William Esty Company, led the way into primetime network programming sponsorships. This was in response to the overwhelming presence in daytime programming of its nemesis, Procter & Gamble, who sponsored several daytime soap operas. Early on, Colgate was able to tap into the exploding trend of women working out of the home, which inherently forced a change in their media viewing habits and provided the Company with a significant competitive advantage.

Procter remained rooted in its history of "stay-at-home" moms, while the more flamboyant Colgate, under Ruben Mark's tutelage, focused on the future trend of "working" moms. The competitive impact of the toothpaste and laundry care wars cannot be overestimated.

Trailmaster

Every westward-ho wagon train had a trailmaster to guide the farmers and the city slickers. The "boss" harnessed a combination of mental trail maps, Indian scouts and pathfinders, and kept the sunset dead ahead on a constant bearing.

And now, "maverick" marketers have yet another tool with the rapidly escalating Global Positioning System. With GPS now readily available and affordable, a new marketing endeavor called "geocaching" is building up across the country. Geocaching is a well-organized mobile scavenger hunt. This harnesses the GPS to "hide" or to "find" certain objects as an involving pastime. There are numerous clubs, rules and websites such as www.geocaching. com. This is a whole new world of "benchmarks" (physical geodetic control points) and "travel buys" (a moveable, trackable marker) that has become a geographic hide-and-seek.

One of the first "mavericks" to connect its brand to geocaching is Jeep, which is repeating with its "Geocaching Challenge." This is a great match of a Brand and an addictive pastime with many engagement points of brand contact with a very profitable, self-selected potential customers.

Jeep is even engaging the Consumer to participate and to "hide" over 5,000 Jeep-branded "travel buys" in caches across the lower forty-eight states. The process and rules are quite elaborate and require a very committed and involved Consumer. As a Marketer, the degree of engagement by the Consumer in pure adult fun is extremely impressive. The "Challenge" runs for a year with top prize being a new Jeep.

The rapid growth of technology and the sheer number of personal navigational devices is opening the opportunities for the "mavericks."

Industry experts are predicting a ten-fold increase over the next two years. Already some retailers are purchasing "real estate" on the navigational map with suppliers, such as Tom-Tom.

Utilizing a new and different media is opening a different door into the Consumer's mind and garnering renewed attention. This can be a new pathway of establishing a more productive relationship.

Viral

A proof point of success in "maverick" marketing is sufficiently avoiding or overcoming the Consumer's proactive defense to marketing to such an extent that the reluctant Consumer becomes a member of the marketing team. If the Consumer becomes an advocate for the Brand, "maverick" marketing has certainly achieved the desired objective.

Traditional marketing, including the most provocative advertising, rarely induces the Consumer to spread the message of the Brand. It is a passive, one-dimensional process. The Consumer receives, processes, accepts or rejects, and internalizes the traditional marketing message. It is a private conversation.

Successful "maverick" marketing often solicits, openly or obliquely, the Consumer to become a part of the messaging process. People who can be induced to spread the word become a part of the "team" and are themselves therefore more committed to the Brand. The dynamic is a public conversation and dialogue between the Marketer and the Consumer.

And in today's jaded and over media-stimulated world, nothing is more effective than an endorsing message from an objective third-party. Perhaps the only traditional marketing event that comes even close to third party messaging is the Super Bowl. Over time, the "Bowl" advertising has become inculcated as an important component of the event itself. A number of Consumers look for, view, discuss, and comment on the Super Bowl advertising. They make the commercials in the game a public or social communication or event... rather than a private matter. "Did you see the commercial for GoDaddy.com?" is a reaction and conversation rarely achieved in any other media event. But of course, to make your message a subject of discussion, Marketers have invested immense quantities of currency and talent to participate in the most promoted, hyped, anticipated, and watched media event of the year. Advertising has become as much a part of the Super Bowl Party as the Star Spangled Banner, the half-time show, or the Budweiser Clydesdales.

In order to promote and foster creativity, Procter & Gamble has offered a commercial appearance in the Super Bowl as an incentive for internal Brand Groups and advertising agencies. The prize is being "marketing famous," ... or perhaps, infamous. Wonder why they didn't offer an obscure website as the venue?

There are a few marketers who do not wish to have this intense public spotlight and evisceration of their adverting. They conspicuously avoid the Super Bowl and its about 100 million plus viewers.

"Maverick" marketing seeks to create a viral situation where Consumers become the conduit to expand the exposure of the message. This can be achieved by inducing a very specific appeal that is so aligned with the targeted Consumer's belief... or attitude preference that they, in turn, pass it on engaging other Consumers.

⋔ Promotion

While not always the case, "maverick" marketing is often a spike or flurry of activities which are shorter in duration and smaller in scale than traditional marketing. The focus of attention is a subset of the

Brand's usual target audience. This enables a unique appeal most appropriate and tailored to that specific segment.

"Maverick" marketing tends to be more promotional than traditional methodologies.

It is a matter of attitude and focus rather than different or specialized techniques. "Mavericks" utilize the same ancient array of promotional guns... contests, couponing, free offers, sweepstakes, events, and grassroots activities or just name your poison. The difference between "mavericks" and base-line marketers is exemplified in three arenas: intensity, flamboyance of execution, and degree of integration.

The degree of integration is a key issue related to the organization and execution "Mavericks" tend to value "promotion" and "advertising" on a more equal basis. In contrast, traditional and larger marketing companies often treat both the function and the personnel of "Promotions" as second-class citizens.

Starbucks experienced the connectivity of digital promotions when it posted on the Net a coupon for a free iced coffee for their employees' family members only in the Southeast. The necessary promotional restrictions were somewhat lax. Suddenly, the "free" coupons rocketed around the entire country, far beyond Starbuck's intent but not their legal obligations. Deciding to take a "PR hit," Starbucks announced that they would stop honoring the coupons. This action generated a $100 plus million class action suit initiated by loyal Starbuck users with too much time on their hands. Herein lies the dangers of promotions executed via the Net... suddenly the "one" becomes "many." The Net unifies individual voices into an evangelical chorus that Marketers cannot ignore.

To compound the carnage, Caribou Coffee, direct competitor and distant "maverick" runner up, publicized that it would accept the very coupons disavowed by Starbucks.

Though somewhat archaic, couponing, invested with the greatest expenditure of marketing dollars, looms as a substantial opportunity for digital execution. It has huge potential for digital conversion, with costs of $6 billion a year in a complex and costly means of distribution, antiquated "hard copy" redemptions, and an excess of 300 billion coupons spreading across The Great Plains.

Online or Net-distributed coupons are increasing rapidly but currently represent less than 1% of total coupon distribution. Coupon usage is "mass" and thus, so is the means of distribution. Virtually all households make use some form of coupons, as does virtually every major consumer marketing company.

Coupon inserts rank only second to the front page in terms of newspaper readership. And we often recommend inclusion of a coupon in any print ad merely to enhance its readership. An included coupon normally "lifts" the readership of a typical magazine ad by 10%. This makes the expense of the coupon, albeit at very low redemption levels, a superlative ROI. A number of online companies, including Google, Coupons Inc., and others, continue to rail at hard copy coupons. The key selling differences are the ability to effectively target very narrow niche segments. The Net enables personalized coupon offers and values down to the granular level of individuals. Coupon-based and other promotional websites such as for sweepstakes are gaining unique visitors at double-digit rates but off a small base. They are among the top ten gainers in the key metrics of unique visitors.

There are major and multiple interface issues redeeming coupons. Currently, online coupons must be printed out and converted into the Gutenberg format for retail redemption, which incurs typical clearinghouse fees.

Once again, the new digital technologies now permit a much more effective, efficient and timely means to execute promotional programs. The Net has infused new marketing value into the old stalwart techniques of promotion. And the "mavericks" have quickly seized the reins. As the pioneer wedding saying goes, "Something old, something new."

Secret Message

The westward winding settlers would leave behind encrypted messages for the next passing wagon train... who, what, and where they were heading.

Promotions based around a specific "code" have been greatly simplified and enabled by the Net. It is now just easier to administer, promote, and track code-based promotions. Entry codes are promulgated on and off the Net in a variety of carriers leading to specific actions.

I feel so special and with a tinge of expectation when American Airlines provides me with a special enabling code to rack up a few more miles. I mean, I only have 2,951, 283 miles and could always use a few more. But American can execute these programs in a highly customized but efficient turnkey manner. No human being actually intercedes between the codes and my activities to engage. It is all on autopilot.

The Net is an ideal environment for code-based promotions and the linkage of hard copy distribution of the codes via advertising, packaging, and retail availability with digital execution. The codes in traditional media drive traffic to the website with the intent of engaging with the Brand. As an example, Hershey is harnessing the media power and exposure on over one billion candy packages to communicate their "Wrapper Cash" promotion. That will generate some traffic!

Blood On The Saddle

In terms of promotion, Adidas explores new promotional frontiers and often sets an extraordinary standard of pushing the envelope... which, of course, is the primary objective.

The promotion, "Bonded by Blood" for the New Zealand All Blacks Ruby Team, literally captures and implants the DNA of the team into the ink of posters that accompany the Adidas jersey. Actual blood from every member of the team is mixed into the poster ink. As the Honda commercial said, "You can't make this stuff up." What more could a sponsor ask but for the Team to bleed for promoting jersey sales!

The "blood" promotion is further exploded in an integrated campaign of advertising as well as an online site where the Consumer can watch a video of the Team members actually giving blood. Now, this is commitment. The result... a hundred thousand hits to the website and a sell-out of Adidas "All Blacks" jersey.

Following suit was the promoter of the "torture porn," horror-genre film, *Saw II,* which involves more on-screen blood than *The Fight at OK Corral.* The star and major "bad cowboy" was coerced into shedding his own blood, which was incorporated into the movies promotional posters. Tying into a related cause, the *Saw* movie series sponsored blood drives for the Red Cross collecting over 10,000 pints of blood. At this rate, when *Saw 5* hits theaters next year, organ donors will be trading kidneys for a pair of movie tickets. This is Consumer engagement.

Canyon Ecko

Marc Ecko Enterprises, a leading urban youth lifestyle Company is based on what the thirty-something eclectic and independent founder nicknamed the "promotion of graf," as in graffiti culture.

While a product of urban New Jersey, Marc Ecko could have been from New Hampshire with its Wild West license plate slogan, "Live Free or Die." The video, "Still Free," which promotes Ecko's "Getting Up" video game, became a viral explosion, ignited with all the subtlety of a military mission,.

His highly successful and extensive line of apparel, watches, and other accoutrements totals over $1 billion in sales and rests on a "maverick" foundation and an anti-establishment Company motto. Marc Ecko and the Company milk that attitude to the ultimate degree by harnessing graffiti as their promotional cause. The Company equates graffiti, not as a crime or vandalism, but as freedom of speech. The impacted property owners may not agree but, apparently, "brandalism" does not bother the youth culture as they scoop up his clothes.

Ecko has successfully fought legal injunctions against their conducting and celebrating the works of renowned graffiti artists. It also fought and won against New York legislation prohibiting people under twenty-one from possessing spray paint or broad-tipped markers. In interviews, Ecko readily acknowledges a graffiti marketing strategy and says his support of graffiti is the equivalent of Nike funding an after school sports program.

So after that, why not spray paint Air Force One?

Paint the Wagon

While somewhat slow on the draw, the global galactic advertising agencies are now following the promotional dollars online. They are increasing their presence with multiple strategies... "building" internally... buying externally... and "borrowing" in strategic alliances.

WPP has paired up with Live World, "M90," Omnicom, EVB, and the litany goes on. Yet independent specialty agencies online have a technological head start and a well-deserved reputation for being more knowledgeable and innovative. Online advertising and promotion require a different, more difficult skill set, which is more expensive to plan, execute, and audit than traditional mass media. The creative content is an entirely another matter.

As further evidence of the exploding online interest, the number of promotional online campaigns entered at the prestigious Cannes Awards numbered in the thousands and was up over a third, when compared with last year.

One of the top winners illustrated considerable "maverick" tendencies and garnered the judges' attention with a clever, promotional short for a hip-hop clothier's video game. A graffiti artist who spray paints Air Force One is featured. It is so realistic that the Department of Defense actually had to issue a press release to reassure the public that this defacement actually never happened. This is, of course, every "maverick" marketer's dream. The ensuing media coverage generated more impressions and promotional value than the original online promo. Good "maverick" marketers search for such leverage.

Silver Dollar

Ricola cough drops, best known for their annoying but highly memorable television commercial (RI-CO-LA) wafting across the Swiss mountains, recently changed their approach to be more edgy. The catalyst for a more "maverick" shift was the Brand's seventy-fifth anniversary, which called for new promotional thinking.

Ricola brought together a totally integrated promotional program designed to generate a "buzz." The Brand promoted the opportunity to win a million dollars for offering a Ricola lozenge to a "Mystery Cougher" as the solution to his or her distress. Radio commercials supported the "Mystery Cougher" and provided local clues as did their website. Additional mediums were utilized, including newspapers, public relations, and in store displays.

The entire package of communications behind this integrated promotion helped separate Ricola from the herd of other cough and cold treatments in the clutter of the key cold-cough season.

Load Yer Six-Gun!

Under competitive pressure for the first time since it invented the new disease, EDS or erectile dysfunction syndrome, Pfizer set up a "maverick" promotional program for Viagra. Much like an airline Marketer, it created a rewards program called the Value Card. Just like a frequent flier program or Starbucks Card, the Consumer is rewarded for sexual usage and loyalty.

Viagra's Value Card provides a free prescription for six or seven pills after six prior qualifying prescriptions. This is a real financial benefit to the user, since most health plans do not cover or severely limit coverage for Erectile Dysfunction Syndrome (EDS) treatment. Politicians and medical cost-cutters, who pejoratively label EDS as a mere "lifestyle" issue, have never conducted emotional focus groups and interviews with sufferers and their partners. If sexuality is not extremely high on Maslow's hierarchy of human needs, what is? And such programs are well received by their direct customers, physicians. The sawbones of the world will alter their prescribing behavior if it will enable the patient with a valuable discount for an expensive self-pay prescription.

Wagon Train

In pursuit of direct engagement with the Consumer beyond the sterility of the Net, "maverick" marketers are resurrecting road events promoting Brands across America. This is a re-invented means of "connecting" in a Brand-controlled, positive environment.

Furthermore, this promotional engagement with the Consumer can alter attitudes and behavior more so than a 30-second commercial.

Brands participating in this "wagon train" of events, mobilize a wide array of promotional venues, techniques, and target audiences. *Scholastic* magazine is promoting a new *Captain Underpants* book with a road show that uses a seven-foot purple potty prop and includes activities, like squeezing a group of kids into a rather large pair of underpants. Jack Daniels has a Whisky Mobile, complete with a bar and grill. Ocean Spray Cranberries sets up depictions of a cranberry bog under a promotional theme of "Straight From The Bog" in its traveling educational exhibit.

How about taking a "Parade on Parade" as Macy's does in twenty markets as it converts the May Company Department Stores to the Macy's brand name. They are replicating the traditional Thanksgiving Parade experience across America, including live handling of the balloons. The "event" has defined and created a national brand, well beyond the original geographic footprint of Metro New York through the years of televising the *Macy's Thanksgiving Day Parade*.

The Oscar Mayer Weiner mobile has been joined by the Johnsonville "Big Grill" and the Planters Nut Mobile. These "up close and personal" encounters provide a unique means of interaction between the Consumer and the Brand. The impact ripples throughout the marketing dynamics. A recent research study by Jack Morton Worldwide indicates that such live events double the sales impact, over traditional advertising alone. Furthermore, the study reports that 9 out of 10 Consumers agree that live marketing experiences make them more receptive to future advertising for the Brand.

That's selling horsepower!

Recognizing the growing importance of promotional execution versus advertising, the prestigious Cannes organization has added a new competitive category called, "Promo Lions." These are awarded for creative concepts directed at producing more immediate purchase behavior.

Ⓜ Opt-In Marketing

Much of the objective for "maverick" marketing is driven at inducing the Consumer to put down his buffalo-hide war shield and invite himself to our marketing campfire.

Back in the "day," there were two means to hunt buffalo. As so eloquently filmed in *Dances with Wolves*, one way was to furiously chase the buffalo like a crazy predator until you were able, at great risk of life and limb, to bring down the prey. Romantic and flashy like network television. The other means was to find a watering hole or a particular luxuriant pasture and wait with your Sharps .50 caliber rifle. As the buffalo voluntarily gathered, you were able to claim your prize because your quarry "opted-in."

There are both great synergies and efficiencies with opt-in "maverick" marketing. If the Consumer has made a concrete action to move toward our Brand, not only will the desired response rate improve but also the degree of personal commitment. Achieving an opt-in attitude greatly enhances the reception and acceptability of our messaging.

Let us sound a cautionary note regarding "opt-in marketing" or "opt-in advertising." Much of what is being promulgated in the marketing trade press, marketing books, and by Internet vendors regarding opt-in marketing revolves around how to avoid recent privacy legislation, which prohibits invasive solicitations by mail, email, or phone.

There is a general preoccupation with how to avoid or end-run legal fences with various technologies or solicitations. The aggressive pursuit and arrest of a few mass spammers has gotten every marketer's attention and raised the bar for creative solicitations and avoidance techniques. Despite the imposed penalties, there are numerous clever "re-sellers" of people who have, in fact, "opted-in" ... but to a different and/or multiple solicitations. The true value of the second-hand contacts generated by another party is greatly diminished.

Many of the current opt-in marketers are focused on legalities, whereas "maverick" marketers concentrate on achieving a "mental handshake" with proactively interested Consumer.

Come On Into the Saloon

A great example of true, voluntary, opt-in advertising comes from TiVo. That's like appointing Butch Cassidy as the Sheriff of Tombstone.

TiVo, the nemesis of advertisers, has just begun selling and promoting "Product Watch," whereby the Consumers proactively view advertising for "categories of interest" while continuing to block the unwanted messaging. This is a "maverick" marketing "win-win." The Consumer has control and has proactively "raised their hand" to receive your advertising messaging. This is among TiVo users who are most adamant about avoiding unwanted marketing.

This is a valuable service and marketing real estate for advertisers, particularly for those whose product is considered for service.

Launch a search for key words, "opt-in marketing", and you will receive a plethora of vendors and contacts. Virtually all regale us with various techniques and offers by which to "pay" people to opt-in. The currency of opting-in ranges from free newsletters, points, cash, and merchandise, on-line services, and frequent flyer miles to organizational memberships. We hold that there is an important distinction between being paid or drafted, as compared to volunteering to join a brand around the "tribal campfire." "Maverick" marketing goes after the volunteer rather than the mercenary Brand soldier.

Some refer to opt-in marketing with various euphuisms like "permission" marketing, "consensual" marketing, or "welcome marketing." In our opinion, this attitude is entirely too benign and passive. Good "maverick" marketing requires a more proactive approach. It is "fishing" but you must still bait the hook with an appealing lure and drop it right where the fish must react. Consumers who pre-qualify themselves and volunteer are almost always the most valuable in terms of lifetime revenue.

Campfire Coffee

"Not only did it get picked up in blogs, throughout the world, but it also got picked up in the press in Canada, Europe, Latin America. That's testament to the power of the interactive space to allow ideas to spread real quickly."

"It started with some word of mouth so nothing kind of happened in the first few weeks that it came into the online community. What was covered in the blogs has made its way through the Internet. We even see a lot of media picking that up showing the interest of traditional media, so it had a spillover effect, step-by-step."

Tami Yamashita
Director of Marketing

Trail Markers

 Exploit your competitive advantages with the agility and fierceness of a "maverick."

 To achieve the "maverick" factor, insist that your organization takes all marketing and business strategies to the next level of planning and execution.

 Assume and prepare for the day when the Company, its brands, and business sectors take a negative digital hit.

 Understand and ensure that sheer size does and not preclude your organization from effectively utilizing innovative approaches to operational issues.

 Relax and prepare to be as uncomfortable as a tenderhorn on a wild horse with the "maverick" function. Yes,… even consider advertising in church bulletins.

 Loosen up on the corporate reins. Empower and delegate downward in the organization for greater "maverickness."

CHAPTER THREE

THE CORRAL

The Wild Bunch

Sam Peckinpah's movie *The Wild Bunch* portrayed an eclectic group of banditos in an environment of violent hyperactivity. Not too different from the players in "maverick" marketing.

They are certainly eclectic. The players are at least slightly on the "outlaw" side of traditional marketing. The Wild West of New Marketing is a hyperactive environment of marketing opportunities and issues.

By necessity, the number of players in "maverick" marketing is increasing exponentially. At one time, it was only the third or fourth tier marketers who were forced into "maverick" marketing. Many had no real alternative but to "zig" when the more powerful herd leaders "zagged." In today's steroidal media environment, many traditional marketers have joined the fray and are vying for intensified Consumer engagement.

Even as grizzled marketing managers, we have to admit that the "messenger" colors our acceptance of the message or credibility in completing the task. If you need a coordinated messaging in seventeen countries, you are more likely to look to the global, galactic and established WPP, Havas, Publicis networks, with proven and documented results on major brands.

On the other hand, weighing the inherent bias, are we more willing to accept out-of-the-box and wacky ideas and executions of "maverick" marketing from smaller and more specialized boutiques? It becomes a balancing act.

From which organization do you buy a "maverick" idea?

Strawberry Frog ... or WPP

Wild Tangent ... or Grey Worldwide

Big Idea Group ... or Google

Bazaarvoice ... or Bain

Renegade Marketing ... or BBDO

Inventa ... or Leo Burnett

Cunning Stunts ... or Young & Rubican

Le Tigre ... or Time Warner

Viral Factory ... or McKinsey

The answer is: any ... and all.

Our analysis and a review of recent "maverick" marketers and their tactical activities indicate a distillation into several key buckets or functions:

Product
Placement

Youthenization

Emotion
Promotion

Integration

Interaction

Venue
Promotion

 Product Placement

Much has changed since Reese's Pieces candy appeared serendipitously in *ET,* way back in the "Dark Ages" of marketing. Product placement within media programming and entertainment vehicles has become formalized, complete with self-designated experts and agencies. There has been a shift from the "free" placement of Windex in *My Big Fat Greek Wedding* to multi-million dollar, cash-for-time deals representing Ford, Nabisco, and other major brands in Donald Trump's *The Apprentice.*

PQ Media estimated the product placement value … note, not cash outlay … in 2006 was $7.5 billion and expects it to double by 2010. As a viable new and energized medium for "mavericks," it retains a great deal of horsepower. The theory is that the Consumer cannot TiVo through commercial messaging inculcated into the program.

As oblique and obtuse as "maverick" marketing can be, Jaguar is quite confident in its product and brand *gestalt*. It simply "places" its cars with solicited "A" and "B+" personalities. Like fashion, just being seen in the desirable venues of restaurants, nightclubs, and an upscale daily life creates buzz and positive associations. However, the real benefit of "cars sold" is absolutely impossible to document or even begin to measure. Sometimes, you just have to "believe."

There is a formal conference for a confluence of a hundred or more marketers and forty entertainment companies to meet and discuss the future opportunities and issues of product placement. A key issue is the long lead-time required for major entertainment events. This includes television, music, movies, and even gaming. Over the years there has been a growing realization that, beyond dollars, the environment must be productive for both the program content as well as commercial messaging. Product placement has reached such a level that Consumers are beginning to notice and resent the intrusion of commercial messages and being "marketed to."

This has not slowed the expansion of product placement's territorial footprint into novels and books. Some Marketers are commissioning books in advance with a specific plan or storyline, which incorporates their Brands. In many cases, these books and novels are directed at specific, hard-to-reach target audiences. Other Marketers have made post-development deals to have their Brands inserted or substituted in books readying for publication. In-book marketing has attracted top-notch marketers such as Ford, Procter & Gamble, and publishers Doubleday and Ballantine. Some progressive authors are utilizing paid product placement as a means of partially funding the publishing of their treasured manuscripts. They proactively reach out to likely and appropriate marketers for such inclusion.

Marketers have an insatiable appetite for sports venues and are offering sufficient financial incentives to break down the historical resistance to commercial messaging. Major League Soccer will be the first professional sports league in the U.S. to permit corporate logos on game uniforms. Major League Baseball and Basketball continue to consider and evaluate similar displays in exchange for a significant infusion of advertising dollars.

Pony Express

Alas, we have news: product placement is not new. Back in the day, Edward R. Murrow puffed away on Camels during his most high-brow and intellectual on-camera dissertations. Ronald Reagan promoted GE products within programming with the same determination as his focus on the Berlin Wall.

However, the focus on and investment in product placement has become much more intense. This has been prompted by the TiVo threat and a general uneasiness with the public's attentiveness to advertising within the standard commercial pods.

Integration into any valuable property, from a television program to a video game, requires long lead time planning and upfront financial commitments of substantial dollar investments. The ability and attitude to engage in very early negotiations to integrate Brands into entertainment content is a characteristic of a brave-hearted Marketer... and not the orientation of most very impatient and large marketing corporations. Vision and the willingness to ride into risky situations mark the "maverick."

Building trustworthy relationships with producers, in advance, greatly expedites the ability to obtain placement in the most desirable properties. And even then, one must accept the inevitability of a series of "dusty roads" before hitting the "mother lode," like AT&T and Coca-Cola's placement in *American Idol*. They took a chance early on and pre-empted the competition to achieve an enviable, competitive advantage.

In a few rare cases, a brand is so contemporary and representative of current society that it is included without a multi-digit fee. Due to its pop icon status McDonald's French Fries were included without a treasured ransom in the modernized version of the Monopoly Game.

Product placement as a new, or rather re-discovered, media has become much more formalized as a process. Specialty agents and advertising agencies along with measurement companies have developed along with its increased importance. The higher-level projects, like cans of Coke prominently displayed on the *American Idol* judge's table require an ROI assessment. Even product placement in popular video games can exceed a $500,000 investment.

And once again, a new media available to "mavericks" has been further empowered by the Net. These are often low-level and affordable opportunities for "mavericks," in contrast to network and Hollywood blockbuster movies, which involve larger multi-million dollar deals requiring long lead times of months or maybe years.

Much of the buzz and industry press focuses on the new digital and video world. Those of us with pre-Net perspective need to point out that two of the most enduring and prominent product placements can be found on the NFL playing field, Gatorade and Motorola. Their collective exposure and advertising value is unprecedented. Recently, Motorola re-upped its on-field agreement for the next five years, paying $250 million. It is ironical that Motorola does not even make headsets and that Gatorade is not necessarily in the ubiquitous green buckets.

In a recent study by prominent public relations firm, Manning Selvage and Lee, a prominent public relations firm revealed that almost half of senior marketing executives paid for the insertion of marketing information into broadcast or print editorials. The supporting rationale of blurring the "Church and State" of editorial and selling function revolved around the necessity of serving up a message that would cut through the clutter of the fragmented media landscape. The Net was singled out as the enabling factor for marketers in the battle with the Consumer to control their marketing and media environment.

Young Guns

"Maverick" marketing is often harnessed to "youthenize" a brand.

"Youthenize" is a consulting word originated by the New England Consulting Group. It essentially means that unless you keep a Brand fresh and contemporary with emerging age cohorts, eventually you will have to euthanize it. "Youthenize or euthanize" your Brand.

Everyone wants the up-and-coming "Young Guns." And nothing has focused more marketing interest than the digital revolution and young people's growing distain for traditional marketing and media. The provocative distancing from today's marketing is directly linked to age and youth:

- Less broadcast ... more blogs

- Less magazines ... more mobile

- Less video ... more video gaming

- Less big-screen ... more little-screen

- Less CBS ... more cell phone

These trends have "stampeded" Marketers into a panic in terms of how to regain these wayward media cowboys. College age and younger Consumers have grown up not in the years A.D. or B.C., but P.C. The personal computer has become a standard fixture in the nursery. This age cohort views the PC as common as indoor plumbing. They may "share" the TV with friends or family members, but the computer experience is up-close and personal. TV is passive. Computers are interactive. TV and Internet on one screen... better.

Digital communication of all genres continues to expand and divert eyeball and mind from traditional media. Computer and cell phone usage is occurring at an earlier and earlier age, ensuring the internalization and more in-depth programming as an alternative medium of communication. The hours spent online by college students has increased 50% in the past four years, with no flattening of growth in sight. A great majority of teens produce and publish their own communication, utilizing self-generated media content.

More than a few marketers have begun to feel and sense a proactive reaction among Consumers, who distance themselves from traditional marketers, traditional marketing techniques, and traditional Media. This frightening phenomenon appears to be more pronounced in younger age segments. This aversion to being "marketed to," increases as more children, tweens and teens become walking billboards, decorated with more logos than a NASCAR driver. The current fashion in some sets is not to wear one flipped-collar Lacoste but rather two color coordinated alligator shirts at the same time. Consumer initiated... marketer, embraced.

As we have discussed, the digital world has empowered the Consumer to modify, reduce, or even avoid the normal channels of selling messages. And then, there is the Oldsmobile factor: Due to the sheer cost and high risk of creating totally new mega-brands, many Brands in CPG, health and beauty aids, Consumer electronics, cars, beer, apparel and other categories are aging away from younger Consumers. These brands have become dated, tired, and too often, closely associated to older generations.

    ... Oreo is almost 100 years old

    ... Nike is 42 years old

... Gap and Abercrombie are 37 and 114 years, respectively

... Coors has been in national distribution for 15 years

... Sprint is 20 years as a brand

Even MTV glosses over its 25th anniversary of being hip and young. A long and venerable heritage for a brand like Hershey, Ford, or Campbell's can be both an asset and a potential liability with age cohorts, whose trends last "days" instead of "decades."

Grand Pa

Across an array of categories, over years and years of "age cohort marketing" for our Clients, we have observed a phenomenon called the "skip-generation generation." The old adage that we are more similar to our grandparents than our parents is often true.

Many children rebel against or deliberately choose to be opposite of their parents. It is how we ferret (another Western critter), out our own identity using our parents as a foil. If John knows his dad's favorite color is red, he will often select blue. The dad, like his son, rejected the choices of his father and, as such, John may be more like his grandfather. This "skip-generation syndrome" is equally applicable to the preferred brand of computer, the first car purchased, type of home desired, career chosen, or brand of beer. As the extremely successful Drug-Free America campaign proclaimed, "Never underestimate the power of a grandparent."

Given the potential disastrous results of these factors, major Marketers have embraced "maverick" activities to reach out to younger age segments. It is not just reaching them but rather "touching" and "engaging" the younger Consumers on their terms. Once again, digital media allows a Marketer to be bolder with their message, since very small niches of Consumers can be "touched" in a compartmentalized fashion. A commercial on network television must inherently appeal to a broad spectrum of ages and attitudes. On the other hand, "maverick" marketing can be segmented down to an individual basis and, importantly, "blinded" from others.

Like its younger adherents, "maverick" marketing can and should be riskier, bolder, and more rebellious. It should be less reverent... but not less relevant... to the Brand. More salsa... less white bread. It should mirror the attitudes of a very narrow and pre-selected target group. The best of "maverick" marketing can move closer to a very specific, younger age segment in a manner that invites, not demands, an "opt-in."

The Kaiser Family Foundation recently released a landmark study regarding online marketing of food brands to children. Fully 85% of the major children food television advertisers have very specific and targeted websites. This was Kaiser's attempt to "weigh" in on the issue of childhood obesity and the use of the Net to market food to children. The real Kaiser objective was to be politically critical of and to nudge the major kid food advertisers... but cloaked in scientific research.

Whatever the purpose, the research (analyzing 77 websites with over 12 million hits by kids under 11 years of age in a three-month period) examines and details the power and flexibility of the Internet for "maverick" marketers. These kid-directed websites utilize the full gamut of techniques to enhance the important involvement and engagement difficult goal to achieve in traditional media.

It is important to note that the best of Net marketing is not isolated, but integrated with other components of the Brand's Marketing Plan. Most Brand commercials, ads, and virtually all packages carry the website address. In turn, more than half of kid-centered websites in the Kaiser study were also embedded in at least one companion television commercial. Virtually all had one or more online promotion like free gifts, branded downloads, sweepstakes, contests, etc.

As one would expect, one of the most prominent techniques used on these websites was Brand-based video games or "advergaming." These are fun, age-appropriate games with a high degree of brand exposure and rather explicit brand-sell. The average website had six plus branded video games. Advergaming is essentially an engaging, faster paced, and subtle version of an infomercial. In contrast to a thirty-second television commercial, the typical video game provides twenty-seven minutes of interactive Brand engagement.

Viral (aka "buzz" and "diffusion") marketing was another key technique in two-thirds of these websites. Viral marketing encourages the little cowboys and cowgirls to become a spokesperson, marketing the Brand experience to their peers. This can take the form of online game challenges, e-mails, invitations to join the membership, or research polls.

Viral is even better than "opting-in;" it is "copting-in," by having a known and trusted friend invite them into the Brand experience. As we know, kids and tweens are peer-driven, herd animals like the pronghorn antelope. Website memberships are particularly appealing as they can "join" the Brand's club, further enhancing the marketing bond.

In order to reach younger viewers who are being diverted from television, the networks are fighting back by uploading their television content to the digital world. CBS and ABC are offering some of their top-rated shows free online, but advertiser-supported. Other networks have provided essentially pay-for-view TV for hit shows, downloadable onto iPods.

While seemingly revolutionary, this is merely "delayed" or additional broadcast venue techniques that the TV networks utilized successfully as cable emerged as a viable competitor in many years past. Increasingly, neither the Consumer nor the Advertisers care if the commercial messaging is seen on a 72-inch flat-panel TV, a PC monitor, or a Sprint cell phone.

Marketers are even "youthenizing" their Brand icons in order to maintain their relevance. Many are carefully crafting a younger profile and shaving a few years off personas like Aunt Jemima, The Michelin Man, Fabio, and Lassie, and Juan Valdez.

In many cases, as a part of youthenizing, the icons have been placed on a strict diet too. While, Americans grew larger and heavier, our younger and more aspirational brand icons have been slimmed by contemporary.

Perception is reality, and many marketers believe that receptivity to Net marketing is directly inverse to age. A survey directed toward five hundred major marketers asked, "For what group is the Net most effective?"

Estimate of Net Effectiveness

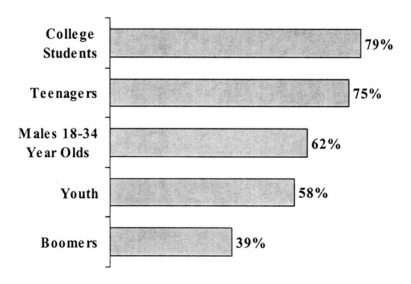

Emotion Promotion

	Brand/Company		Execution
Emotion Promotion:	3M	–	3M set up a website that shared "secret" ways the Company used Post-it products. On the website, viewers can obtain "secret" tips better to organize their lives, as well as enter sweepstakes and request free samples of Post-its.
Emotion Promotion:	Brawny	–	To update their image, Brawny held a competition where women could write in and nominate a person to be the real-life Brawny man. More then 4,000 women participated in the competition, with the real life Brawny men ranging anywhere from body builders and firefighters to flabby fathers and balding husbands. Sexy.
Emotion Promotion:	Dawn Dishwashing Liquid	–	For over 20 years, Dawn has been used by wildlife groups to rescue oil-covered birds, most notably during the Exxon Valdez incident. In order to maintain their momentum as a market leader in dishwashing soap, Dawn unleashed a new campaign emphasizing their soap as mild enough to help the environment. One of many ads depicts a duck with the words, "If this bird could talk, he'd tell you how this soap saved his life."

Emotion Promotion:	De Beers Group —	De Beers is targeting 30-54 year-old women with an income of $100,000+, with a campaign dedicated to at persuading them to wear more than one expensive wedding ring. The campaign's message is that women have two hands and therefore both should have more than one expensive ring.
Emotion Promotion:	Diet Coke and Mentos —	A couple of frustrated film-makers discovered that mixing Mentos and Diet Coke creates a huge, gushing flow coming from the Diet Coke. They sparked a viral and unanticipated campaign by filling the Internet with homemade short films of fountains of fun.
Emotion Promotion:	General Electric —	GE's corporate advertising campaign is working to advertise their "College Bound" program, sensitively and without bragging. The College Bound program sponsors students and GE employee volunteers who serve pancakes to the elderly, clean playgrounds, and read to kindergartners. With this technique, GE is garnering well-deserved recognition as a community leader and supporter of local causes.

Emotion Promotion:	Hershey	–	Hershey supplied our troops overseas with candy in order to generate an emotional connection to the Brand. The Hershey candy reminds the soldiers of their childhood and home. The candy is being treated in card games as currency. Supportive rather than exploitive, appealing to the "troops" is... a proven technique.
Emotion Promotion:	Hooters	–	When faced with a barrage of feminist complaints, Hooters, charged with a counter publicity campaign, rather than retreating. Rush Limbaugh, in jest, called for a rally of all "feminazis," "environmentalist wackos," and other politically correct groups. Hooters knows its core constituencies and "connects."
Emotion Promotion:	Hormel Stagg Chili	–	Hormel Foods sponsored a marketing vehicle called "Staggmobile" to "Shaqtacular," a charity carnival sponsored by Shaquille O'Neal. While the Staggmobile handed out samples, coupons, and T-shirts, the goal of sponsoring the Staggmobile was to make a positive mental connection with the Brand and its cause.

Emotion Promotion:	Jagermeister	–	When launched in the U.S., Jagermeister targeted college students and the "buzz" often referred to the liquor as "Liquid Valium." Jagermeister denied drug rumors, but later played on the "rumor" and the "humor" that it contained opium by distributing an article obliquely suggesting such a message, across college bars and campuses.
Emotion Promotion:	Milk-Bone	–	Milk-Bone's 100th Anniversary provided an opportunity for anthropomorphic bonding among the Brand and Consumers and their dogs. Milk-Bone pulled out the entire emotional arsenal with celebrities and their dogs, building the World's Largest Dog House made of Milk-Bones. The dramatic touch was a $1 million donation to Milk-Bone's Canine Heroes Program, which trains dogs to assist the disabled and law enforcement.

Emotion Promotion:	Neiman Marcus —	Neiman Marcus featured a fantasy trip for six passengers in their holiday catalog of truly fantasy gifts. This outrageous trip was priced at $1.76 million and included medical assessments, training, and a ride on the Virgin Galactic spaceship. As just one of the "can you believe this" fantasy gifts in the catalog, the trip drives buzz for Neiman Marcus and, subsequently, the sales of their merely over-the-top products.
Emotion Promotion:	Oasys Mobile —	Oasys Mobile created a campaign with a fake doctor and website, claiming that certain proprietary ringtones, named Pherotones, would increase a person's sex appeal. While the Pherotones were tongue-in-check, the campaign became a very successful viral campaign and increased general sales for Oasys Mobile. Humor works.

Emotion Promotion:	Pantene	–	Pantene launched hair donation campaign, Pantene Beautiful Lengths, to inspire women and men to make a gift of healthy hair. The campaign was to benefit cancer patients by using high-quality wigs to help them maintain their self-esteem and body image after chemotherapy. It doesn't get any more emotional than this.
Emotion Promotion:	Starbucks	–	Starbucks expanded its marketspace by selling CDs of children's stories narrated by Meryl Streep. The CD's are sold in Starbuck's across the country and are a step to further the belief that Starbucks is more than just a coffee shop.
Emotion Promotion:	Time Warner Cable	–	After studies showed that 60% of mothers decide which package to buy, Time Warner Cable started targeting their advertising of cable and internet packages to mothers after studies showed that 60% of household's mothers decide which package to buy. The new campaign focused on showing the packages through a mother's eyes, featuring characters with a hectic lives and loving families. Channel alignment.

Emotion Promotion:	Tyson Foods	–	Tyson has now started offering free, downloadable, multi-dimensional prayer books for religions. What started as an internal religious mission, expanded to equate Tyson as a faith-friendly Brand for Consumers in a proactive manner.
Emotion Promotion	Unilever	–	Unilever teamed up with Albertsons Supermarket for a bowl-a-thon for battered children. At the event, a life-size version of the Snuggle bear donated a check for $25,000 from Albertsons and Unilever. The Snuggle bear and an assistant then read books to children and gave out free, miniature stuffed animals.

🪣 Integration

Integration:	Philips Electronics —	Philips Electronics sponsored access to premium content on the *Wall Street Journal* online and ESPN websites. On selective Fridays, instead of viewers having to subscribe or enter their login-ins, they had to watch a Philips Electronics ad to gain access to the news stories.
Integration:	Anheuser-Busch —	Anheuser-Busch launched an online entertainment network in order to produce branded entertainment. The network hopes to further develop advertiser control of the media, thus counteracting the growing trend of Consumers using DVR to skip or avoid conventional 30-second advertisements.

Integration:	Bud Light	–	Bud Light utilized a technology that allowed Consumers to go online and insert their own picture into specific Bud Light ads. Once the image is completed, it is branded with a Bud Light logo and users can invite people to see their creations via email. The "chain" campaign will be promoted through email and is intended to add a personal experience of the Brand with the Consumer.
Integration:	ClipSyndicate	–	ClipSyndicate developed a system that takes various newscasts and niche stories from across the country and archives them. People are then allowed to search the archive for video clip reruns, with the producers of the video paying ClipSyndicate to show their own ads with the clip.

Integration:	GM	–	This campaign seeks to contemporize the Brand's infamous "Baseball, Hot Dogs, Apple Pie, and Chevrolet" slogan. Advertisements circulate on the TV, radio, newsprint, and video blogs, cause-related tie-into the Boys' and Girls' Clubs, and numerous linked websites. Local promotions have some ballparks singing the new Chevrolet theme song for real "buzz."
Integration:	Home Shopping Network	–	The Home Shopping Network grew significantly by switching to an auto-ship initiative, where product refills are automatically sent to previous Customers. The process locks buyers into an arrangement where they no longer have to remember when it is time to repurchase. This innovative program benefits the seller by having a minimal inventory at risk.
Integration:	Kraft	–	Kraft created online games for about 17 of its brands, plus classic games such as chess, mah-jongg, and backgammon to attract young Consumers. The advergaming technique exposes a series of Brand images during the game.

Integration:	MTV	–	MTV developed a broadband channel that capitalized on the rising trend of student-produced short films, music videos, and sitcoms. The channel is used as a testing mechanism for mainstream shows, which can be further developed for broader distribution. The broadband channel is exclusively available in dorm rooms on college campuses.
Integration:	Nestlé Coffee Mate	–	Coffee Mate started calling back all the people who had called the 800 number and began interviewing them for advice. By doing so, they were able to engage very opinionated Consumers and gain valuable insights.
Integration:	Procter & Gamble	–	P&G has a deal with Sony Music where girls can download songs from various artists on their website, beinggirl.com. The strategy is to connect popular artists with brands like Secret, Tampax, and Cover Girl.

Integration:	Petco	–	Petco is adding a ratings and review system for their best Customers. They found that Consumers tend to trust other Consumers more than advertisements. This rating system greatly improved their visitor-to-purchase ratio on the website.
Integration:	Royal Caribbean International	–	Royal Caribbean targeted its cruise ship advertisements to cold weather environments. Bad weather or snow-targeted locations automatically trigger a wave of marketing support. Advertisements were also displayed on sites like Accuweather.com, especially when a search originated from regions with temperatures 20 degrees Fahrenheit or lower.
Integration:	Super Stop & Shop	–	Super Stop & Shop has adopted the use of a device named "My Shopping Buddy," in order to distinguish their shopping experience from other stores. "My Shopping Buddy" is positioned on the handle of a shopping cart and offers shoppers such services as alerts on deals, store maps, and special promotions for the deli.

Integration: Vogue Magazine —   *Vogue* launched a website shopvogue.com that only sells merchandise from companies who advertise in the magazine. The agreement gives advertisers better exclusivity with *Vogue* shoppers, as well as encourages more advertisers to place their ads in the monthly editions.

Integration: 7-Eleven   —   With the release of *Simpson's The Movie*, 7-Elevens were converted to the famed "Quik-E-Mart." In addition to this name change, they also carried products featured in the series, such as Krusty-Os cereal and Buzz cola. Large cutouts of Homer, Marge, and other characters graced these promotional retail outlets.

🪣 Interaction

Interaction: Burger King — Burger King started a campaign named, the "Big Bucking Chicken," in which a chicken does crazy stunts on a motorcycle. The more people who viewed the website, the crazier were the stunts that the chicken performed, providing both an incentive and a degree of control to the participants.

Interaction: CBS — CBS hid $2 million in gold across the country to promote their new reality show, *Gold Rush*. During the show, commercials gave clues as to where the gold was hidden. As added value, during the upfront, Advertising companies were allowed to bid on whether their commercials contained the hint to generate better message attention and retention.

Interaction: Dove, McDonald's, Nexxus, Etc. — Many companies including Dove, McDonald's, and Nexxus are starting to have contests to get ordinary people on their packages and in their advertisements. People are becoming bored with looking at glossy celebrities. Companies are responding. An excellent example is Jones Soda, which places real people on the bottles. Real soda for real people.

Interaction: Ford — Ford created its own spin-off reality show, similar to *American Idol,* in order to connect with a younger audience. In the show, car designers compete and the ultimate prize is that Ford produces their car design concept.

Interaction: JetBlue — JetBlue has set up "story booths" in eight cities for fliers to record their recent flight experiences. The testimonials can then be replayed to other Consumers and utilized for internal JetBlue improvements. Consumers become the message.

Interaction: Kraft — Kraft designed a family game show called, "Be a Cheesillionaire," which was promoted on 7 million packages of Kraft Singles. The contest prizes included a year's worth of allowances and family vacations to Los Angeles in order to compete for the grand prize of a $20,000 scholarship. To support the campaign, Kraft created trivia contests in ten key markets, gave away free grilled cheese sandwiches, in the stores, and harnessed dedicated TV tags.

Interaction: MTV Networks — MTV pushed further into reality series further by introducing a site named Virtual Laguna Beach. On the site, fans can become three-dimensional, digital characters in a virtual version of *Laguna Beach*. Characters can club-hop neighborhoods, buy music, watch videos, sing karaoke, and start their own bands as a means to enhance the depth of engagement.

Interaction: Planters Peanuts — Planters Peanuts held a voting contest to decide what new piece of clothing should be added to their mascot, Mr. Peanut. Votes are tallied online, with participants choosing from a predetermined set of clothing. The winning piece of clothing will be added to the mascot on future packaging.

Interaction: Ricola — Ricola offered $1 million in cash to Consumers who could find the "mystery cougher" and come to their aid with a Ricola cough drop. After it was advertised during an episode of *Friends*, the campaign created such buzz that anyone in New York who were seen coughing were rushed by people looking to help and claim their prize.

Interaction: Ruffles — Ruffles had a nationwide contest to award a $50,000 scholarship to parents who named their newborn after the Ruffles mascot, "Horton." In order to be eligible for the competition, couples had to both deliver their child by the promotion deadline and legally have Horton be the child's first name in order to be eligible for the competition. Out of 1,000 hits on the website, 49 parents applied. Apparently, the $50,000 scholarship was a significant interaction.

Interaction: Sony Ericsson — To support the introduction of their new picture phone, Sony Ericsson generated an "embarrassing picture" campaign which utilized a contest to support the introduction of a new picture phone. "Shameacademy.com" and advertising named "Drool" were the key comments. Consumers were encouraged to send in pictures of themselves with long pieces of drool hanging off their mouths. The campaign generated considerable buzz as well as encouraging a number of independent sites eager to display their own hanging phlegm.

Interaction: Tripmates.com — Tripmates.com emerged as a travel-oriented social network. Through the network, travelers can search for recommendations on restaurants, hotels, and entertainment. The network permits others to see personal profiles, such as favorite places to visit and favorite music, so that other viewers can determine if their tastes are similar.

Interaction: ThisNext.com — ThisNext.com combined shopping and social networking into a single community where shoppers can swap shopping ideas, browse, and blog. The site focuses on unsure Consumers who are looking for Consumer-generated ideas to get a better idea of what to buy. The website allows visitors to grab photos from various websites and distribute them across the online community.

🪣 Product Placement

Product Placement:	Applebee's	—	Applebee's became an integral component of the *Friday Night Lights* primetime soap opera as the setting for numerous plots. It is impossible to miss in the show as "the meeting place" in the small West Texas town.
Product Placement:	Burger King	—	Burger King entered into video game marketing by developing its own video games for the Xbox 360, starring their freaky mascot, the "King," as the main character. The three new BK-specific Xbox 360 titles, *Big Bumpin*, *Sneak King*, and *PocketBike Racer*, were priced at $3.99 in restaurants with the purchase of a value meal.
Product Placement:	Cadillac	—	Cadillac struck a deal with Xbox Live which allowed users to download free versions of their top model cars for different driving games. Electronic games have traditionally only featured high-end cars and Cadillac is trying to be seen among them. Lowering the age appeal of the Brand is another key objective.

Product Placement:	Cover Girl	–	Cover Girl was featured in a young adult novel where the heroine wears LipSlicks, a brand by Cover Girl. In return for placement, P&G featured the book on beinggirl.com to generate sales for the book... and advertising which is indirect but difficult to miss.
Product Placement:	Febreze	–	Febreze sponsored a series of Nick at Night short sitcoms titled, *At the Poocharellis.* The show is not solely about Febreze. However, the product is intrinsically woven into the plot of several episodes. The series contains eight micro episodes, which simulates and collapses the experience of watching a sitcom of normal length.
Product Placement:	Ford	–	Ford sponsored a 90-minute theatrical film to promote the Lincoln Zephyr and Mercury Milan. Lincolns and Mercurys made dramatic cameo appearances in the film, while larger roles were comprised of imaginary brands.

| **Product Placement:** | KFC | — | KFC made an attempt to place its product into the actual Super Bowl game by offering a quarter million dollar donation, in the name of the player who did the "Chicken Dance" for three seconds in the end zone. The players "chickened out" but KFC received its due in buzz. |
| **Product Placement:** | Procter & Gamble | — | Procter & Gamble worked with the CW Network to have mini-magazine shows featuring Herbal Essence to link with 30-second ads on the show, *America's Next Top Model*. The mini-magazine shows have three different segments regarding what's "hip," "hot," or "happening." depending on which segment is being shown and hopes to draw more viewing from the entertainment factor. Herbal Essence is integrated into the behind-the scene preparation for Fashion Week. |

| **Product Placement:** | Quiksilver | – | Quicksilver added to its sponsoring and dressing of extreme sports athletics, by placing its clothing line into top-selling video games produced by Activision. While Quicksilver is currently a niche Company and does not sell through Target or Wal-Mart, using its clothing in video games sold in those stores provides a means to get their marketing message in a unique venue. |
| **Product Placement:** | Revlon | – | Revlon has partnered its way into a three-month plot on the soap opera, *All My Children,* in exchange for a major advertising commitment. Different from many product placements, Revlon products are not just included in the series. The Company is actually written into the episode as the antagonist. Though positioned as an evil foil, Revlon is using this technique as innovative means to generate Brand recognition. |

Product Placement:	Smirnoff	–	Smirnoff has re-positioned itself to be associated with James Bond to establish a sophisticated image. In forthcoming James Bond movies, Smirnoff will become Bond's favorite martini vodka. The campaign is accompanied by a website named "Shaken & Stirred," and allows visitors to create "Bond" music mixes.
Product Placement:	24 Hour Fitness	–	One million dollars in equipment and integration fees were paid by 24 Hour Fitness to be the club of choice for NBC's show, *The Biggest Loser*. The Company has also been tagging its commercials, asking people to watch the show.
Product Placement:	Volkswagen	–	Volkswagen teamed up with the producers of *Bourne Ultimatum*, creating a movie trailer that featured the Volkswagen Toureg. This use of placement makes advertising more gripping, with less focus on selling the care and more on the building of Brand recognition.

Venue Promotion

Venue Promotion:	AT&T	–	AT&T unleashed a mass of French poodles on Bastille Day to dramatize their new global long-distance plan. Each of the poodles was trained to grab people's attention and was strapped with a mass of brochures for people to take.
Venue Promotion:	Adidas, American Apparel	–	Adidas and American Apparel are utilizing Linden Lab's virtual world, *Second Life* to advertise their real world products. In *Second Life*, virtual characters called avatars can purchase virtual items to dress their characters and show off their clothing. The Retailers are using the virtual world in order to develop Brand image and attract the users in the real world.
Venue Promotion:	Broadway Musical *The Wedding Singer*	–	The play partnered with large wedding web sites like "The Knot" and magazines like *Modern Bride*. Targeting also focused on bachelorette parties and giving away tickets at wedding stores.

Venue Promotion:	CBS	–	CBS used egg-vertising to advertise its primetime shows on eggs bought at grocery stores. The information is lasered onto the eggshells, with featured show times and quotes from the different shows in the primetime lineup.
Venue Promotion:	Charmin	–	To generate trial, Charmin is replacing the normal, cheap, one-ply toilet paper at state fairs with Charmin Ultra. The campaign is connecting to masses of people at once, in a moment when the softness of Charmin Ultra demonstrates its biggest differentiation from normal toilet paper. Carrying this even further, Charmin sponsors public restrooms in such visible sites as New York's Times Square.
Venue Promotion:	Clear Channel Communications	–	Clear Channel Outdoor worked with leading mall operators to create see-through tables in food courts that display advertising while Consumers eat. The table-size advertisements are designed to be non-disposable, waterproof, and safeguarded from stains to maximize durability.

Venue Promotion:	Epic Records —	In order to combat declining CD sales, Epic Records connected with street teams to sell records and hype names, at the grassroots level. Popular DJ's and other "cool" people promoted different albums at nightclubs and local concerts to build a strong fan foundation at the local level.
Venue Promotion:	FHM —	FHM uses a new technique called "headvertising" that places Companylogosorbrandnameson student's heads, using temporary tattoos. Students become living, walking, advertising venues. The students are paid to hang around in key public locations and are on duty three to four hours at a time. They are allowed to shower, but not to rub their foreheads.

Venue Promotion:	Hershey Foods –	Hershey wanted to take the experience beyond the remoteness of Pennsylvania and bring it to life with a Hershey factory, towering fifteen floors above Broadway. The tower contains more than four thousand chasing lights, four steam machines, three hundred and eighty feet of neon lighting, and a moving message board for people to flash messages to loved ones. This Hershey store is packed with tourists and locals alike, and turns adults into chocolate-seeking adolescents.
Venue Promotion:	Hewlett-Packard –	USPS has removed a law prohibiting the personalization of stamps by corporations and people. The reversal of the law allows corporations to place advertising graphics on stamps. Hewlett-Packard was one of the first marketers to experiment with personalized stamps.
Venue Promotion:	Independent –	A creative director named Steve Babcock put the "right side of his brain" up for auction in order to get paid for his creative talents.

Venue Promotion:	ING Direct	–	ING Direct, an Internet bank, hired the firm Inventa to take to the streets in attention getting, bright, orange outfits, matching the Company's corporate colors. People in orange colored uniforms flooded the streets, rode orange mountain bikes, and even handed out orange Tic Tacs to stimulate brand awareness.
Venue Promotion:	Le Tigre	–	Le Tigre placed about three thousand static-cling tiger logos and two hundred fifty wash-away graffiti logos around New York City, in a single night, to advertise the Brand. The advertisements, which only lasted a few days, were placed anywhere from subways to posters containing products ads. Street presence can be a powerful tool.

Venue Promotion:	Monster.com	–	Monster.com deployed five slime-green vehicles across the nation in movie theater parking lots. Before and after movies Monster.com representatives encouraged people to search for new jobs. Paying less than $1,500 for access to each theater parking lot, a large number of people in a short period of time can be reached and actually experience the service.
Venue Promotion:	Motorola	–	To demonstrate the new T193 mobile phone, Motorola hired a crew of pitchmen dressed in gaudy 1970's attire to visit more than 1,000 theaters showing New Line Cinema's, *Austin Powers in Goldmember*. The pitchmen worked the lines at the cinema, giving moviegoers hands-on experience with the phone and letting them see its functions.
Venue Promotion:	Palm	–	Palm generated a smaller, cheaper PDA, called the Zire that allowed it to enter into new markets previously unavailable. From QVC to grocery stores, Palm is tapping into the lower income market, positioning its product as an impulse-buy. Palm is hoping to break free of their image as niche gadgets for businessmen and geeks.

Venue Promotion:	Smirnoff Ice —	In order to gain a presence, real or associated, in the Super Bowl, Smirnoff Ice is purchasing advertising time in local markets. The process, named "ambush advertising," takes advantage of national networks selling time to local stations and enables advertisers to undermine the official sponsors of such events.
Venue Promotion:	Snapple —	Snapple promoted its new drink, Diet Peach Snapple, by using office voice-mail advertising. The campaign called offices in metro areas, mass voice-mailing employees in this most unusual venue.
Venue Promotion:	Sportsbook.com —	Sportsbook.com actually displayed $100,000 cash in $1 bills on a billboard in Las Vegas to promote contests on their website. The money was placed in a plexiglass box near a hired security guard, so that anyone who drove by in the car would be tempted. In an additional public relations move, Sportsbook.com also offered 6 to 1 odds that the money would be stolen from the billboard... <u>it was</u>.

Venue Promotion:	Target —	Target advertised its back-to-college supplies by branding movie theater popcorn bags with ads. The advertisements shown during the summer were at 104 theaters in 10 major cities and portrayed a woman snuggled under her colorful stripped blanket with Target's red bull's eye logo in the middle of the bag.
Venue Promotion:	Tim Hortons —	Tim Hortons Donuts opened up a store in Afghanistan in order to gain awareness from Canadian troops stationed there. The overseas store came at a time when Tim Hortons was aiming to open 200 new coffee shops throughout Canada.
Venue Promotion:	YouTube, Warner — Music Group	YouTube.com reached a deal with Warner Music Group to post a catalog of music videos on YouTube, in return for Warner Music Group receiving a percentage of revenue from advertising next to the video. The deal promotes artists and allows home videos of people lip-synching to be legally distributed.

Venue Promotion:	Nivea	–	To promote its new cellulite reduction products, Nivea has a forty-five minute class at New York Sports Clubs, designed to target and tone cellulite prone areas. It is called the "Nivea Goodbye Cellulite Workout." Now that's placing your message in a target-rich environment.
Venue Promotion:	Head & Shoulders	–	Head & Shoulders placed special shower mats in gyms across the country. When the hot water hits these seemingly normal mats, an advertisement for the Brand appears where there was previously just a black and white mat... right under your feet.

🪣 Youthenization

Youthenization: 7Up   —   7Up revitalized its brand by partnering with the Grammy's and aiming a promotion, "Sit Your Can At The Grammy's" directly at the 12-24 year-old market. The promotion included designing the official logo for the 43rd Grammy Awards, Grammy voting games, and "Under the Cap" competitions to win a trip to the show.

Youthenization: Bacardi   —   Bacardi launched a service to turn your house into a retro bar. Upon request, a list of bartenders and DJ's in the area would be contracted to turn a house into a party atmosphere.

Youthenization: Churchill Downs — Churchill Downs sponsored events to attract younger people to the races and change the image of horse racing as only being for older generations. Activities included a Family Fun Festival, cookouts, pony rides, and the center attraction of a Beerfest in the oval.

Youthenization: Dr. Pepper — Dr. Pepper, in a continuing effort to create a "maverick" differentiation between the Brand and other CSDs, encapsulated the punk band "Cartel" in a transparent bubble for three weeks. The breakout became a mega event with both media coverage and active Cartel Band enthusiasts. This reinforced Dr. Pepper as something on the edge.

Youthenization: Hawaiian Punch — Hawaiian Punch held an online competition to allow teens to update the five-year-old design of the Brand. Four finalist ideas were chosen, refined, and posted on a youth-oriented website, where teens were allowed to choose the final design. Instead of focus groups, the Brand went straight to the teens for the Company's future direction.

Youthenization: Hershey — Hershey shunned away from classic TV campaigns to promote their new Take Five chocolate bar as a "maverick." Sending out 69,000 "evangelists" to distribute samples of the candy it targeted the 18-34 year old age group. The campaign encouraged the "evangelists" to record people preaching about how Take Five is the "greatest candy bar ever," in hopes that Hershey could use the footage in future commercials.

Youthenization: Hewlett-Packard — Hewlett-Packard originated a viral campaign at the website FingerSkilz.tv, featuring close-up videos of a hand painted as a soccer player that performed soccer tricks with a wadded-up paper ball. The site generated more than 180,000 unique visitors, as well as prompted widespread blog discussion and imitators. The site was part of a campaign to "youthenize" and gain the "cool" factor, vastly dominated by Apple.

Youthenization: Hewlett-Packard — Hewlett-Packard sponsored a show on MTV called *Meet or Delete*, where young people decided whether they want to date candidates based on the content of their hard drive, videos watched, and websites visited.

Youthenization: *Maxim* — *Maxim* magazine signed a deal to have its name on a casino. The casino, backed by the Maxim image, is designed to compete with the Palms Hotel and Casino by focusing on a younger, more vibrant Consumer.

Youthenization: New York Health — New York Health and Racquet and Racquet Club Club hired six attractive young men and women to advertise the facility near Grand Central Terminal. As people walked by, the hires flashed their underwear to the strangers, revealing the club logo and a fitness class named "Booty Call" appearing on the garment.

Youthenization: Old Spice — Old Spice is targeting young adults in order to revitalize its brand from an older image to a new more youthful one. To do so, P&G is dispatching skimpily clad "towel girls" during Spring Break. It is also passing out samples of its new product Cool Contact with rental tuxedos and at high schools on prom time.

Youthenization: Puma — "Together Again for the First Time" a concert in Toronto with indie bands. It was staged in a run down warehouse in an up and coming district. This was an attempt to stay under the radar and maintain the "coolness" factor. The objective was to be the "party of the summer," even if only a few hundred people could attend.

Youthenization: Tylenol — Tylenol targeted younger, active demographics of 18-34 year olds with their new Tylenol 8-Hour product, by targeting gyms and athletic facilities. Partnering with Bally's fitness, they were able to have national gym distribution and market to their target audience upon release.

Youthenization:	Tylenol	–	In order to develop a younger "hipper" image, Tylenol had girls in fur skirts hand out free samples of the new Cool Caplets in order to develop a younger "hipper" image. Tylenol utilized the campaign as an opportunity to reclaim the title of innovator, as it is the first OTC pain medicine to experiment with flavorings.
Youthenization:	United Parcel Service	–	UPS hired models to drive some of their trucks during fashion week in order to generate buzz. The hired drivers had to be over 6 feet tall and have a 32-inch waist and bright eyes. Designer Miguel Androver also showed off a collection of fashionable reinterpretations of the UPS gear on the runway. What will Brown do for you?

And how should we classify a start-up company called Thrillist.com, which lived up to its name? In an attempt to generate "buzz," the Company hired a professional knife thrower. Various attendees, I assume, the less sober of the participants, at the Company's party stood as a target while the knife thrower practiced his art. "Maverick"? Absolutely. Smart? Debatable!

"We're very pleased to see that it actually received quite a bit of buzz. The installation itself was planned, the amount of buzz that it received not only in the U.S. but around the world was certainly not directly planned, but an outcome of a very inventive marketing approach."

Tami Yamashita
Director of Marketing

Picture is a cup of Folgers painted on a New York City manhole cover.

Trail Markers

 Ensure that "who" the messenger is does not color or reduce the probability that your company will accept or take action on a "maverick" idea.

 Beg, borrow, and steal shamelessly from your competitors, as well as others beyond your business category or business sectors.

 Study other marketers and their entry into "maverickness," including how their executions can be adapted and changed to leverage your Brand or business. What assets are required?

Demand that your staff and marketing teams analyze, learn, and dissect what other marketers have done before proceeding with a project.

 Recognize that the mistakes others make in "maverick" marketing are often the greatest source of learning.

 Be wary and ensure that any marketing programs to "youthenize" do not alienate a core franchise with mixed messages.

 Remember that the 50+ population constitutes one-third of all disposable income and 10% of all condom purchases.

AARP branded condoms... now that's a "maverick" idea!

CHAPTER FOUR

ROPING AND RIDING

Every cowboy or settler seeking a "Don't fence me in" lifestyle had to master the basics of roping and riding. As with most physical or mental endeavors, a wide differential existed between the available skill levels and their actual performance.

Pick Your Poison

Every cowboy learned, improved, and adapted various techniques, which seemed to work best for him and his set of talents. The equipment to conquer and hold the West, from saddles to firearms and hats to lariats, evolved and became specialized for certain tasks and terrains.

Similarly, today's "maverick" marketers employ a wide array of powerful techniques, many of which perfected through trial and error. As a "maverick," one is enabled to conduct more small-scale experiments than a traditional manager following corporate guidelines. This provides a substantial advantage and corporate adaptation.

"Maverick" marketing involves a more even blend or campfire stew of both art and science. It is an acquired taste for many marketing organizations and senior marketing executives. The functions or marketing approaches currently being utilized vary considerably, given the task at hand and the specific organization. Some techniques are totally new-to-the-world... others are adaptations of traditional marketing methods. The stable of "maverick" techniques is continuously changing and adapting, but often includes:

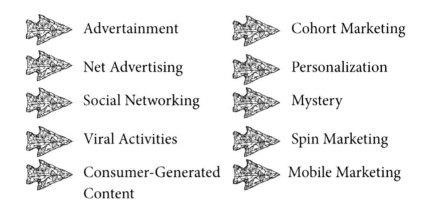

Advertainment

Net Advertising

Social Networking

Viral Activities

Consumer-Generated
Content

Cohort Marketing

Personalization

Mystery

Spin Marketing

Mobile Marketing

and a long wagon train of other powerful marketing approaches.

 **Advertainment**

Confluence Of The Mississippi And The Missouri

Some critics regard the accelerated blurring of media as corruption of the bright line between the Church, editorial, State, and commercial messaging. However, we regard this phenomenon merely as a pragmatic reaction of Marketers and the traditional media toward the objective of engaging the Consumer to "buy-in." It represents just one of the many defenses against the TiVo fast-forward habit.

The mutual fund of Marketers utilizing "advertainment" grows more prestigious everyday, with joining companies like ESPN, GM, BMW, and FTD. Programming becomes both editorial and advertising. Today's Consumer makes much less distinction between the two than has been the case in the past, leaving that debate to the purists.

These advertainments are essentially a more sophisticated, less obvious, and, usually, shorter version of infomercials. The selling is oblique rather than eliciting a direct response. It has been exploded beyond mere sponsorship, to actual inclusion within the storyline. There exists a heavier weight on entertainment and therefore, hopefully, more engaging to Consumers defiantly avoiding commercial messaging.

It is a paradox that today's Consumers who are creating a moat between themselves and advertising are more accepting of blurring of commercial messaging and editorial... the latter being less sacrosanct than historically true. Advertainment has become a tool believed to be effective, but is yet unproven by objective measurement.

 Net Advertising

Eagle-Eyed

At the first sighting of a prairie dog den, kids in the wagon train would attempt to count these wily little creatures. Confronted by the thousands of beady eyes popping up and disappearing down their intricate set of holes, the young pioneers quickly became frustrated and gave up.

… ditto, measuring Net advertising

The measurement and auditing of traditional media has become relatively refined over the years. Traditional media is public and therefore, the metrics are more easily captured by observational techniques. This situation is further improved by intra-media and marketer cooperation to provide coding that enables a relatively accurate tracking of invested dollars. The auditors are objective, third party companies, providing syndicated data at a price. Due to the use of rate card costs in the calculations, our own experience and a number of "reported versus "actual" spending tests reveal that the standard sources tend to over-estimate the advertising expenditures by 10–15%. Not bad and within an acceptable range for good management.

On the other hand, "maverick" marketing activities and, specifically, the Net are notoriously difficult to monitor and value. Virtually every deal on the Net is subject to wide negotiation of rates and rarely disclosed. The Net advertising buying process, including rates, is private and murky. Much of the data is derived, estimated, and incestuous, being repeated over and over again until it morphs into fact. Attempting to quantify the amount of advertising on the Net is like counting prairie dogs.

The following are a few estimates; take your pick:

"Internet advertising is a $12.5 billion market."

– eMarketer

"The investment in Internet advertising is less than $7 billion and accounts for 2.6% of total advertising spending."

– Leading National Advertiser Report

"Advertising on search engines is already a $14 billion-a-year business."

– New York Times

"Internet ad revenue is on track to hit $16 billion."

– IAB/Pricewaterhouse

"The advertising dollars invested in Internet is $7.9 billion."

– Universal McCann

"In 2005, Internet Advertising reached $10.1 billion."

– Jack Myers Report

"Digital advertising will be $18 to $15 billion."

– McKinsey & Co.

"The Internet media (excluding retail transactions) in $16.92 billion."

– Ad Age Annual Media Report

While the quantification of the size of the Net advertising market remains elusive as a prairie dog, the fact remains that it continues to grow rapidly and provides a real alternative to traditional media.

No doubt, considerably more "smoke" than "fire" exists regarding Net advertising... but the "fire" is roaring.

Survival Of The Fittest

Only the strong survived the migration westward, and the same might be said of traditional media.

Charles Coutier, Executive Chairman of Mediaedge CIA, a leading global media planning and buying company, relates that, "The dynamics of marketing have changed. Empowered Consumers are continually re-defining the media landscape. Now, the challenge for brands is to find ways to participate in media rather than simply impose themselves on it."

The "mavericks" tend to find newer and more innovative media opportunities, which siphon away advertising dollars at a rapid rate. Marginal Media are endangered.

The latest network television upfront season has been tagged as the "last upfront" season, due to the rise of alternative, Internet media. A number of major advertisers like J&J, Coca Cola, and Verizon have loudly and publicly elected to sit out the upfront buys. In fact, the last upfront season was off only 5% and all of this is likely to be recouped in later, scatter buys. However, the big Six-Shooter advertisers have effectively harnessed the threat of digital media as a cost containment strategy and negotiating tool, just as they have with the emergence new media over the years in the never-ending struggle between buyers and sellers.

We should keep in mind the reality, rather than the perception, of the negotiating aspects of public relations surrounding the impact of digital media. Recently, the reduction in network TV upfront sales has been impacted equally as much by the leveling of the pharmaceutical companies support for Direct-to-Consumer advertising.

Virtually all of the "buzz" and trade press focuses on the Net and the damage it has wrecked on traditional media. However, the impact of the diversion of traditional media dollars to Hispanic media is often overlooked because of the newness and coolness of the new digital world. We at the New England Consulting Group are often accused of confusing people with the facts. Hispanic media has been growing at double-digit rates and outpacing the dollar growth of traditional media. Hispanic media investments exceed $4.2 billion and are projected to grow, with 80% of advertisers planning to increase their investment to this key segment as an alternative to traditional network... or non-traditional ecommunication.

Railroad Business?

The "sucking sound" of dollars leaving traditional media companies for digital media is forcing a serious re-definition of their business model. It is the age-old question, "Are railroads in the railroad business or are they in the transportation business?" The late Ted Levitt would be fascinated at how relevant his 1960's treatise of business definition is today.

You know a media is in for a hard time when *Ad Age* launches a survey to determine if the decline in newspaper readership is terminal.

Similarly, and beginning to take on the courage of a wounded cougar, traditional media is finally beginning to operate with an "eyeball" business definition of their business space. There are truly no more pure-play newspapers, magazines, or television companies... or rather, very few that will survive. The surviving and successful traditional media forms are and will become "communication brands," executed across a multitude of channels. *Glamour* magazine is now into branding films. *Teen People* converts from a magazine to a website platform. *Maxim* is licensing in a number of categories, from hair care to bedding products.

It is encouraging and very telling when traditional media begins to act with "maverick" tendencies in utilizing innovative media themselves. Some are just too clever and new to pass up.

The classic CBS Network of *Edward R. Murrow* and *The Golden Girls* promoted its new fall lineup with "egg-vertising." Today's re-invented CBS laser-etched over thirty-five million eggs with their logo and pithy phrases. These egg-themed phrases carried reminder ads related to the new shows such *CSI's*, "Crack the Case on CBS," and *Shark's*, "Hardboiled Drama." A cereal box may have been more appropriate, but not nearly as startling.

Whether this egg-ecution actually catches on with the Consumer and generates ratings remains to be seen. What is vitally important is that the CBS Marketing Group is thinking "outside the tube" and utilizing innovative media. They, correctly, seem to be having fun with their egg-vertising and certainly are generating important "buzz."

Gold Discovered!

About the time of the California Gold Rush, gold was also discovered in New York media. The venerable, 155 year-old, *New York Times* is illustrative of the impact on and the reaction of traditional media to the changing media-marketing environment.

Here are just a few confessional snippets from the *Times'* Annual Report:

> "Moving in a new direction."

> "Building a 21st century media organization."

"Creating a research and development group that concentrates on new media."

"To stay ahead of the technological and consumer curve."

The New York Times Company is like a "duck" on the traditional media surface, gliding serenely but peddling like crazy underneath. To its credit, the *Times* has supplemented the traditional staple of newspapers, TV, and radio stations with innovations, addressing both Consumer "wants" and Marketer "needs." It owns at least four "dotcoms," delivering over a billion monthly page hits. One, About.com, has the tenth largest traffic on the Internet. And a few years ago, who would have guessed *The New York Times* would own a daily give-away paper, or publish regional travel guides, or associate itself with the plebian Super Bowl, or be an "electronic" purveyor.

"Times" is a changing!

Similarly, back in the day of the 1800s as the wagon trains snaked ever westward, a young man founded what has become the media empire, E.W. Scripps Company. For over a hundred years, the Company has demonstrated an uncanny ability to evolve and continuously re-define its business.

An early adopter and "maverick," the Scripps Company harnessed emerging technology and changing environments to move over the century from cold-type newspaper, to telegraph, to syndicated content, and new digital media. It has been a forerunner in diversification to narrowcast cable networks and, more recently, the Net. Scripps built a digital portfolio including "Shopzilla," "Uswitch," and dotcoms linked to its print and television properties.

Prairie Chicken

Fighting back, the NBC Prairie Chicken or Peacock is beginning to be more erratic and to strut its stuff.

For those of us with an age-advantaged perspective, the idea of NBC running fourth in revenues and ratings seems truly staggering. But from adversity is forged steel. The "Peacock" has launched a "maverick" attack utilizing an eclectic *NFL Sunday Night* program as the warehouse of TV time to promote its run-of-schedule programming. NBC hired away the "Mouth" and "Mind" of John Madden to carry the pigskin and Cavalry charge toward a ratings improvement.

NBC has embarked on an aggressive promotional and marketing program to build Sunday Night Football as an engine of growth. The NBC-NFL contract is itself innovative. NBC has a flexible option to select the match-up only a week in advance, in order to generate the maximum ratings impact — a "maverick" advantage.

This previously staid media company is kicking up its heels and fostering its new investment in the NFL, with grass roots advertising at subway stops, on pizza boxes, and in Wal-Mart and Circuit City's in-store television networks.

Media, specifically print, has been "eating dust" as advertisers and agencies were out front in "maverick" marketing. However, the media community has raced ahead not only to address the advertisers needs but also to market themselves.

Having invested the entire cost of constructing the country's transcontinental railroad to obtain the first official baby picture of Angelina and Brad's baby, *People* magazine embarked on an integrated market and sales program. First, *People* raised its newsstand price by 15% and increased the print run by almost half. Then, the Sales Group went to work to sell Chrysler on an exclusive multiple-page buy for its Dodge SUV within the special Jolie-Pitt baby photo section... virtually guaranteed to generate high readership.

Some may feel this is an intrusion or maybe even an invasion of commercial messaging into editorial. But the integration and weaving of the Chrysler advertising into this "must read" section makes it difficult for readers to miss the commercial message.

Teen People, a raging print success of 1.6 million in circulation at one time providing a distinctively teen-tween point of view, succumbed to the diversion of ad dollars into online advertising. Somehow, using print to reach teens seems archaic to many twenty-something media buyers.

Two recently discontinued teen magazines, *Elle Girl* and *Teen People,* remain active as websites. Establishing the Brand in broader distribution creates an excellent strategy, with a much more efficient delivery system. Time Warner's *Sports Illustrated on Campus,* another hard print magazine targeted to college students from the Time Warner stable, *Sports Illustrated on Campus,* suffered a similar fate and remains active only as an online magazine.

It remains to be seen if a "pure-play" website magazine can be sustained and attract the levels of required advertising support. Merely having a presence on the Net is somewhat like standing in the darkness of a The Great Plains night, waiting for someone to find you.

While it is easy to attribute the recent declines in traditional magazine revenue solely to online advertising, there are certainly other factors of equal importance. For example, the magazine industry's Audit Bureau of Circulations has forced a re-statement of circulations that deleted "public-based" circulations from the total paid for by advertisers. For some magazines strongly reliant on doctors offices, barbershops, and office waiting rooms, this could mean up to a ten percent loss in revenue.

School House

Bucking the trend of an early death among print vehicles targeted to the emerging generations are college newspapers. Being a "must-read" on the majority of campuses, college newspapers have been surprisingly resilient with this most tech savvy of groups. Two-thirds of college students read the hard copy version of their college newspaper "connector" even though a parallel website is always available. In a few smaller college towns, the circulation and revenues of the local college newspapers exceed that of the local "townie" newspaper.

We conducted a survey of recent college graduates and there was general concurrence about the strong appeal of hard copy college newspapers, which are more convenient when a PC is not appropriate. Digging deeper, our panels delineated the real appeal: a highly visible badge of being involved with campus life. No one knows if you are reading the college gazette online.

Group Sing-Along

Having been in the marketing and advertising business since Certs were "two mints in one... with retsin" and before an English supermarket cart maker acquired such glorious companies as J. Walter Thompson, Grey, and Ogilvy & Mather, provides one a textured perspective.

The traditional print and broadcast media have long utilized ancillary events, alongside their primary mission of the delivery of "eyeballs." For many years, these events were designed as merely entertainment and a reward for those advertisers investing their dollars... Super Bowl Week parties for the advertisers, golf outings in exotic locales, and upfront television show previews.

Morphing with the times, the various media companies have entered a phase of "event" marketing, in an effort to engage the Consumer. These events, ranging from Spring Break extravaganzas to the Z-100 radio station "Jingle Ball" concert in Madison Square Garden, add value to the base media buys. The advertisers are afforded the opportunity to interact with, talk to, and sample their wares to the crowd generated by the media organization. The media is normally very successful at leveraging its power to bring Consumers to a centralized event.

While both successful and fun for all involved, the physical site events have proven to be costly due to the many inefficiencies. Advertisers have begun to calculate their ROI on these interactive events. Their additional investment, in terms of production, staffing, and samples, make these events more difficult to rationalize.

The more innovative and "maverick" media properties have taken such events to the next level with the efficiencies and penetration of the Net. These Net-enabled events are more distant and independent of the parent media property, taking on a life and value of their own. These have become independent profit centers and a multi-media alternative in their own right. The gamut of properties include fashion shows, teen events, cause venues, and concerts. The difference is that now, with the Net, these events have become content for broadcast, Net video, and extended promotions. Advertisers appreciate the multi-media nature of these new and innovative media properties, which have proven to appeal to specific targets... and at a more efficient cost than previously the case.

Bling! Bling! Ricochets

Blinks! Not bling! Another media "maverick" leading the cavalry charge is Clear Channel Radio. To assist its stable of "maverick" advertisers, Clear Channel, who has tested the reduction of commercial time within its radio programming, now has initiated a test of "blinks." "Blinks" are essentially ultra-short, almost illegal subliminal commercials. These one to five second commercials serve as "commercial interrupters" for a simple and pre-established commercial messaging.

The intent is to be startling and just plain "new" to Consumers. Hopefully, the commercials will have the Consumer "leaning forward" to accept and catch the next blink for the Brand. And to tell your friends, "Did you hear the blink between songs on Z-100?" The blink can be a joke, website, or slogan.

Clear Channel is the largest single radio station company with twelve hundred stations across the country and often bumps up against the FCC rules of concentrated market ownership. Clear Channel has been in the forefront of offering "maverick" marketers innovative programs and integrated cross-channel media platforms, from TV to rock concerts.

An independent radio station, KFYE-FM, in the badlands of the California Valley, has given its listeners whiplash. From years as a religious format, it suddenly repositioned itself as "Porn Radio." As you can imagine the song selection revolves around any possible connection to or innuendo of sex. Its theme line is "All Sex Radio."

KFYE is even adding special erotic sound effects over the sound tracks, if the song is not sufficiently linked to sexual activities. And they are certainly creating great awareness and noise for a station of its size. There is some speculation this is just a transitional play to publicize a format change. Now that's "maverick."

The impact of the Net on traditional media is nowhere more apparent than on local television stations. Long admired and sought for their cash flow, margins, and market share dominance, local stations may now appear as endangered buzzards in the new digital world. Once vital as the primary distribution channel for the networks, local stations have been subjected to an end-run by three forces... cable, satellites, and the Net. Local stations are now responsible for less than 20% of network programming delivery.

Rather than relying on network distribution fees, local stations have been forced to adapt themselves, becoming "mavericks" and acting out of character for the industry. Sometimes, when fighting a forest fire, the most expedient action is to set a backfire yourself. Local stations are, for perhaps the first time, going "local" ... their one true point of differentiation with local news, local promotions for local advertisers, local websites and local video webcasts.

Storm Signals

While the debate rages over the current program ratings, which determine the cost of television time versus the actual commercial ratings, the Weather Channel has stormed ahead to take the lead. It guarantees certain achievement levels of audiences during the advertiser's, actual specific commercial.

This represents the nirvana advertisers have been demanding in to counter the remote skipping and TiVo avoidance of advertising. Historically, Nielsen provided the viewer ratings only for the "average" commercial viewing in television coverage. This is not perfect but is a dramatic step forward that provides substantial new angles of attack for "maverick" marketers.

This new standard metric has two organizations very nervous... the television networks and the creative agencies who develop the commercials. Both are "at risk" when the advertiser can see just how many people are actually viewing specific commercials.

Treaty Negotiations

"That will be $12 worth of beads, cloth, and knives for the Isle of Manhattan."

We have to assume that in any transaction, two negotiating parties have reached equilibrium and achieved partial satisfaction. The agreement is not difficult... it is the negotiations that are the hard part. A key strategy of any good negotiator is to have another viable option and ensure that your opponent knows your options. "Maverick" marketing has been, and will continue to be, an integral component in the negotiation of pricing for traditional media.

Many years ago, the evangelical Ted Turner, disheveled with socks falling down around his ankles, was in my office extolling the value of his emerging cable TV networks... none of which registered a half a rating point. With Clients like MasterCard, Warner-Lambert, Union Carbide, and Nissan, we had to assist them to move millions of units, which could not be achieved by reaching a very limited number of people on cable. Ted was very persuasive and did make the sale, but not for the standard rationale. Turner made a very provocative argument that we would actually "save" money for our Clients through using our cable buy as a negotiating tool with the traditional networks. We made known to the TV networks of our buy in cable, along with the costs, early in our negotiations. The strategy proved very successful. Thanks Ted! And thanks, Ted, for almost singled-handedly saving the American bison as a species.

Similarly today, a substantial reason for "maverick" media innovation is to pressure and dampen the cost of traditional media. It is very difficult for NBC or *Time* Magazine to increase their rates in the face of media innovations that are simply more fun. Every press release about a new, cool means to reach Consumers contributes to the steady drumbeat on the pricing and profitability for traditional Media, particularly network television.

Friend or Foe

Regarding the continued blurring of media, the traditional television networks harness the retailer's in-store television in promotional deals to promote their own new shows. As professionals, we are keenly interested in such "sleeping with the enemy" activities. However, in today's media-saturated world, the Consumer hardly bats an eyelash.

Both the brick-and-mortar and the "pure play" Internet retailers continue to view advertising sales on their websites as a vibrant revenue stream. In our judgment, this will continue to be very successful, unless it becomes, essentially, a newly required advertising slotting fee with little real value to the marketer.

Walmart.com, one of our Clients, Home Depot, and others are opening their websites to suppliers. In the absence of "forced play," advertising on a retailer site should be a "win-win." Reaching a self-selected, interested Consumer within a retail environment is "as good as it gets."

For the first time, Wal-Mart has appointed an agency of record, Saatchi and Saatchi, to handle its shopper and in-store communication. The overall objective is "connecting and communicating" at various points of contact between the Wal-Mart store and its shoppers. With over 120 million shoppers spending forty-five minutes within the store each week, Wal-Mart TV alone would rank in the top tiers of any media ranking.

Epic

A highly recommended online movie made for the Museum of Media entitled, *EPIC 2015,* takes an ominous view of the future and the centralization of news. The movie leads off with a basic premise.

"In the year 2014 *The New York Times* has gone offline.

The Fourth Estate's fortunes have waned.

What happened to the news and what is EPIC?"

The movie has the thought-provoking attitude of *1984* but updated to include the impact of the digital world on traditional news sources. The development of the Net is portrayed, past and future, culminating in the merger of Google and Amazon into "Googlezon" as the sole source of news.

Definitely worth a view... and a later reflection on the basic premise.

Set 'Em Up, Barkeep

Even brands built with superlative creative in television must now face the current pragmatics of budget levels relative to the cost of traditional Media. A two-digit, million dollar media expenditure is borderline, and particularly so if the Brand is targeting smaller niches or age segments. And Cable provides little relief.

On my last venture to Australia skiing Tredbo, not bad for summer skiing, and diving on the Great Barrier Reef at Cairns, I expected to find Foster's as ubiquitous as Budweisers are in the U.S. The long-running "Foster's... Australian for Beer" campaign had convinced me, as someone experienced in the marketing business, this was true. I was wrong and, in fact, it was actually difficult to find a Foster's to go with my Australian special meal of "Hop, Skip, Hump, Jump." That's Australian speak for Surf and Turf but really means a delicious medley of kangaroo, crocodile, camel and ostrich.

Despite the strength of the Foster's U.S. advertised equivalization to Australian beer, the difficulty of reaching young men, only 21 years of age of course, has been compounded as this age segment spends a greater and greater share of leisure time in non-traditional media and gaming. This greatly decreases the efficiency and reach-of-audience by traditional television.

Foster's shifted its TV-built brand into an all-Net strategy. Importantly, there exists an even more fundamental and underlying market quake. Media strategy and how to reach an audience on the consumer's terms and in their own media set now drives the Creative strategy. The "Crazy Creatives" are forewarned... the next round of advertising agency presidents may very well be Media Directors, who actually know how to reach out and touch someone.

Foster's was a "maverick" in its original TV Creative. Foster's is now a "maverick" in its media strategy. The Internet creative approach continues to be rather "cheeky" and Australian in tone. The focal point is the heavy.com website, featuring a heavy dose of movies, videos, and music. The advertising is essentially the tried-and-true promise, "win a trip to Australia and meet beautiful women." The digital twist induces the viewer to weave his way through a number of video clips to access the needed clues.

"Stealth" marketing is also in Foster's arsenal of "maverick" techniques. Foster's is foisting a viral advertising campaign of Consumer-generated, homemade videos. These are, in fact, professionally produced commercials under the banner of "crack open a friendly."

This approach seems very current and on-trend. However, the practicalities remain. Can you sustain adequate movement of a plucky, imported beer based on advertising on a single website and airing a few "homemade" commercials? Can you get your fair share against the Anheuser-Busch stable of brands and the Coors "Cold Express?"

House Advantage

Whether you are gambling in Dodge City in the mid 1800's or at the Bellagio in Las Vegas today, the "House" always has the advantage. The dealer has "hole" cards and rules to which you are not privy. The same advantage is true in Search advertising. I asked a few questions to Udayan Bose, Founder and Chief Executive Officer of NetElixir, a highly successful company that manages Search on a 24/7 real time basis.

Tom: "Could you briefly describe the unknown factors in the bidding process for a Search term? It is really much more complex than meets the eye, right?"

Udayan: "Google, and now Yahoo and MSN, have made the bidding system into a black box by adding a quality score dimension to the ranking process. The quality score can be interpreted simply as Google's way of gauging the relevance of an ad copy per the keyword typed. The factors that influence Quality score are listed by Google at: http://adwords.google.com/support/bin/answer. py?hl=en&answer=10215."

Tom: "Given the dominance of Google, we might as well address them directly. When I have bid and purchased a Search word or term, what have I really bought?"

Udayan: "It is not really clear, even to the experts. You have purchased a Search phrase and your text ad listing appears on the phrase. How much you bid (per click cost you are willing to pay to Google when someone clicks on the ad listing) determines your position on the Search page along with the Quality Score. As an example, you decide to buy the keyword "hotel" by bidding $0.01 (minimum bid). Your ad probably appears on the 20th page of Google search result for the keyword "hotel." After a week you decide to increase the bid to $3 per click. The ad moves from page 20 to page 2 or maybe bottom of page 1. Then it starts getting clicks and impressions and the Google Quality Score for your listing starts increasing. And so does your position, from 12th to 7th to 5th etc. However, one must remember that just because I am able to see your ad listing on the 5th position in Princeton, NJ, does not mean that someone else would able to see it in 5th position in Connecticut or LA or Chicago. This is because Google has many huge server farms delivering the ads."

Tom: "Udayan, there was a recent report that the investment in paid Search was continuing to increase at an even faster rate, while the growth rate of the other methodologies such as banner advertising was slowing. To what would you attribute this trend?"

Udayan: "Paid Search has been growing at an explosive pace because of four key reasons. One, it is measurable from "click to purchase" and the entire engagement cycle can be mapped. Second, it is non-intrusive. Searchers click on your ad because they want to with what we call "searcher intent". Third, paid Search is inexpensive and controllable. A mom and pop store can compete with the Fortune 500! Also, it does not cost much to run a basic campaign. Lastly, the average lifetime value of a customer acquired through paid search is about 70% higher than a customer acquired through other channels or sources. All this is based on our in-house research on five search advertiser campaigns on Google, Yahoo and MSN for the period March 2006 to March 2008."

Tom: "How do you see the Search advertising methodologies evolving or changing over the next five years?"

Udayan: "I would be very bullish. Local Search is becoming more and more important and combination ads, rather than pure text ads (video + text), are gaining importance with potential enhancement to the user experience. Mobile ads have become more important with greater global acceptance and usage of Search as part of life. Social networking should be connected with Search advertising. Say you are searching for an Italian restaurant in New

Delhi, the search results you get are listed based on your connections' recommendations along with pure relevance on which Google bases its listings. Global search advertising would grow at an explosive pace. At NetElixir, we firmly believe that managing a global search advertising account requires a deep understanding of local cultures, solid delivery systems, and an ability to adapt. The think global and act local dictum has become a necessity."

Google's dominance in Search is at an inflection point which cannot... absolutely should not... be permitted to last. The major advertisers from Unilever to McDonald's to Glaxo simply cannot tolerate the current dominance of Google in Search. Draw your six-gun!

What if a TV network had an 80% share and dictated such onerous terms that would favor the "House"? What if a single newspaper or magazine controlled 80% of the advertising space? If a single radio organization owned 80% of the airwaves, the alphabet soup of the ANA to the 4As would find a means to change that situation. Google was recently named by the Harris study as the most reputable Company in the U.S., among Consumers. Marketers may not be so trusting and should not be sanguine regarding Google's dominance.

It is only a matter of time before the advertising powers that be decide to "feed" alternative Search options beyond Google, even at the expense of efficiency. As the major advertisers harnessed the emergence of cable to bludgeon the TV networks and the Net to corral traditional media, they must now lasso and tame Google. Yahoo!

New-Fangled

The latest new-fangled Net mutation that will compound the complexity is the growth of "ad networks." Multiple Web sites join in a confederation to sell each other's ad space and share content. The intent is to amalgamate an audience of sufficient size to interest advertisers. It is increasingly difficult for digital media buyers to ascertain what they are actually getting for their Clients. It is as if your television buy on NBC was some unknown combination of ad time on CBS, ABC, Fox and a few cable networks. The Client is losing control of placement and selectivity within these ad networks.

Social Networking

Square Dance

"And swing your partner." Social networking sites offer "mavericks" yet another highly leverageable opportunity to connect with its Consumers.

Led by MySpace, social networking has exploded on to the Internet stage with a big bang. While much of the Net focuses on isolated and lonely individuals plugging into global galactic resources of data, social networking is exactly what it says: connecting one-on-one, in a social environment. It is a rather private conversation, in which some commercial "mavericks" are beginning to intrude.

Almost two billion dollars is being invested into the infancy of social networking advertising. That is more than the ad revenues for *The New York Times*. The enormous popularity of social networks indicates that we have a high proportion of the population who are digitally empowered for at least a portion of their social life.

Small Town

The West was settled by the seeding of small towns and local communities by the flotsam and dropouts from the wagon trains.

Numerous "maverick" marketers are following in the footsteps of very successful, pioneering social networks like MySpace, YouTube, and the college-based Facebook in creating electronic communities. Companies are setting up their own "social" networks that have varying degrees of transparency. Some sponsorships are obfuscated, others tend to be blatantly branded and focused on the brand experience.

Branded social networks were born out of the recognition that your Customer base has now been empowered to "talk" online about your product or service, whether you like it or not. The Brand can choose to remain out of the fray and ignore the discussion. Or, the marketer can guide and foster communication among its Customers. The latter, at least, positions the Brand as an active participant in the discussion, gaining knowledge of the topics. A branded social network helps create the "buzz."

Live World, a leading creator of branded social networks, reports the results of a comprehensive survey it has conducted. Its research indicates that participants in an online branded community return to the site nine times more often and for much longer periods of time than non-participants. Live World, of course, sells its services but makes a very good case for enhancing Brand loyalty. We would only add that the people utilizing your branded site are likely to have been your most ardent brand loyalists, well before joining your social networks. Subject matter and content certainly govern the success and tonality of any branded network.

Social networking finally reached the necessary scale to be of value to marketers. Of particular appeal to advertisers is that all "members" have fully opted-in, openly displaying such sensitive information as their commitment.

Pitched Battle

	Year Founded	Registered Users	Target Market	Exclusivity	Of Note
facebook*	2004	70 Million	All Ages	Not Exclusive	Microsoft purchased 1.6% stake for $250MM
myspace.com.* a place for friends	2003	110 Million	All Ages	Not Exclusive	$900MM deal to provide a Google search facility and advertising
friendster*	2001	36 Million	All Ages (Emphasis on Teens)	Not Exclusive	Currently valued at one-twentieth its valuation in 2003
Linked in	2005	19 Million	Business Professionals	Exclusive	Growing at an annual rate of 485%
Xuqacom	2005	1 Million	Young Adults/ College Students	Not Exclusive	Markets sex, gambling, music, richness
aSmallWorld	2004	300M	Rich and Famous	Most Exclusive	Patrolled for users who are not connected enough to the Social Register

We find "facebook.com" very interesting, not only for its rapid success but also for the unique characteristics and targeting. Despite its enormous membership base, it has retained a sense of selectivity whereby acceptance of messaging and making one's profile is only available to a friend's friend. It is the Net's version of "seven degrees of separation."

Facebook is a privately owned, online social networking service for high school and college communities with a strong emphasis on the college market... and expanding outward, via alum as they join the real world beyond.

It allows, or rather, encourages members to post personal information, share pictures, send private messages, join social groups, and advertises internally to the network. Facebook fosters exclusivity by offering memberships only to individuals with valid e-mail addresses (i.e. name@college.edu). For example, a general name @ aol.com address is not accepted.

The site provides extensive privacy options for profile viewing, but students show little or no "inhibition" and a great deal of "exhibition."

It is extremely visual and the format virtually insists that the member post pictures, hence the name, of themselves, their dog, room, and friends. Herein lie its unique appeal and the edginess. The students have literally "dropped their pants" and posted every parent's nightmare of exuberance reserved for college.

With the speed of the Net, it took only one day to achieve a thousand members at Harvard, on Facebook's initial launch. That base has exploded to now include over seven million users in 2,500 colleges, 22,000 high schools, and a thousand businesses. The site ranks #1 on the Net in terms of "photos posted" and the average number of page-views per visit, and thirteenth on "unique visitors."

Facebook is so pervasive on college campuses that not to be on Facebook would definitely be anti-social behavior. Some colleges attempted to fight Facebook but quickly retreated. Now they settle for warning students of the downside of posting certain photos, subjects, and personal data. The sheriffs... namely parents, potential employers, and religious organizations... have also discovered and gained access.

Facebook is the Wild West, fresh and percolating, making it a favorable environment for "maverick" advertisers. The micro-targeting capabilities are excellent, both demographically and attitudinally. A smaller marketer can have banner ads targeted to single females who like Billy Joel and really enjoy the *American Pie*, in one or all twenty colleges in Boston .

Microsoft has become Facebook's only provider of banner and sponsored links advertising. Facebook has grown into an adult media company, and this mutually advantageous arrangement with Microsoft benefits both organizations.

Even the Chinese Premier Wen Jiabao now has an official profile on Facebook, with thousands of "supporters." Viewed positively, this is one more indication of its ubiquity. However, the "cool factor" of this social network for a teen is substantially diminished. Interviewing on a number of colleges for talent, I am finding that more and more students are avoiding or being very restrictive in their use of Facebook.

> *"I confess, I have not read for myself the application essays for the members of the class... but I do feel I know you, for I have been browsing on Facebook.com."*

> – Lawrence H. Summers, President Harvard University

 ## Consumer-Generated Content

Homespun

Homespun calico on the Western drive was a luxury possible, only after safety and the basic necessities of life were achieved.

The same is true for Consumer-Generated Content (CGC), which is emerging as a true embodiment of the Net and its power-shifting capabilities. CGC is an amalgamation of online content, of a wide variety which originates with the Consumer and encompasses commercial messaging. Consumer-Generated Content can be pro or con... fact or opinion... video or text... smart or dumb... dull or entertaining.

CGC is a new, fancy, Net-enhanced acronym for an ancient marketing technique of involving the Consumer in developing the Brand's advertising. The digital world has simply made CGC easier to execute in smaller and more rapid events.

The stampeding popularity of Consumer Generated Content is illustrated by "Current TV." This is an entire television network based on viewer-produced commercials, authorized or expropriated. The Consumer-producer of the commercial content collects substantial fees, depending on the ultimate use beyond "Current TV."

Considerable debate exists in the industry as well entrenched camps on whether CGC must arise spontaneously from the Consumer or can be initiated, fostered and incentivized by the Marketer. We would certainly take the latter position that a Marketer can induce CGC. This technique is growing rapidly as Marketers leverage the Consumer's willingness to be proactively included and engaged in the commercial messaging process.

Peter Blackshaw, Chief Executive Officer at Nielsen's Buzzmetrics Company and headquartered a rifle shot from his alma mater, Procter & Gamble, invented the Consumer-Generated Content terminology. Peter's prolific stream of ideas is matched only by his typing skills to generate a cataract of information and insight on the Net. He relates "I keep hearing folks from the agency world talk about the new rules or the importance of 'listening.' And yet the solutions or next step rarely hit the strike zone. This is not listening. Kevin Roberts, CEO, of Saatchi is spot-on about 'Love Mark,' but to what extent is that core philosophy of encouraging and embracing 'feedback' actively practiced within Saatchi brands? At the end of the day, the fastest growing media is that which Consumers create and shape themselves. It's TiVo resistant and presents long lasting sources of influence. It cannot be controlled, but it can be influenced."

Much of the current marketing efforts behind CGC are targeted on engaging the Consumer in preparing video advertising for a specific brand or company. This blends the Consumer's desire to express their ideas and share or "publish" them in social mediums. This video emphasis has only recently been enabled by new technologies and informational capacity.

Marketers embracing CGC online and in traditional media, include a "who's who" of marketers, such as MasterCard, Frito Lay, Absolut, Procter & Gamble, Jet Blue, Sony, and even Yahoo!. A number of CGC commercials will be appearing on the Super Bowl, courtesy of marketers such as Chevrolet, Doritos, and Alka-Seltzer, who built an entire promotional campaign around the CGC process. Consumers appear not only willing, but also anxious to invest considerable time and energy to participate. Even the NFL, who guards their Brand experience like a Mama Grizzly, has joined the "amateur parade" with similar Consumer originated advertising. At $2.7 million for a 30-second commercial, the extra promotional value must be substantial.

But how different is the exotic and hip technique called CGC and Doritos' Super Bowl program from the "Ozzie and Harriet" era of recipe or slogan contests? Or the Pillsbury "Bake-Off?" Not much in fact — other than the digital ease and efficiency in execution, versus hard copy contests "back in the day." I will concede that the target audience has shifted from the "30s something" CEO of the nuclear family household to a much younger profile.

Shake Hands, Partner

One of Pete Blackshaw's most "maverick" concepts regarding "CRM" is that it should begin with a Company's Consumer Affairs Group. Organizationally, it should belong to the Marketing organization and not Corporate. The premise, with which I concur, is that the digital world has so altered and blurred the communication patterns between Marketer and Consumer, that the Company has no choice but to speak with a single voice. Consumer Affair Groups tend to have the objective of restricting the "conversation" ... while Marketers desire to promote it.

There is a good reason the phrase, "I've been AOL'd" became a generic lament for proactively bad Consumer service. Did you ever try to cancel your AOL account? You'll need more luck than a card counter in a short deck in a Western saloon.

It is imperative that CRM does not offset or overwhelm CGC in a battle of the acronyms. In today's digital world with near perfect knowledge of a company, an alignment of "prospecting" for new customers and addressing the needs of existing customers is absolutely imperative. Marketers want to engage and create a Consumer dialogue. In most companies, Consumer Service Groups need to be re-oriented to comprehend that they are on "offense," not "defense" in the marketing of the total company.

Bowie Knife

Empowerment is a two-edged Bowie knife. Whether spontaneously originated by the Consumer or induced by the "maverick" marketer, the reins of CGC clearly rest in the hands of the Consumer. Any marketer, particularly one providing the digital content and inviting manipulation, may be horrified by the chain of events he has initiated. Video advertising is highly susceptible to unflattering parody, proactive negativity, and pornographic reproduction of your Brand's cherished "Kodak Moment." That messaging lives on in electronic infamy. Even mild derision or ridicule can erode a Brand's equity when ricocheted repeatedly around the world in cyberspace.

Consumer-Generated Content is a risky endeavor and even a "maverick" must weigh the potential positives and negatives in a thorough and objective risk-assessment. Furthermore, CGC is best utilized as a consistent, long-term strategy and not as an "in-and-out" tactic.

A recent major industry conference, titled "Turning Advertising Into Content," drew a crowd of almost 500 marketing executives, including strategists from companies such as Coca-Cola and AOL.

This calls into question if a technique such as CGC becomes so prevalent that it has a major conference with numerous Fortune 500 companies. Is it still a "maverick" application. Ditto, the "Mobile Marketing Forum."

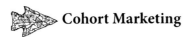 ## Cohort Marketing

Tombstone

As much as all of us wish our brands, and ourselves to be young and hip, marketers ignoring or refusing to address the older, 50+ years of age group do so at their marketing peril. This age cohort is larger than the adult population of the UK, Canada, Ireland, and New Zealand combined.

And the 50+ group is larger and growing more rapidly than all minority groups — Hispanics, African-Americans, and Asians... combined!

It is much too early to write this age cohort's tombstone and, if it were time, the epithet or bumper sticker on their Lexus might be: Spending the Kids' Inheritance. This market enjoys significant discretionary income per capita, and that does not even peak until after 65 years of age... net worth... not until post-75 years. This segment controls two-thirds of the country's entire wealth. Worth a marketing campaign? Many Marketers and advertisers continue to resist embracing the facts — and the 50+ age segment. They just do not want to be associated with the older population... even though 43% of all adult shoppers are sitting around this campfire.

And how do you execute "maverick" marketing to this age group? Just ask Anheuser-Busch who developed and tested Michelob Ultra, their low carbohydrate, pre-Atkins beer for the 50+ crowd. The initial marketing was at the grass roots level, through retirement communities and veteran groups.

And ask the Viagra team at Pfizer!

Boom! Boom!

No, that's not gunfire or a posse chasing bank robbers. That is the thud of so-called "baby boomers" turning 60, at the rate of four million a year. We have strong reservations and warnings regarding Baby Boomer marketing mentality, as this so-called homogeneous segment is actually multiple segments.

Utilize the "Baby Boomer" term only at your businesses' peril. It is a myth!

Originally, "Baby Boomer" implied no homogeneity. But this term has been corrupted into a homogenous monolith with a common purpose and behavior. "Boomers" as a group have not been proven to be any more or less similar than any other 18 years-of-birth cohort, in terms of attitudes or transactional behavior.

"Boomer" is not a "generation." It is multiple generations, since some "Boomers" are children of other "Boomers." Approximately ten percent of "Baby Boomers" are foreign born, with a concentration at the lower end of the age spectrum. Fully 23% are minorities, with greater affinity towards their ethnic group than an age cohort.

Amalgamating such a body of population under a common or homogeneous banner tends to hide the actual differences at the polar extremes. Comprising 37% of all adults, the group identified as "Baby Boomers," tends to look demographically like the general population. This is just one of the marketing dangers of "believing" in the "Baby Boomer" myth.

Whether marketing food products or pharmaceuticals or financial services, we have found the "presence of children" in the household to be the dominant demographic. This factor changes how, when, and where a household invests its resources... financially and time-wise. If considered as a distinct segment, 44% of "Baby Boomers" have children in their households. They are more likely to be preoccupied with school and soccer than reminiscing about "Woodstock."

The next time your own organization, your advertising agency, or your consultant presents a plan or position paper under a "Baby Boomer" banner, stop the meeting and shoot out the lights! And send them back for a more correct and appropriate assessment.

With Facebook and MySpace on one end of the online social network phenomenon, now emerging are the "Eons" of social networks for the older population. This social network has been started by Jeff Taylor, founder of Monster.com and, therefore, we must give it instant credibility. Eons.com is developing as less "photos" and "get a date" and more toward "information" and "connecting."

After all, *AARP the Magazine* and its various editions remains the largest circulation magazine in the world. For "maverick" marketers willing to go against the tide of youth and the embrace the older age segments, there is a growing list of media alternatives. These new availabilities have advantages of being discretely targeted so there is little or no image contamination of the younger segments. Furthermore, these alternatives are both affordable and relatively efficient.

Hold The Stagecoach

Cadillac is a brand that has struggled for many years with the age dilemma. Despite its recent success (30%+ increase) in a reversal of downward fortunes, the Brand is making some "maverick" moves.

Cadillac, even with successful market achievements under its belt, remains schizophrenic regarding the target audience and specifically the desired age demographic. Is Cadillac the urban bling-bling Escalade? Or is the Brand better represented by the luxury STS sedan? How far can the multi-hued crest logo stretch?

At least from the outside, it appears that Cadillac's efforts to address the bipolar age nature of its purchasers are highly over-reliant on traditional media. It is much more difficult to have differing creative on various sub-brands within non-discrete general media. With over $225 million in advertising investments in measured media, Cadillac has the luxury of affording specific and segregated media for sub-branded models, which vary so greatly in appeal.

Experiencing a few flat sales periods, the Brand's Marketing Group suddenly dumped the established advertising agency, Leo Burnett, for a "new" agency appropriately called Modernista. The drive is to appeal to younger and potentially more female purchasers. Along with a totally divergent advertising strategy, Cadillac is shifting its target from urban bling-bling to suburban doctors and housewives.

As with so many marketers, Cadillac's issue will be how to "youthenize," while holding its core of older purchasers. The good news is that the Net is a superlative tool for segmented delivery of commercial messaging to discrete demographics, which Cadillac is utilizing to a substantial degree.

A "maverick" marketer would have a field day with the Escalade! The most Escalades I have even seen in one location was at a combined auto show and hip-hop convention in Miami's South Beach. The reflections from both the jewelry and the "rims" made sunglasses a necessity. Give that brand to a "maverick!"

The age of Consumers is one of the most challenging dilemmas faced by marketers today. As we indicated in our years of working with many sophisticated marketers on age cohorts, it is vital to "youthenize" or keeps your brand current with the emerging consumer base. Many of today's most powerful brands are beginning to become "dated." "Aged" is ok... "dated" is not.

Even the older age segments do not want to be associated with a "dated" or behind-the-times brand. Being current and state-of-the-art is a valuable attribute in all age cohorts.

Our population and purchasing power are becoming bi-polar creating a number of marketing issues. Brands must, pragmatically, deal with widely varying age cohorts.

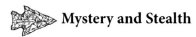 Mystery and Stealth

3:10 to Yuma

In this 1957 classic starring a young Glenn Ford, everyone on the "3:10" train had a troubling secret.

The Internet, as conceived and invented by Al Gore, was intended as a populist and open exchange of information and connectivity. There was to be free flow of trusted communication in a relative pure environment.

The Net, not unlike the original, pristine Western settlements, quickly became corrupted by "wine, women, and song." It is a dance-hall woman with exposed secrets and stealthy, disguised characters operating freely.

The major search engines have come to understand that, in contrast to traditional media, their future lies in selling "behavior" rather than "eyeballs." In order to accomplish this task, search engines Yahoo!, MSN, AOL, etc. are accumulating massive information and data regarding specific individuals and their Net behavior... pages read, ads clicked, subjects searched. Mass algorithms encircle any Net activity and corral targets for its contextual commercial messaging. With a "digital LoJack," a comprehensive landscape of a person's most private behavior can be traced, documented, and sold. Such behavioral data is a "boomtown" for "maverick" marketers, enabling them to accurately target specific niches, even where and when the commercial messaging to that specific individual is most timely. The last bastion of video and audio are falling to new technologies enabling mining and searches, and the linkage of advertising to key words or "text tags."

Go to aolpsycho.com for a sobering reveal.

Some "mavericks" are pushing the outer frontiers, learning more about individual Consumers and their informational and transactional behavior. What a smart Marketer can learn about each of us is alarming. Shortly after buying my first house, I was horrified to receive a direct mail solicitation that included my exact mortgage amount. Little did I know this information was public record, as are many data points — including your auto license number in some states.

The Net empowers the Consumer with information regarding a marketer, but this is a two-way flow of information. The Net provides the richest possible gold mine for "mavericks," with their intent to know the "Market of One" … the individual Consumer. When the Consumer enters any "door" or portal to the Net, someone is watching, recording, and amalgamating "what," "when," and "where." Behavioral targeting enables the marketer to skip the implied or indirect influences of demographics and to concentrate on actual, direct behavior.

Interestingly, some of the thrill and appeal of the Net, particularly among the younger age segments, involves the "transparency of danger." Avoiding the intrusion of Marketers has become just another video game of competing with the electronic Jesse James' of the Internet world.

Spyware and the much more mercenary, adware, are growing at an exponential rate, essentially exposing the Net users' most intimate patterns. Behavioral targeting companies are highly active and increasingly sophisticated. These technology "tricks" are <u>not</u> considered by us to represent "mavericks," but rather outlaws.

Dynamite

In today's digital world, sometimes the "maverick" can be a Consumer or even a mysterious and unknown party who puts your Brand "in play," without your knowledge of agreement. One of the most successful examples has been the independent viral video, "Diet Coke and Mentos Experiments," put together by Stephen Voltz and Fritz Grobe. This video, akin to a high school chemistry prank, presents an irreverent and hilarious series of explosions timed to pulsating music, resulting from Mentos being dropped into Diet Coke.

Neither Mentos nor the Coke folks would have dared to have so much fun with their brands... or garnered over five million hits and valuable network television exposure. The Mentos Brand seemed to see the humor, enjoyed the fortuitous exposure, and even ended up sponsoring the video on some sites. Originally, Coca-Cola was less than thrilled and their reaction was chilly. Under the onslaught of such contemporary and favorable "maverick" exposure, the Coke Company had to relax and enjoy the explosion of their product synchronized to music. It was dynamite!

Masked Man

Well, of course, the "masked" man was a bank robber in the Wild West. But... who on the Net?

The Net offers a degree of anonymity as one of its most powerful characteristics. Consumers like the anonymous nature, and Marketers have exploited it fully. Marketers utilize their own Net-savvy employees or engage outside freelancers to further cloak their activities. In fairness, except for the very youngest, the Consumer recognizes that not all is as it appears as the Net.

Of all MySpace profiles, a million or more are believed to be fictitious and created by marketers for Brands... their iconic characters... spokesperson... cars... or even movie and television programs... actors and characters. Many assume these are Consumer-generated rather than sponsored by marketers. Virtually all of the open social networks... YouTube to Facebook... are infiltrated by "stealth" marketing activities and much of it is camouflaged commercial messaging. Some of these "false fronts" are very expensive paid space while, others manage to avoid the site's sheriff.

Some Marketers slip video content onto the Net, without indicating their role in what is essentially a camouflaged viral campaign. If "accepted" by the viewers as Consumer-Generated Content, the messaging has more power and traction as genuine word-of-mouth.

Assigning designated but unbranded bloggers, not identified, to initiate reviews and a catalytic opinion offers another popular but often not discussed technique. The Net, unlike regulated traditional television, has no requirement to specifically identify the advertiser or sponsor of the commercial messaging. No "promotional consideration given" notification is required on the Net. This is a digital Wild West, and no one wears a "White" or "Black" hat as identification... and the trust in the validity of Net information is being greatly eroded.

Some Marketers will even have internal people or outside contracted personnel click on competitive websites to bump them out of the search engine's triage, after the threshold number of paid clicks. This leaves the competitor with useless clicks and a second or third tier positioning. Like the pedophile being successfully rounded up by a forty-nine year old sheriff, posing as a vulnerable and nubile teen girl, the Net masks much of the intent and identity of many participants. Being a "maverick" is one thing... being a "masked man" is another that we do not recommend.

Town Marshall

Ultimately, the outlaws always get caught, or at least in Western movies. Sometimes the outlaw is the one you might least expect... the Town Marshall. Some newspapers and magazines have canned or disciplined writers and editors for anonymously creating misleading blog content. In one case, the editor praised himself on the magazine's blog under an assumed name.

And then there is the case of an employee, of the prestigious Edelman public relations firm, who got caught. A paid employee created a fake blog, "Wal-Marting Across America," for their Client and deliberately concealed any connection. What makes this so egregious is Edelman's role in writing the "Word of Mouth Marketing Association" code of ethics, which specifically prohibits such subterfuge.

Marshall Dillon, bring the handcuffs.

Sony suffered a considerable backlash from young gamers when it anonymously launched an outdoor campaign. Street artists were commissioned to create graffiti-type ads of kids using their game devices. That it was, in fact, advertising and who sponsored the message was masked. A couple of bloggers, who happened to be "street artists" themselves, led the attack. Sony trespassed into the graffiti culture as an unidentified interloper and had to retreat.

 Viral

Wildfire

Making their way westward, the settlers discovered a new phenomenon... wildfire spontaneously sweeping across The Great

Plains. It was both dangerous and productive, as the destruction elicited new growth and fresh grass.

Today's "maverick" marketers have found viral marketing to have many of the same characteristics as a wild fire: free, powerful, dangerous, productive, and, once initiated, has a personality of its own. Every event is unique and is subject to an incredible number of variables governing its direction, mass, and speed. Handle with considerable care.

Viral marketing has particular appeal to "mavericks" willing to balance the marketing risks versus the rewards. As it is often classified as "zero cost" marketing, the viral technique can be very affordable for a Company or brand facing budget issues. We strongly caution Viral is not free, as the out-of-pocket management time and production costs are often much more than initially planned.

The basic concept is to induce or encourage Consumers to do the heavy lifting by passing along commercial messaging or hidden branding. With the Net, the traditional idea of "telling a friend" has exploded into "telling everyone." In an age where information is social and professional currency, people tend to desire to "share" to a much greater extent than in the past. This enables viral marketing and massive communication easy and pleasurable activities.

Viral marketing generally has two time dimensions, immediate and long-term. The latter are viral marketing plans more oriented toward customer relationship-building and on-going research or feedback. Viral-based research is particularly valuable in providing product and marketing input and garnering objective observations in an unstructured format from interested Consumers, who have not only opted-in but made a series of proactive contributions.

The dialogue among Consumers, when they are communicating to each other... and not you, as the Marketer, is raw but likely to be more informative. Many successful marketers now talk less... and listen more. Consumers have become attuned to proactively sharing their input.

Shorter-term viral campaigns tend to focus more on promotional, one-hit videos or spoof commercials that ricochet around the world through word-of-mouth. These campaigns most often revolve around video, music, or a specific promotion. The flames of Consumer referral roar around the Net and are quickly extinguished only by the wet blanket of familiarity. When you receive a "forward" you have already sent out, the half-life of the viral campaign is over.

How do "mavericks" fan the flames of viral campaigns? It takes some degree of financial investment and a great deal of dedicated effort. Some of the employed "sparks" include:

- Planting information in related blogs

- Providing product samples to active bloggers

- Playback of changes made in response to encourage Consumer input

- Incentive or "reward" systems for proactive participation

- Quoting and providing links to supportive bloggers

- Publicizing the results of prior such programs

- Providing a "tell-a-friend" mechanism on sites

- Providing provocative videos or spoof-like commercials

- Multiple re-broadcasting of "forwarded" material to expand the reach

- Offering online games, sweepstakes, contests, or surveys

- Appeals based on charities or popular causes

The marketer may initiate the "infection." In other cases, the wildfire is sparked by natural causes. Whoever is the "infector," the spread is related to the "contagion" of the content.

Marketers are often able to spark a conflagration across the prairie, but particularly on the Net and once ignited, control has passed. The masses may bend, distort, spoof, or even make obscure your commercial message. Even a "maverick" marketer cannot be faint-of-heart in handling viral marketing. Control of the message is just not possible. We recommend that a viral plan be considered a political campaign. Not being proactive in Viral is letting your opponent accuse you of multiple aggressions and weaknesses without responding or counteracting the message. Sooner or later, the marketer is likely to find his Brand in viral space, whether he initiated it or not.

"Thank The Lord for Unanswered Prayers"

Remember, there is a Country Western song with that philosophical title.

In some instances, Consumers seize control of a Brand's advertising creative and its media delivery. "Head On," a topical headache remedy with directions to "Apply directly to the forehead," had equally weird advertising. The advertising so intrigued the Consumer that "special" and customized versions with disapproved claims began ricocheting around the Net in ever expanding circles. Even after the regulators put a kibosh on the errant claims, the "Head On has a major advertising campaign operating outside the purview of the regulatory sheriffs. The media reach of the Consumer-adapted advertising is probably greater than the impressions generated for the actual campaign in traditional media.

Did the company make it happen? No. Did the company promote this new viral advertising? No. But, it did benefit.

"Maverick" marketers looking for a "zero cost" marketing technique will be disappointed in a viral campaign. Viral costs money and management time. If beyond your organization's capability, you may need dedicated Net experts, PR agencies, or promotional agencies. Even with new streaming video technologies that have reduced the costs, video clips remain a substantial expense. Furthermore, the Consumer's expectation of production values for viral catalysts has increased exponentially and measurement technologies also require significant investment.

Furthermore, viral marketing has suffered from its own "buzz." The press, trade, and consumer tend to cover a few outrageous successful campaigns, which has created the general impression that viral marketing is cheap, easy, and almost always a homerun. We do not learn about the high percentage of failures that just never catch fire. In fact, a recent survey among 2,000+ marketers indicates that those who have never conducted a viral campaign have a much higher opinion of the technique than those who have substantial experience with the technique. Prior experience in viral marketing tends to dampen sales expectation as well as the anticipated probability of success.

Differing viral techniques generally experience varying results... varying from eureka to dismal. Video clips, tell-a-friend offers, and independent micro sites tended to perform best. The strengths of various techniques have evolved over time, as viral participants have grown more sophisticated.

Even "mavericks" need to be wary. Viral marketing campaigns tend to fall into two classifications, a raging success or "cow chips." Even a major investment in viral activities will not ensure results. It helps to be both lucky and provocative.

Fire Starter

A few very brave "mavericks" are willing to take the risk of starting the fire, or planting "infector" advertising on sites known to appeal to video aficionados such as Google Video, YouTube, and iFilm. The result is a viral spreading of the Brand's commercial concept through Consumer-produced commercials, varying in production value from pseudo professional to a seventh grade homework assignment. Those commercial concepts, normally very strong creative which has a definitive concept or executional technique, lend themselves to such viral parody... MasterCard's "Priceless," Burger King's very weird "King," and Vonage.

In many cases, these Consumer-generated versions take the creative concept and drive it to the extreme. Most such Consumer-generated commercials are more humorous than the original.

However, the adage that "copying is the sincerest form of flattery" is not necessarily true of "infector" commercials. While the original commercial may be copied, the commercial messaging is not and may have been hijacked. A successful commercial in traditional media or a planted "infector" commercial may be twisted, tortured, and burned at the stake.

The resulting commercial careening around the Net may be an advertiser's worst nightmare, which exposes or opposes the Brand to a strong anti-message. Think about a version of the anti-tobacco campaign, "True," applied to your own brand. In the reality of the digital world, the advertiser has little or no control over Consumer-generated messaging. That is its power, pro or con.

We recommend that advertisers accept and virtually ignore any resulting negative commercials. Attempting to counteract or take legal action would only fan the flames and drive the wildfire faster.

 **Personalization**

Brokeback Mountain

Every marketer wants to make the marketing equation a closer one-to-one relationship. The current rage is the personal pronoun or marketers seek to create a close relationship that acknowledges the Consumer's personalized interests and importantly, their control of the situation. Everyone is attempting to get up close and very personal with the Consumer.

Witness just a few trademarked, personalized concepts examples:

- Youtube.com
- myspace.com
- My Life
- myTunes
- My World
- youchoose.com
- my eon

- mynews.com
- mylocalbrands.com
- my 9TV
- My Fries
- My Fave
- myflavia.com
- KYOUR Radio

The "I" and "me" strategy employed in "maverick" marketing techniques is carried over in other categories, ranging from computers to condiments and confections. More food marketers like Heinz are turning toward "my packages" with a high degree of targeting and offering very specific personalized messages on Heinz Ketchup bottles. Hershey and Mars sell customized chocolates and Jones Soda makes available personalized photos on their soda labels, all at a premium cost. A Consumer involved enough to pay a substantial premium for a mundane product is definitely engaged with the Brand.

The Net has been a great enabling agent in offering personalized and branded products. Every Consumer or small business owner can now be an art director and printer. Various websites provide a myriad of personalized options for calendars, note pads, candies, stamps, business cards, and every other conceivable printed item.

Country Western Song

There is a Country Western song that represents this point of view. But then again, there's a Country Western song to represent virtually every emotion... "Born to be an American," "She Got the Gold Mine and I Got the Shaft," "Friends in Low Places," and my favorite, "The Redneck Yacht Club."

Toby Keith emotes the feelings of today's online generation with these lyrics, written by songster Bobby Braddock:

"I wanna talk about me, I wanna talk about I,

Wanna talk about number 1 oh my, me, my,

What I think, What I like, What I know, What I want, What I see."

Despite a realistic and growing fear of identity theft, Consumer interest in personalized Net use is very high. To some degree, the Consumer remains open to sharing specific information in exchange for personalized solicitations. According to Choice Stream, which is a consultant in Net personalization techniques, 79% of Consumers indicate a willingness to view personalized content based on prior searches.

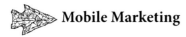 ## Mobile Marketing

Tom Hayes

Battle On The Open Plains

The "horse" greatly expanded the range of conflict rendered the battle of the open Plains into one of fluidity. Whether the conflicts involved the wagon train versus the various Indian tribes, or the settlers versus the outlaws, mobility was the key distinguishing element.

And so, Mobile marketing is a continuing battle out on The Great Plains of Marketing. On one hand, ESPN waves the white flag of surrender. Yet the four battle-hardened veterans, AT&T, Verizon, T-Mobile, and Sprint, compete for leadership in a business plan of continuing upgrades to carry on the battle across all fronts.

The spoils of this war are the hearts and pocketbooks of Generation X and Y, tech-savvy generations of 18–35 year olds who are connected to their phones twenty-four hours, seven days a week. This segment of Consumers is fleeing newspapers and zapping past commercials on

TV at a faster rate than other age cohorts. The one critical apparatus that this target cannot escape from, however, is their cell phone.

About 30% of the two hundred million U.S. cell phone subscribers text message at least once a month. At least 55% of the highly sought 13–24 year olds regularly send text messages. Already 10% of cell phone users, or about 22 million people in the U.S. are regularly browsing the wireless web. My own teenager regards voice mail and even email as somewhat archaic, relative to texting.

Although the mobile channel continues to be heavily endorsed by both providers and "maverick" marketers, how far the growth will continue is still speculation. The battle continues to rage on, but questions remains if all these bells and whistles and added costs will end up as just the ante to stay in the mobile marketing poker game. Only an estimated 1% of subscribers choose service based on entertainment options. Out of those, only about a fourth are estimated as eligible to switch due to the fortress of prior service contracts.

Exactly how much does it cost to continue the "standard" of technology? Just to stay competitive, T-Mobile, fourth place nationally, had to vow $2.7 billion to upgrade their system for advanced services and $4.2 billion for licenses to operate their network. ESPN forfeited the $150 million in start-up capital from Disney when they left the race. Billions and billions of dollars will be spent by companies just to stay alive and competitive. However, the "size" of the prize in governing a massive new medium that is clearly "on trend" is staggering in its appeal.

A Consumer can subscribe to Sprint's Power View Internet packages for $15-25 a month in addition to their normal Talk plans. Sprint also has created its own sports and entertainment network, where monthly prices can easily range from $50-100. Nokia, who spends about $1 billion a year in developing high-end multimedia devices, charges \$450–700 for their "multimedia computer" phones that have music, Internet, and email capabilities. Adding on the costs of novel ringers and music downloads, the Consumer costs can quickly become astronomical and dampen the appeal.

To subsidize and reduce the potential costs, mobile marketing and its advertising revenue stream will have to grow rapidly. However, it must maintain relevance to the Consumer with interactive means of engagement. In a recent survey, over 40% of mobile customers said they would be open to mobile advertising if it was relevant, asked for, or offered coupons.

The delivery of coupons via mobile phones is on the cusp of a major expansion. This promotion offer is very appealing to both Consumers and Marketers. The delivery of mobile coupons is perfected and can be highly targeted by individuals, locations, and connected to specific retail locations. Browsing coupon sites, text messaging, or placing the coupon on the individual phone are ways to execute coupons.

However, actual redemption of mobile-delivered coupons is currently much more problematic. Mass retail locations are not yet adept at accepting these digital format coupons. Providing coupon code numbers is not widely accepted and few front-end scanners can read the UPC codes directly from the phone. This will change quickly.

Similar to the Internet, mobile consumers are dynamically searching for attention-grabbing content, as long as it is configured in shorter time bursts and formatted for the smaller screen.

While mobile Consumers may be tech-savvy and on-the-go, there's still is no motivation more appealing than "something for nothing." No matter what generation, everyone loves something for free. The marketing agency Traffix offered ad-supported ring tones and movie clips for free as a way to reach Consumers. Progressive Insurance sponsored free video games including their ads to mobile users.

Even on the low end, Dunkin' Donuts found success by texting 99-cent latte coupons, which increased store traffic by more than twenty percent.

Though most mobile campaigns are simple, short, and experimental in nature, a few brands are looking to make a pre-emptive strike with multi-channel campaigns focused exclusively on mobile medium. P&G, emotionally connecting to people in situations where fresh breath is a must, unleashed a mobile "maverick" campaign for Crest called "Irresistibility IQ." The campaign focused around a mobile quiz with questions for the modern day Casanova. Accessing the quiz was as easy as texting the word "IQ" or "Extreme" to the number 27378, or C-R-E-S-T. Word of the campaign was spread throughout the hottest dating scenes using of bar napkins, bathroom signs, and the Internet. Youthful icons, "Celebrity Matchmaker" Samantha Daniels, and MTV's Nick Cannon were hired as spokespersons. Even a sweepstakes giving out CDs and iPods was created to help generate buzz. As a finishing touch, a quiz Internet site was also created with a link to promote participants' "Irresistible" scores on their MySpace pages.

Elle magazine's campaign took much more of an integrated approach between mobile phones and the Internet. Estimating that 99% of *Elle's* target audience was likely to have a cell phone, the magazine saw mobile marketing as a clear channel to get readers engaged in the advertised products. Consumers were able to create a virtual "wish list" by using camera phones to take pictures of ads, which could later be viewed in collection at *Elle's* website. The products listed were accompanied by information on how and where to buy each product. As an added bonus, each reader also was entered into a sweepstakes for a gift certificate to purchase the entire wish list.

But if camera phones, text messaging, and mobile videos are the quick-drawn six-shooters of today, what are the weapons of tomorrow? What does the future hold for the mobile "maverick?" NeoMedia, a newcomer to the battlefront, has been hedging bets with new technologies. Their software, PaperClick, enables Internet accessible cell phones to read bar codes on products and magazines, directing them immediately to a weblink for coupons.

Consumers can instantly retrieve information or special pricing on products. A second technology allows a Consumer's mobile camera phone to read a newspaper, poster, or magazine ad. The cell phone then instantly connects to any relevant information from that image. For instance, a picture of a movie poster would produce related movie times, tickets, theme songs, and reviews and allow you to purchase tickets. A picture of a team logo would produce game results, stats, and paraphernalia. As pictures become connected with information, relevance to the consumer will drastically increase.

Over 500 million new wireless connections are made globally. Some analysts predict that mobile television advertising alone could be worth more than $25 billion by 2010. If technology continues its current trend to conglomerate technological gadgets into all-in-one devices, the spoils, as well as the number of opponents, will continue to increase faster than a buffalo stampede.

 Spin

Custard's Last Stand

Can a "maverick" break ranks with the parent company, which owns it outright... even making the parent a foil and public fool? The answer is "yes" when the corporate strategy at Unilever is to give "free reins" to its wholly-own "maverick" subsidiary, Ben & Jerry's Ice Cream.

Unilever has developed a new technology, which would actually make the consumption of ice cream healthier by providing satiation at lower levels of butterfat and calories. This technology is based on a protein from an Artic pout which was then cloned and, unfortunately, making it technically genetically modified... even though from a natural source. The resulting ingredient is an ice-structuring protein widely used in the U.S.

Ben & Jerry's took very public umbrage to its parent company's action of genetic modification and distanced itself from Unilever. Ben & Jerry's is consistent in its "maverick" strategy and positioning. It gains credibility with the fringe "Organic Consumer Association," as well as the more mainstream consumers.

Similarly, the Company has launched a Fair Trade vanilla ice cream and wears such causes on its sleeve — or rather carton. While certainly altruistic, capitalizing on the fair trade foods trend, up 40% last year, is another smart marketing and "maverick" move, which aligns with its social responsibility strategy.

As a result of this positioning, Ben & Jerry's also set themselves up for the six-shooters from various other advocacy groups. Under the threat of the Humane Society and a looming boycott, the Company capitulated and dropped Michael Foods, the country's largest processor of commercial eggs, as its supplier. The animal welfare groups were ready to pull the trigger on a campaign called "Scoop of Lies... Ben & Jerry's and Factory Farm Cruelty." Ben & Jerry's had little choice. The Humane Society indicated it would only be satisfied with a free-range egg supplier which, as Ben & Jerry's discovered, can be a supply chain nightmare at higher costs. It will take the company four years to make the conversion.

Renegade

Another Ben & Jerry cause, "Lick Global Warming," advocates fighting industries and governments on the reduction of carbon emissions. Whoa Nellie! Did anyone at the Company consider that cows, producing milk for Jerry Garcia and other Ben & Jerry's flavors, are among the World's largest sources of methane and global warming? As one marketing philosopher remarked, "It is not our job to confuse Consumers with facts."

In another bold attempt to recapture a successful "maverick" positioning, the global conglomerate and among the largest CPG companies in the World, Unilever is bringing back the "hippies of old" ... Ben Cohen and Jerry Greenfield. The "Ben & Jerry Combo," who personally collected $300+ million, are structured as if they have some modicum of control. All of this is to launch a variety of ice cream called "America's Pie," with a local market campaign to be coordinated with the website. The theme transcends social activism into the political and military arena, and calls for a reduction of U.S. nuclear military armament.

This is the case of a company may be just trying too hard to be a "maverick" marketer. It strains the bounds of believability. In the good ole' days, a company might be able to pull off such a ruse. In today's sophisticated and transparent digital world, actions such as Ben & Jerry, Inc. may not be believable or relevant. After all, in an environment of rampant obesity in adults and children, a protest against nuclear protection by high cholesterol, high caloric brand is likely to be viewed with considerable skepticism. Furthermore, only the U.S. government is targeted, not the other global nuclear powers including the U.K., France, Russia, Iran, India, Pakistan, Israel, etc. Nuclear armament versus butterfat.

Nevertheless, Unilever is smartly exhibiting a solid and productive strategy of supporting this "maverick" Division. It is a good business to have a mix of "mustangs" and trained, traditional business sectors.

Buffalo Chips Into Firewood?

As the wagon trains snaked across the Plains and over the Great Divide, one of the primary duties of the "westward ho" kids was to collect dried buffalo droppings for the campfire. I kid you not.

Similarly, in some cases, "maverick" marketing can be harnessed proactively by going on the offense, turning "trash" to "cash."

Let's examine take the parallel and recent example of two retailers, Whole Foods and Safeway. Both were selling live lobsters from tanks at retail locations. This is a very difficult business proposition. Demand fluctuates widely, there are maintenance issues, consumer resist buying lobster in mass environments, and the list goes on. Selling live lobster in a retail environment is just not profitable by any analysis.

The Safeway chain, with ten times the retail stores as Whole Foods, quickly retreated from a bad business proposition and the live lobster tanks were replaced with a much more profitable offering and utilization of valuable floor space.

In contrast, Whole Foods smartly takes the offense and wraps itself in a flag of "ethical sourcing." It utilized a study from a European Animal Authority, think PETA, which indicates that lobsters may have feelings and can learn. This is despite the great weight of evidence from biologists and oceanographers, from numerous prestigious marine science universities, who point out that lobster have no brains and only an insect-crude nervous system. Positioning and appealing to one's customer base trumps science... everyday.

Therefore, not because selling live lobster is not profitable, but because it is unethical, Whole Foods launches a major public relations campaign to communicate why it is ceasing to sell live lobster as being consistent with its vision and set of values. Put some points on the board for Whole Foods! It is smart, "maverick" thinking to reinforce your position and uniqueness while eliminating an unprofitable business.

Now, Whole Foods proudly announces it will sell only frozen lobster. Ironically, some crustacean experts point out that frozen lobster often is sourced from the larger, migratory lobster breeders rather than the smaller, geographic lobsters, which typically occupy the fresh tanks. In expressing its "animal compassion," Whole Foods' action may very well have the unintended impact of harming the entire species. In fact in Maine, it is illegal to sell these "breeders," which are most likely to be sold, frozen, by Whole Foods.

Perception versus reality.

A "maverick" turns buffalo chips into firewood.

Campfire Coffee

Trail Markers

Select and choose from the stable of the numerous "maverick" techniques and approaches available in a manner that complements more traditional marketing.

Do not permit your organization to be stampeded by the great deal of hype of digital advertising, as if you are being frozen out. Many of the Net pundits have a vested interest in building a bigger campfire.

Leverage the substantial distress of traditional Media to your advantage in obtaining both cost efficiencies and added value.

Insist that your organization allocate a substantial portion of your paid search budget to non-Google sources in order to slow their dangerous dominance.

Be wary in the use of viral or Consumer-Generated Content, fully weighing the risk-reward equation in a thorough assessment. Playing with a rattlesnake has its thrills.

Insist that your marketers, agencies, advisors, and accountants expunge the term "Boomers" from their vocabulary.

Make sure your organization understands and abides by the dictum that "maverick" programs have no less legal, moral, and ethical standards than more traditional marketing.

Turn "trash" to "cash" and disasters into successes with "maverick" marketing.

CHAPTER FIVE

RODEO

As Willie Nelson might relate, "There's no reason to stage a rodeo, unless you keep score." Unfortunately, with the complexity of the ever-expanding Wild West of New Marketing and the average consumer seeing over 5,000 advertisements or commercial messages each day, the means of measurement have become increasingly numerous and complex. The traditional forms of measurement become less defining and relevant to the Media alternatives available. Metrics are becoming a blend of statistics and just pure old-fashioned judgment on the marketing frontier.

Launching a new product or service can no longer be concentrated on merely one front or medium. A new product attack must be formulated to address resistance and barriers in the Consumer's mind. With each new media or channel innovation, it may very well take an innovative way to measure the impact of any marketing campaign. Can the world be simplified into a few numbers on transactional data? Doubtful! After all, "close" only counts with horseshoes.

The Culpepper Cattle Company

While many debates exist on whether traditional forms of marketing metrics are dead like the buffalo, or just wounded, I would argue that these metrics must continue to function as a solid foundation for decision-making. Traditional methods and metrics have stood the test of time and should not be discarded, but instead supplemented, specialized, and adapted to the new mediums or channels of communication and new channels of distribution.

It has been long recognized by Marketers that one of their greatest friends and worst enemies can be the Media or vehicles of commercial messaging. From sunrise to sunset, the Media, traditional and non-traditional, are developing new abilities and avenues to shape a consumer's mind with an exponential number of formats from MySpace.com to movies... barf bags to blogs. A new innovative media opportunity can start a wild stampede that overwhelms mere logic and marketing metrics.

Of course, one cannot forget the Marketing 101 favorite of Return on Investment (ROI). In more traditional words, "the bottom-line." While other factors will always weigh-in, "How much did I spend versus how much did I make," will always be the dominant issue. We have to ask ourselves, on any project, did it contribute to the future of my company? There have been "mavericks" questioning this as well.

"Marketing is a $450 billion industry, and we are making decisions with less data and discipline than we apply to $100,000 decisions in other aspects of our business," relates none other than the CMO of Procter & Gamble.

There will be continued utilization and needed refinement of the traditional metrics. Ad Awareness, Cannibalization, Lifetime Value, Sales Force Effectiveness, Out-of-Stock, Residual Elasticity, Deal Depth, and the list goes on. The question remains, how do we relate the acronym-dominated, campfire soup of ACV, BDI, CAGR, DPP, GMROII, etc., to the Net and other "maverick" marketing activities?

While these are just a few of the numerous traditional measurement methods, let's take a moment to point them out. We still consider them vital when looking at metrics of successful "maverick" marketing. However always heading towards new frontiers of measurement, you cannot set up camp just around these factors alone. They are just one ingredient in the recipe of a successful "maverick."

Clickety Clop ... Clickety Click

The one metric for technology that has become the golden standard for the Internet is the infamous Click. The Click on the Internet appears to be the undeniable marketing action, which forms the basis of diversion dollars out of traditional media of so many marketing dollars. The metrics of traditional media continue to revolve around "indirect" or interim steps including exposure, awareness, and attitude and imply, but do not necessarily measure action.

We regard the Net as "digital direct mail" and the Click is the measure of the Consumer's opening of the electronic envelope. But again, a click is not necessarily the purchase or even a serious consideration. The Click is merely a measure of action taken by the Consumer to enter the Marketer's world of messaging. It is there that the marketer must engage and persuade the Consumer, with targeting and creativity, to take the many steps toward purchase or engagement.

The Net, its "mouse" mentality, and the use of the Click as its currency tends to minimize what must be accomplished after the electronic envelope has been opened. Yes... a Net Click does place the marketer in the enviable position of being much closer in the sequence to a purchase, physically or a mental buy-in, than a television or magazine ad exposure. But a Click merely opens the door of communication. A Click is not an end in itself. Involving and convincing the "clicker" remains a difficult task, despite an initial step in your direction.

Clicking is the equivalent of flipping television channels to see what may be of interest. "Mouse marketing" places too much emphasis on the Click rather than purchase behavior.

Like the circulation or ratings of traditional media, the Click is not nearly the direct measure many Net marketers believe it to be. The prevailing attitude that traditional media is not measurable while the Net is fully measurable. This attitude may be a reflection of anger and frustration at traditional media.

The Internet Advertising Bureau defines an "ad impression" of a display ad actually reaching the Consumer's browser. Yes...but! The fact is an ad or commercial is registered on the Consumer's screen... TV, computer, or phone... does not translate into viewing or communicating. All media suffers from the gap between communication, attitudes, and actual purchase action.

A search Click is not concrete but rather comes in numerous flavors and values:

- "Nuisance" Clicks – "just get it off my screen"

- "Informational" Clicks – "just searching for more information"

- "Paid" Clicks – fraudulent Clicks to inflate traffic

- "Competitor" Clicks – Clicks by competitors to clear out the position

- "Half" Clicks – Clicks that do not fully load to the browser

- "Random" Clicks – "oops ... didn't mean to do that"

- "International" Clicks – from Tibet, Thailand, and Timbuktu

Some experts, based on intense tech research, place the "bad" Clicks in a wide range of 20 to 60% of total Clicks.

So, while the Click can remain a standard practice for advertisements for simplicity, a "maverick" must look beyond the constant "clickety clop ... clickety click" over the horizon.

DILBERT: © Scott Adams/Dist. by United Feature Syndicate, Inc.

I turned again to Udayan Bose, CEO of NetElixer, for additional insight and perspective on metrics.

Tom: "There has been considerable industry angst about the development of more definitive Net advertising metrics. What should the metrics be for Search advertising?"

Udayan: "This has drawn significant discussions already. Here is my take: Metrics are created within a context, a frame of reference. If Search advertising is considered to be a customer acquisition tool, the metric would be conversion rates (clicks to sales/conversions) and cost per conversion. If it is tied to profitability and bottom-line, then the most relevant metric would be ROAS (Return on Ad Spend) and if the goal is visibility the metric can be impressions and clicks."

Tom: "Who do you think is a real successful 'maverick' in Search advertising and what techniques have they utilized?"

Udayan: "This is a tough one! Successful Search advertising management needs discipline in planning and execution. There is honestly no magic involved. It is just setting strategy, drawing up a plan for execution, using the relevant technology for scale and optimization, and tireless 24x7x365 execution. Deep pocket advertisers like eBay buy millions of keywords, but do a great job in testing and constantly refreshing the campaign. Smart use of Search advertising involves seamlessly connecting the different channels and building the users' excitement and involvement at each level. Search advertising can serve as a useful connector."

Wild West Show

Product placement in movies, theaters, and video games is continuing to explode. Just how difficult is it to measure such non-advertising advertising exposure? ITVx, the leader in measuring product placement, now uses over 60 different factors to examine how effective an actor holding a can of soda in a sitcom is worth. Let's examine the process as explained by their Chief Executive Officer, Frank Zazza, to get a better understanding:

> "Fully 60 different factors are harnessed to compute a standard metric called the Q-ratio, a decimal fraction or a multiple of a 30-second commercial. The value of the product placement is the multiple of the Q-factor times the average cost of a commercial. A Q-ratio of 0.5 would mean that the quality of the product placement was worth half that of a commercial for the same product."

The Q-factor, however, must be weighed against the average cost of a commercial and the number of viewers. For example, if you were to have a show on Fox and the same show on the Weather Channel, then the quality of the placement (i.e., the Q-ratio) would not change, because the product placement did not change. Only the number of viewers and the cost of the commercial would differ, changing the overall value of the product placement.

While the process is proprietary, here are just a few of the sixty data points shared with us:

- Type of placement used
- Market spending
- Brand Resonance
- Engagement
- Background
- Effectiveness
- Psychographics of the audience
- Involvement
- Foreground

- When it occurred
- Demographics
- Integration
- Number of other products seen
- Where it occurred
- Audience Size
- Context, Clarity
- Government Regulations
- Hands-on

If it takes 60 factors to measure an actor driving a car in a movie, how many does it take if the entire show is about the car? For instance, Meow Mix ran a show called the *Meow Mix House*, a parody on the reality series *Big Brother* and *The Real World*. Does it have to be an eccentric process to predict success? Well, um... kind of. Let's take a look at the classic measurements to see why.

A normal pilot for a TV show is difficult enough to manage, test, and predict results. Hollywood has tried for years and is still working on perfecting the techniques, with millions of dollars invested. Sometimes the shows are a success... other times they are a flop. For commercials, testing a spot can be equally difficult to execute from the testing of the animatics to the testing of the finished spots. In this product placement scenario, there is a complex hybrid of the two.

First, you must test for the show's actual likeability to the viewer, as well as the puns, jokes, and humor portrayed. Next, you must test the message delivered by the show itself. Did the show reach the target audience? Was the Brand impacted by the show and vice versa? Did the show push the Brand name too much? Because of the unique approach to obfuscate the sponsoring Brand, this last question is perhaps the most important. If consumers see this approach as just another long commercial, then the execution was flawed. In essence, copy testing for this product placement lies somewhere in between that for your average sitcom and standard commercial testing. This will require the use of a hybrid of both methods to determine success.

Pre-testing the "Meow Mix Hour" will involve getting together several diverse groups and measuring their pre-disposition to the Brand, similar to the testing of an average commercial. However, metrics will also need to be included, as to their preference of characters, shows, and average TV viewing habits. You almost need to breakdown the lifestyle of the individual to completely understand his overall disposition... a nearly impossible task.

Even with a little tweaking, a few exceptions, and some intellectual creativity, these classic methods still provide only the foundation of metrics for "maverick" marketing, as executed in product placement.

Piebald

The piebald horse was a favorite horse for the cowboy due to its intensity and stamina. The patches of different colors were an evolutionary adaptation, like the zebra's stripes, to protect this prey animal.

"Maverick" marketers, too, have evolved for survival, with Marketing and Media innovation. "Mavericks" tend to blaze their own trails alone.

Investing management and marketing time in "maverick" campaigns can be quite draining to the organization, mentally, financially, and physically. But as you can count your Company's grueling hours of time that were invested into your campaign, so can you use others' time to measure the fruits of your labor. "Do Consumers take the time to engage and slow down with your campaign?" If the answer is yes and the target audience is taking the time to glance, talk, write, think, or even pass along what you communicated, then you can be reassured that your technique worked to some degree.

With the cacophony of advertisements consumers are exposed to each day, people do not take any time to care about what they are seeing. Consumers are interacting with Brand names more and more, but in turn, are caring less and less. We challenge you to even ask yourself when the last time was that you took extra effort to pay specific attention to an advertisement. Unfortunately, a Consumer has only twenty-four hours in a day, and as Marketers, we are always going to be fighting for the same limited and valuable commodity of their time. All marketers are competing for S.O.E. or "Share of Eyeball."

Measuring Consumers' energy investment into your product or Brand proves to be very beneficial to "maverick" marketers. Energy investment is becoming so important now that at this year's Promotion Marketing Association's annual conference, the buzz word was "engagement." Everyone sought to learn new techniques of getting consumers intimately involved with their Brand. When counting, their president, Claire Rosenzweig, is reported to have heard the engagement word 44 times within the first two hours of the conference.

"Call it what you want – sweepstakes, contests, music download giveaways – it's all promotion marketing: the mission of getting customers to win, enter, participate, and well, engage."

– Claire Rosenzweig

People tend to remember and associate to a much greater degree with Brands and marketing concepts on which they have taken previous action. Take something as simple as a phone book ad. You may see that same ad 100 times and possibly never think about it. However, if you have called that number even once for any reason, even a wrong number, your chances of retention increase drastically.

No single pathway or trail exists on how to measure the energy an individual invests on your product in "maverick" marketing. Each method of Consumer engagement is usually unique to itself. Take the examples of Brawny and Sony Erikson. The Brawny brand search was designed as a means to reconnect with the middle-aged female. While the Brand had a strong equity, it needed a way to revitalize itself with women of this decade. Thus began a campaign to create a virtual Brawny Man on their website. Over the course of the year, fully 30,000 women logged on to create their virtual Brawny Man... as they, not the marketer, imagined and preferred him.

The success of this idea even lead Brawny to have a contest, called "Do You Know a Brawny Man?," where women could nominate a real-life person who they believed best portrayed the persona of what a Brawny Man should be. Over 4,000 women nominated their ideal man, while countless others waited for the results.

While neither direct sales nor future sales alone can be linked to either of these engagements, the energy and effort expended by these women was monumental. Each of these women took time and the energy to personalize the Brand image in their own way. Only one person could win the contest. Yet the energy commitment once invested, would tie all of them to the Brand.

Unfortunately, it is not enough to just say, "Wow, I really believe that changed the Brand image!" If you can't measure it, you can't manage it. It takes more effort and a few extra steps, beyond counting Clicks.

The Brawny campaign was undoubtedly the work of a "maverick." However, minus a few written letters, the campaign was predominantly conducted online. Being online both complicates and simplifies the matter of measurement. Online metrics have been thoroughly sliced, diced, mixed, and trampled every which way and how. Each company seems to have their own sense of the "best" metric, from "net reach" to "orders per visit." Personally, I like to keep it simple by using the factors generated by Nielsen NetRatings:

- Sessions/visit per person

- Domains visited per person

- PC time per person

- Duration of a web page viewed

- Active digital media universe

- Current digital media universe estimate

Nielsen's six simple measurements can help you infer a wealth of information, by not only determining absolutes but also standards of comparison. Using these measurements, we can even measure against the general Internet behavior of the average surfer. Yes, they will help you get a great idea of success, as long as the campaign is predominantly online. What do you do if the campaign has a large viral aspect?

Spittoon

One of the hygienic problems of the Wild West was how to keep the tobacco juice and "drool" off the saloon floor.

Sony Eriksson had an online campaign, which encompassed a unique approach and marketing strategy utilized for a new phone introduction. The campaign, properly named "Drool," asked for people to send in photos of themselves "drooling" for the phone. The campaign quickly caught on as people reveled at the opportunity to display their prepubescent behavior, with long trails of phlegm dripping from their mouths.

The contest created a wagon train of controversy. Whether the campaign was the most grotesque example of creative thought or a spark of genius, the campaign as a whole worked. On one front and perhaps their original target audience was reached with thousands of pictures from young adults drooling all over themselves, having fun doing it, and taking the energy to send it in. On the other front, the most important was the controversy about the campaign itself. Write-ups and blogs sprung up continuously, either to criticize or promote the campaign. Every time a write-up occurred, so did a prominent mention of the phone. In the end, the phone received tremendous exposure. So, the question must be begged, "Is all publicity really good publicity?" On the Net, maybe.

Telegraph

An innovative company called Marketing Sherpa believes they found a way to tell… or at least measure the effect of a viral campaign. The company, a research firm focused on various marketing techniques, has an emphasis for online campaigns. Marketing Sherpa derived the five following metric techniques as the best for determining viral marketing aspects:

- Track visitors via "cookies" to generate demographics

- Trace incoming emails and resulting site activity and interaction

- Survey and segment visitor on Brand perception and awareness of viral exposure

- Track and analyze blogs and other public forums for group chatter

- Track "unique," "total open," and Click rates (Overall site traffic is too broad)

This remains quite a great deal to monitor at once. The problem with viral campaigns is that they can spread everywhere at once, and keeping comprehensive track of them means you have to watch… a great swath of The Great Plains. Like Marketing Sherpa, a "maverick" must prioritize the arenas that have the greatest concentration and impact on your target audience. It may be quite advantageous to track the source of the viral outbreak so you can be ready for the next opportunity.

Keeps The Herd Moving

While the Internet is certainly the prevalent technology platform at the moment, "maverick" marketers need to notice the increasing number of people who are turning to mobile devices for instant on-the-go information. While the majority of short-code, SMS numbers are now premium services, there are companies emerging who are willing to provide free information to mobile users. As mobile networks advance and convergent devices become more prevalent, it is only a matter of time before this market explodes onto the marketing landscape.

Preparing for this eventual paradigm shift, there are a number of mobile marketing options. How to capitalize on them, and to know if you are getting your silver dollar's worth is another matter.

There was a huge push on behalf of several manufacturers to create a wireless technology standard that could interface devices and take the place of short data wires between devices. While several technologies came out of this effort, one of the clear winners was a wireless protocol with the catchy name of "Bluetooth." While most people had no idea what Bluetooth did or how it worked, it quickly caught on in Europe where it was integrated into cell phones and created an entirely new generation of advanced-techs, who walked around with Star-Trek headsets.

This tech advance also created an inexpensive and easy way to send data and messages from phone to phone. With capability available, it was not long before "maverick" advertisers in Europe originated mobile broadcast units walking around with their phones in their pocket delivering a message to anyone within thirty feet. This practice has taken on the rather burlesque name, "Bluejacking."

Marketing through Bluetooth messages is inexpensive and immediate, but it's fairly clunky and limited to certain geographic areas. Moreover, the target audience for the ad becomes anyone with a Bluetooth enabled phone, which is often too broad for most applications.

However, adding an outgoing message broadcast from a Coke machine that suggests the purchase of a cold Coke on a hot day, might be just the ticket. In this instance, measuring the increased number of sales would be an easy metric to determine effectiveness with a paired location test. Such retail applications make tracing the results much more conclusive.

"Mavericks" need to be prepared to pull the plug quickly on Bluejacking if you find that people are responding negatively to your ads imposed on their phone. Instead of generating a positive association to Coke being refreshing, people can quickly grow numb to your message and may even become annoyed with the constant intrusion of commercial messaging.

Mobile-originated text messages are those that come initially from a mobile phone. The "maverick" is searching to acquire a database of numbers from people who identify themselves as being in a targeted demographic or attitude. Perhaps you are looking for people who would be willing to purchase tickets to a jam-band festival. One easy way to do this would be to offer a Dave Matthews Band music download to people who send your service a text message. You now have a database complete with people who are self-identified as being interested in whatever you are selling… plus a concrete action-related metric.

A Marketer might immediately respond to whoever sends a text message with an offer to purchase concert tickets. This is called "responsive SMS" Messaging, because the response is immediate and directed to the initiator. Measuring the effectiveness of this sort of marketing is possible by adding a purchasing code or specific purchasing method along with the responsive SMS. A specific website (www.my-company.com/SMS) or phone number in the text message would be easiest to track.

Of course, in this age of inexpensive data storage, it is unlikely that you will dispose of that database any time soon and thus a "maverick" can accumulate a longitudinal list of people who are interested in jam-bands. Might you send these same people a text message next year offering to allow them to pre-purchase tickets, before you book the concert? Absolutely! This is where one must look long-term at the impact of SMS spamming and the adverse effects this could have if people start filtering their text messages the way they do their email.

At the moment, there is nothing illegal about SMS response, but abusing an "open-ended" opt-in could certainly create the sort of regulation that the telemarketers and e-mailers now face. In order to avoid controversy, one might want to have those text messengers "opt-in" to your future ads. And in this manner, you know they want to hear what you have to say... and you have not vaporized the good will and engagement created.

Church Social

Even the most grizzled cowboy might attend the local church social to meet girls and share opinions. Not much has changed.

The desire for people to espouse their opinions and spew and share their point-of-view to others has been around long before the Net. It is simply that the Internet provides people with a much larger audience than they might otherwise have if they simply resorted to writing letters to the editor of their local paper. Additionally, shy of being a celebrity or owning a paper or newsletter, it was impossible to ensure that one's efforts would actually make it to "publication." Now, everyone is a publisher.

As soon as the Net allowed people to share their thoughts with the masses, the masses decided to start "sharing back." Initially, this sort of mindless drivel took place in emails, which were sent to an entire address book with instructions to be forwarded. Then, the number of sites and their user populations exploded, as people learned that there were others who shared their interests. It has become easy to make personal websites. From there, it was only a short trail ride away from Google purchasing "Blogger," and the entire world beginning to start their very own personal online journals, better known as web logs or blogs.

The impact or value of any network, digital or analog, social or casual, is based on the number of participants and their activity and interaction level. Robert Metcalf, one of the leaders in digital networking, formulated "Metcalf's Law," which "values" a network by squaring the number of nodes or participants: $V=n^2$

That is a purely mathematical equation, based on one-to-one communication, which does not consider the vital issues of human behavior. We would assert, from working with Clients on specific projects, that the value accelerates more rapidly in the early stages the first thousand sign-ons to engage … and the levels off. At an inflection point where the individual becomes overwhelmed or lost within the Network, the "value" begins to diminish. Such was the case for AOL, Friendster, and others.

Furthermore, much more traffic in a social network increases the connector points. The "value" to a Marketer can now be overwhelming and stale to the consumer. And then there is the human "need for newness" in the digital world. My teenage son once regarded MySpace as "dad's space," whereas Facebook was his... now that social network has been corrupted by sheer size.

Social network programs provide a fair base of metrics and traceability, even back to a specific individual. Many such "maverick" activities based on social networks are often transactional in nature.

Rattlesnake

Viral marketing is like a rattlesnake in that it is well camouflaged, a highly effective hunter, and dangerously difficult to capture and measure.

Back in the day, that is pre-Net, the metrics of viral campaigns were much more ambiguous and indirect. If your advertising slogan was parodied on the *Tonight Show* or picked up in a major magazine, the indications were that you had struck a nerve of Consumer interest. If your advertising became a component of the vernacular like Bud's "Whassup" or Wendy's "Where's The Beef?" you were on the right trail to a cultural touchstone, and not a tombstone.

The concrete, measurable numbers in the digital world create a comfort zone for Marketers. After all, we can count the download or views. However, the numbers can be misleading and not as truly successful as it might initially appear.

Anheuser-Busch posting its Super Bowl commercials on several websites focuses attention on the Consumers' willingness to proactively watch commercial messaging. The Company reported a tremendous success with almost 800,000 views of their commercials. This was achieved with the support of a major public relations campaign and inherent interest in the Super Bowl advertising. However, these were "views" and not necessarily "unique viewers." One person could likely "view" these commercials many times, which inflates the "views." In contrast, the Super Bowl itself delivered 90,000,000 unique viewer of all six-company commercials. The Net and Network TV should not be regarded as competitive "cowboys and Indians," but rather as compatriots.

Like Anheuser-Busch Smirnoff Vodka faces another issue with utilization of the Net. It registered over a million views on YouTube with its "Tea Party," but only over a full years' period of time. More than half of YouTube members are not only under drinking age... but also under 18 years old. Even at that level of viewing, assuming only one view per viewer, which is patently not correct, this represents only 3% of YouTube visitors in the past month.

Many "mouse marketers" assume that any computer viewing has the undivided attention of the clicker. Just as in the traditional television media, Net viewing has many distractions. What if your commercial only receives 50,000 or 5,000 or 500 or 50 or 5 views?

Is viral marketing worth the trail ride?

Texas Hold'em

Emerging as many "mavericks"' new best friend or worst enemy, blogs provide one of the greatest metrics for marketing if you know where to look. "Maverick" marketing is especially appropriate to bloggers because of its innovation and ability to generate buzz. Due to the exploding number of blogs, however, it is very difficult to know where to draw the line for measurements and to know the quality of feedback that is being received. An endless cycle of constant checking and resources could be used to constantly monitor what people are expressing.

Several companies, such as Sprint, have found a way to potentially control measurement of public opinion without sacrificing an inordinate quantity of resources. They are now inviting the domain masters of the most popular blogs to join them in a program of marketing research. By enlisting those who constantly are in "the know" of public opinion, it generates an army of "ghost" employees, now with increased Brand loyalty and a rich source of market research.

A second option that companies have utilized is to generate a product blog site on which consumers can express their feelings. These sites are aimed at points of Company interest and give companies a chance to filter through the endless subjects that may be exposed on other sites. However, validation of this method's unbiased opinion is yet to be proven.

As the relevance of blogs has increased the depositing of false messages on blogs in order to change opinion, called Message Planting, has been increasing as well. Not only is it possible to identify opinions through blogs but you can also change the way people think, both negatively and positively. Additionally, companies are also employing professional bloggers to interact in negative blogs about their companies and lead conversations and topics away from the original author's posting. Referred to as "thread jacking," this technique can defuse a situation quite effectively.

So like a "Texas Hold'em" game full of cheats, how do you know the truth? What is public opinion, what is guided opinion, and what is planted? This mounting problem is making the already unclear world of metrics even hazier. With blogs, it may be impossible to truly tell whether you are in an honest game or someone is slipping an extra card into the deck.

In an attempt to measure the effectiveness of blogs, Stowe Boyd coined the idea of a Conversational Index:

Conversational Index = (Comments+Tradebacks)/Posts.

His form of metric equates the number of comments and tradebacks against the number of posts, and computes a relative number. Stated bluntly, to determine if a blog is active, it should have a larger number of comments and tradebacks than postings to show that viewers visit and interact. A Conversational Index of <1 is considered particularly active, while an index of 3 to 5 shows only moderate participation. Unfortunately, this quick and dirty method has its faults.

People are often quick to regurgitate unintelligible comments. Often, little or no thought is put into writing, and a majority of it is unrelated to the subject at hand. One moment, conversation could be about a new product and its reviews, and the next, it could be about a new book or movie that opened. People naturally have a tendency to divert from the original posting and pursue their own agendas.

The variety of people who post comments is not measured and can be limited to only a few loyal, yet frequent viewers. A blog's activity can be deceivingly high and still be just an aggregate or argument of comments among only very few people. Blog content is not always intended to instigate a large number of comments. Conversational Index is highly skewed toward postings that are controversial and therefore, trigger debates. Other postings, such as news blogs, are frequently checked but rarely require an explicit response.

Researchers are working to factor in these issues, but as of yet, no general standard has been accepted and the Conversational Index remains one of the better tools.

Outhouse Marketing

While there are few advertising mediums that can guarantee undivided seconds of an individual's time, there is one such a location...the outhouse.

Long held as a taboo for marketers, the urinal has recently become recognized as one of the few places where there is little competition for a person's time, and one of the very few locations where a man dare not take his eyes off the ad for the duration of his time. Rarely a call to action, the best ads tend to use offbeat humor to make the Brand more memorable.

Of course, it has been known for years that men will generally pay attention to what is in front of them at urinals. It was in the early 1920s that some bars first began posting newspaper articles or sports' scores above the urinals for men to read while they handled their business. While that practice came and went over the years with various trends, the location was the same… at eye level, straight ahead.

Gradually, newspaper ads were replaced with the ever more ubiquitous LCD displays, which could show full motion video. While this worked as an attention getter, the ads were difficult to produce and costly since they needed to be shown quickly and in rapid succession. A few "mavericks" turned to digital pictures instead of live-motion video, but flashing a picture to an inebriated cowpoke in a bar is rarely a good way to have him recall your product later.

The growing trend in outhouse marketing is toward the interactive ad. While these take on various forms, they all basically work the same in reaction to a directed urine stream.

The great thing about technology is that there is so much of it out there that can be used in so many creative ways. For instance, take the motion detector. When CMT decided that they wanted to have a guerilla campaign to advertise their *Outlaws* show, they installed devices that would detect when the urine stream crossed a beam and then start playing a recorded message that told the men to watch the show because they couldn't hit anything else.

The predecessor, of course, was low-tech devices such as waterproof stickers or branded toilet mints that could be placed in the urinal and were meant as targets. And it is along that line of thinking that the Wizmark was developed. The Wizmark is an electronic mint that sings and plays music when the drop hits the right spot. And, while it is just the first of such devices to hit the market, you can be sure that if Wizmark is successful, there will be many followers.

Perhaps though, none so as ingenious or "maverick" as the urinal campaign undertaken by the carmaker, Mini. While no stranger to unusual or outrageous ads, their urinal ad was perhaps the best example of a well-executed urinal advertising to date. Knowing that men would immediately look straight ahead when approaching a stall, Mini placed a poster above the urinal that showed a picture of a convertible Mini Cooper facing downward, with the caption, "Test your handling skills." While the double entendre was clever, what makes the ad most memorable was the miniature orange driving cones that were attached to the inside of the actual bowl so that while a guy was completing his business, he could, in theory, take some corners.

Of course, one would not expect the conservative U.S. to lead the way in WC ads, and while the rest of the world is off to a slow start, it would be wise to look overseas for the next big thing in "porcelain messaging." In Australia, they have already started to analyze the visual urination patterns of males 18-30 years old to establish where they are most likely to look first in the urinal (upper left corner in case you were wondering) and they are hard at work creating a waterproof pee-playcard that is heat activated so that one has to actually spray the message away to see what it says. The idea is that the cold flush will reset it for the next user.

The value for this ultimate "Maxim Man" advertising is difficult to monitor. The association of urinal advertising is a risky one that few if any Brands can get away with. Though this advertising technique must be approached with only the most delicate touch, you can be certain that this will be one of the few times when you have their undivided attention. "Porcelain messaging" can have a huge advantage over the common poster or billboard, but the metrics are totally non-existent.

No one ever said that "maverick" marketing had to be in good taste.

Branding Iron

The ad agency of Kapust-Allen decided to start applying temporary tattoos to the foreheads of college kids and brought a disturbing new form of advertising into our vernacular... headvertising or human branding. Now that is "maverick" thinking.

While it was slow to catch-on, the first major use of body advertising came when Toyota branded over 20 teenagers with Scion insignias on their foreheads and had them walk around Times Square, answering questions about the new line of vehicles. Of course, it doesn't stop there.

Realizing a gimmick when he saw one, a computer programmer who had survived the Internet boom of the late 1990s posted an eBay ad declaring that he would get a temporary branded tattoo on his head and wear it for 30 days. His auction reached just over $50k.

This kicked off a phenomena and, within days, eBay was flooded with "me too" auctions where upon people not only offered to wear temp tattoos, but actually get permanent tattoos displaying the name or URL of a company. While most traditional companies shied away from that sort of quasi-delinquent behavior, the infamous Golden Palace Casino did not fail to disappoint and promptly paid a woman $10k to have www.goldenpalace.com tattooed across her forehead in large black block type.

On the other end of the spectrum, quite literally, there is "Assvertising." Though not as in your face as a logo plastered across someone's forehead, assvertising typically takes the form of stickers worn on rear jean pockets or underwear that prominently display a company's logo. In the case of underwear, it is common for the person wearing the underwear to not wear any pants, or to pull their pants-down or skirt-up, thus displaying the ad to unsuspecting people. A "maverick" marketer knows that the effectiveness of the ad here will have a lot to do with the frame on which it is displayed. In this case, take extra care to match your exhibitionists to the image you want to portray. Case in point, Stephanie Lerner of New York, New York, a noted underwear model, recently sold her ass for advertising space. The company who purchased the ad stated, "It's taut, it's round, it's perfectly shaped to advertise our product." Their product? Apple pies. What could be more American or "maverick?"

Starkly contrasting that Americana image is the one of famed British streaker, Mark Roberts. At just over 40 years old, he has streaked over 380 events in the eleven years he has been crashing various gatherings in only his birthday suit. Until just recently, it was all for fun but now there's a bounty on his head. No, he's not in any danger... he's just in demand.

In his first working gig, the Golden Palace paid Roberts nearly $100,000 to streak in the Super Bowl, immediately following Janet Jackson's unleashing, and such well-known companies as BMW and Siemens are vying for a spot on his back. He has already appeared in several television commercials and if the money continues to flow, we can certainly expect more acts to follow his. For the sake of all of us though, lets hope there are more Stephanie Lerners than Mark Roberts waiting in the wings.

"Maverick" marketers want to know if such activities are worth the trail ride. With body advertising, it becomes more of a judgment call than perhaps any other form of advertising. Will it get attention? Undoubtedly. Is it the sort of attention you want? Perhaps. Can you convert that attention into a message? Maybe. Toyota made use of its walking billboards by having them answer questions. Though, in retrospect, they might have benefited more by having them pass-out booklets with Scion information printed on them.

Additionally, one of the original web hosting companies to buy a five-year head tattoo placement on eBay has added more than 500 customers in the first 6 months since hiring their human billboard and giving him a ten-second ad to recite. When considering this technique, you need to keep in mind that the effectiveness comes in being able to shock, rather than scare people. The idea should come across as unique and friendly, not something to run away from.

The advantage of body advertising is measured through the wear-in and wear-out of the advertisement's placement. If "wear-in" is defined as the frequency required before a given advertisement achieves a minimal level of effectiveness, then seeing an advertisement on someone's forehead ranks at the top with its perverse appeal. Even though the average person may do a double take to make sure they actually saw what they thought, it will not take seeing headvertising more than once to make an impact and get a point across. Similarly, with "wear-out," I am not sure that we as a society will ever consider body advertising a norm. It is a joke that is funny no matter how many times you see it.

Both the quick wear-in and longer wear-out times help these advertising methods and effective reach and frequency. If properly done in public areas, lots of people will notice… fast. Not only will they remember it, but the better the placement, the more times they will want to keep seeing. The perverse appeal is just human nature.

While a quick Google search will show no less than ten agencies willing to put marketers in touch with tattoo volunteers, the more market friendly way is to use eBay. As of this writing, one can purchase a permanent tattoo on the bicep of a 23 year-old female for the bargain basement price of $150 plus the cost of the tattoo. You don't even have to search hard. Just go to the eBay category quaintly titled "Advertising Opportunities."

Horseshoes

Well, with all those horses around, the pioneers had to do something with the old horseshoes. Throwing them seemed to be a good idea at becoming a common pastime. This game is one of the few where the metrics permit "close" to count.

And "close" might be an excellent description of how Marketers are utilizing the impressive metrics of "maverick" media against traditional media.

Procter & Gamble, currently the largest global advertiser with and the one with greatest $5 billion vested interest in advertising costs, has utilized an effective cost-containment strategy by being a "maverick" marketer. They have consistently supported new and emerging media as a challenger to traditional broad-reach media, where they continue to place the great bulk of their advertising. P&G has done so very proactively and visibly as a long-term negotiating tool.

I remember the great trepidation of the dreaded inquisition of the annual Business Plans for Procter when working on Brands as Pringles, Sure, Citrus Hill and others. One of the main grading points by P&G management was always the inclusion of a portion of the budget to the "maverick media of the year." This became a mandatory allocation to the annually designated media... cable, radio, in-store, Hispanic, and now, digital. This became a "check-off" topic on which to be grilled. The Brand Group that did not include non-traditional media had to defend its action and was "guilty" until proven innocent. The selected "media challenger" of the year was a deliberately open secret to promote and illuminate new innovative avenues of marketing.

However, the corporate intent was to test, validate, and fund innovative media as an alternative to network and spot television and national magazines. Normally, more tight-lipped than a badger, I once helped make 4,000 "Loose Lips Sink Ships" t-shirts for Procter. The Company made sure that its interest in and use of alternative media was well known in the industry, specifically including the sellers of traditional media.

Recently, a few "maverick" marketers including such as Johnson & Johnson, in a very public manner, decided to skip the upfront television buy. Stunt or negotiating strategy? Johnson & Johnson is a "maverick" also in looking to what is dismissively called the "past" success of television, while the great heard of marketers are over-preoccupied with the "future failure" of the television media. J&J is re-investing in greater amounts of advertising into family-friendly, sponsored programs where it has more positive control of the content, including how the commercial messaging relates to the content.

Large marketers are deliberately fueling "maverick" media as a negotiating strategy with traditional media and are utilizing convincing metrics to do so.

Stalking-Horse

Back on The Great Plains, both the Cowboys and the Indians used "stalking-horses," a horse trained to conceal the hunter from approaching game. The buffalo could never figure out why some horses had six legs until it was too late.

In the guerilla or sneak attack, the new player is the "alternative reality game' or ARG. This is a multi-media game, usually online, that deliberately obfuscates the line between a game and reality. A key characteristic is a refusal to acknowledge that it is a "game" until the end or well into the process. Some place the origins of this digital version back to the "Chutes and Ladders" and "Dungeons and Dragons" game craze. ARGs attract a certain breed, with both the time and inclination, to engage in such an involved process.

Historically, many of the more popular and commercial-intent ARGs have been loosely based on movies or television series. Perhaps one of the more interesting commercials was a foray into this technique by General Motors, used to promote the availability of "green," ethanol-ready cars in their franchise. It is a corporate thrust to promote ethanol and to be recognized for such. Their game, "Who is Benjamin Stove?" lasted over a four month period and was about as oblique a sales message as one can justify. The fanciful story involved a young man from Tampa, Florida, a farm in Iowa, a mysterious disappearance, an antique painting, and crop circles. The connection between corn and ethanol is modest and "Who is Benjamin Stove?" is more convoluted than the "Da Vinci Code." General Motors appears to regard this as an experiment to communicate its "green" message.

It did generate about two million page views and four hundred thousand people entering the game site at least once. Yet only one thousand made their way through to the game's end. And if we apply the standard factor of how many people are actually in the market for a new car every year, only a hundred and fifty were hot prospects.

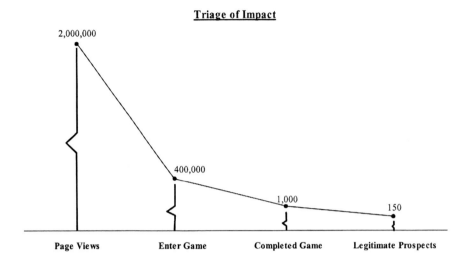

Triage of Impact

Was the investment worth the trailride? Only GM "may" know the real metrics.

Lariat

Cowboys had a personal and valued relationship with their lariat, and it often determined their success in managing the herd of cattle or just staying alive.

With product placement inside television programming becoming one of the fastest growing areas of new media, it was vital that the industry develop comparable metrics. Nielsen, extending its television viewing research, recently conducted a major longitudinal study of the interaction with traditional commercials and in-programming product placement. In general, a Brand's product placement enhanced the Brand awareness achievement of a commercial in the same program by about 20%.

Sarsaparilla

Sarsaparilla was a favorite and treasured drink of the Wild West. The Sarsaparilla name, in addition to Pennington, Wells Fargo, and others, were branded on the boxes and crates that cluttered the floor of every Western general store. This was the in-store marketing of its day.

FrontLine Marketing

A number of in-store alternatives are now available to marketers. One of the major in-store media companies, FrontLine Marketing, offers programs that are simply impossible to miss. A CMO does not have to be concerned with TiVo with this execution right at the checkout lane. FrontLine provides an opportunity for a complete trial program in the most highly trafficked areas of over 8,000 retail supermarkets, including Safeway, Kroger, and Albertsons.

The digital world is not the only medium where Marketers are desperately seeking more refined metrics. More than $17 billion, considerably more than any estimates of Net marketing, is invested in advertising and in-store marketing. Yet, there are virtually no accepted measurements of Consumer interaction and impact. As a result, both pricing and evaluation are truly the Wild West.

As a result, an in-store Metrics Consortium has been created to address this immediate need by a number of major marketers, including Coca-Cola, Kellogg's, and Miller. The first step to date has been a pilot study in several key food, drug, and mass-market chains. The objective is to ultimately have standardized metrics, by Arbitron or Nielsen, on a par with those available for traditional media.

Currently, the metrics are based on documented shopper traffic and are essentially "opportunities to view" in-store advertising and promotions. This would permit in-store activities and investments to be officially accepted by Marketers as media and with comparability to broadcasts and print. The Retailers who own the real estate may be the greatest beneficiaries.

Trail Markers

 Do not expect or insist on the same degree of accurate metrics in "maverick" marketing programs. If a program can be measured and corralled, is it a truly "maverick?"

Insist that your organization does not become overly fixated on the click metric in their "mouse marketing."

 Think of your organization as a "publisher" of media, as well as being a marketer.

 Test your organization to determine how they can successfully utilize Sony Ericksson's "maverick" "Drool" program as an analog.

 Ensure that your entire organization plays together. With the fragmentation of marketing and media, it is prevalent that the internal debate has shifted to "either/or," rather than the most productive mix.

 Spend as much time with your Agency's Media Director as you do the Creative Director... and preferably together.

 Ask your organization if they should be involved in an "outhouse marketing" program. That will certainly communicate to the group your willingness to entertain "maverick" ideas.

Chapter Six

Border Crossing

Stampede?

As previously discussed, "maverick" marketing is often short-lived and focused on an event or a narrow point in time. More often than not, it is harnessed as a "one-off."

Kemo Sabe! That raises an important issue. Can "maverick" marketing be a strategic platform, rather than a purely spontaneous and short-term action? Is it strategic? Or is it just a stampede?

The answer... in the exception... is an emphatic yes! Over the years, we have followed a number of Marketers who utilize a "maverick" approach... "the crowd is going right and I'm going left... in a highly strategic play, with vision of the long trail ahead. These are normally the founders of a totally new venture. They have tended to land on a set of "maverick" and different precepts early in the formation of their Company. And they have rigidly branded and inculcated their own particular and personal "maverick" streak into their organization.

These strong-willed founders ensure that their herd is focused and running in the same direction, together...even as the Company herd takes a different path than its competitors across The Great Plains of Marketing.

Examples of the founding "maverick" marketers include Howard Schultz (Starbucks), Sam Walton (Wal-Mart), Michael Dell (Dell), Gary Erikson (Clif Bar), Ralph Stayer (Johnsonville Sausage), Roseanne Quimby (Burt's Bees), and others. Having worked with many of these companies and "mavericks" as Clients, we have certainly observed them up close and personal.

⑪ Cowboy Bar

No, Not a Cowboy Bar, a Clif Bar.

Clif Bar, Inc. is a fascinating "maverick" and an unlikely story of a bicycle enthusiast who turned into a baking entrepreneur, out of desperation with the energy and sports bars offered at the time. Gary Erickson was clearly a "maverick" well before the first bar was even baked. He has been quite forceful to inculcate a consistent mission within the Company, to "go against the grain" and not behave like his competition or other large corporations. In fact in 2002, he turned down a $60 million buyout in order to maintain an ecologically driven, employee-friendly, "small" Company.

Clif Bar is one of the clear leaders and most successful and profitable companies in the extremely competitive arena of energy and sports bars. This "maverick" goes "where?, when?, and how?" the Krafts, Kellogg's, and Nestlés of the world have difficulty playing. Being the "maverick" is a deliberate and conscious strategy that has insulated the Brand and Clif Bar company from the actions of these much larger competitors.

With its key constituencies of "consumers, customers, and compatriots" (employees), Clif Bar is a small and highly personable Company, and one is favorably disposed to buy their products. After all, the product was first mixed in Gary's mom's kitchen sink, and named after his Dad, Clif. And not rock climbing like most people assume.

"No, this really is Clif." How's that for a corporate switchboard message (510-558-7855) which convinces one you can do business with this Company. If you have a problem or question, Clif himself will get you to the right person. Don't try that at Kellogg's. Or look for a climbing wall in the employee's "time out" room like Clif Bar's at Nestlé.

Not too long ago, I broke a tooth eating a bag of "corn nuts." I was particularly chagrined, since this specific snack Company had been my Client for over twelve very productive years. My dentist wrote a letter explaining, "I sent in the package and a sample of "nuts." I had a laboratory test done which proved the "nuts" were not chewable, at least not by humans." The behemoth Company returned my $310.85 dentist bill with a series of letters from their lawyers.

This is not the treatment one would get from Clif Bar, where being the "maverick" good guy is a strong, deliberate, and competitive advantage.

Clif Bar is unique in its corporate values and culture. The Company is "Committed to making the world a better place to live, work and eat." It sponsors hundreds of non-profit organizations and charitable events annually. Employee perks include indoor climbing walls, a complete workout facility, personal trainers, camping and skiing trips, and volunteer opportunities on Company time. Clif Bar employees commit to working 2,080 volunteer hours of community service, equal to the yearly hours of one full-time employee. Clif Luna sponsors the Luna Chix, a professional women's mountain bike team whose ambassadors run fitness workshops and raise money for breast cancer. A portion of all Luna proceeds go to the Breast Cancer Fund.

Clif prides itself on interaction with and responsiveness to consumers. They proudly include kosher certification, increased soy protein, additional antioxidants, and improved texture and flavors, as direct result of consumer input. Strategically, Clif Bar leads in the category's best practices, nimbly responding to Consumer trends with innovative flavors and products... promoting its brands through event sponsorship and public relations... and building strong brand loyalty. As a result of being an energy bar pioneer and maintaining that philosophy, Clif Bar has an extremely loyal following. Clif Bar's strong societal values and committed support of causes translates into exceptional Brand equity for its target Consumers and sales and margins respect in the Trade.

While holding on to its core and humble beginnings of sports, specialty and natural outlets, the relative growth and size of Food and Drug outlets has greatly altered Clif Bar's distribution channel to the Consumer. The All Commodity Volume distribution is 75%+ in Food, Drug, and Natural Channels.

Despite the dramatic change in "where" the consumer sees and buys Clif Bar products, there is absolutely no evidence that the Brand has lost any of its powerful cachet.

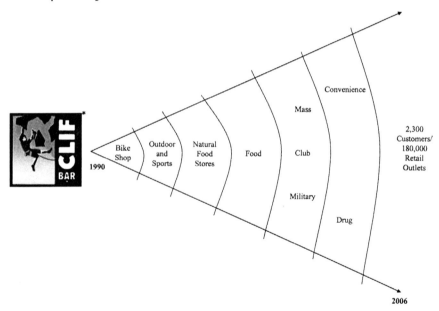

Outdoorsman

The Consumer is quite comfortable carrying out of their local supermarket the Clif Bar image of a rock climber or extreme sports enthusiast. As in so many cases, the difference between perception and reality has a dramatic impact.

Clif Bar Users

Image and Perception	Reality
– Young	– 25-54 years of age
– Struggling	– $75,000+ income
– College students	– Graduate degree
– Unemployed	– Professional/managerial
– Rural	– "A" countries
– Extreme sports	– Walking

While a few users of Clif Bar and Luna participate in the more extreme sports, more than half just walk for their exercise. The users of Clif and Luna are relatively much more mainstream than would be anticipated from the Brand's core positioning. Less than 6% have ever been rock climbing or ridden a mountain bike.

True to its "maverick" nature, Clif Bar continues to refuse to do business with Wal-Mart... more on a philosophical belief. This is certainly not a business decision most marketers would make. Alas, one "maverick" clashes with "another."

Clif Bar was one of the first Marketers to understand that while advertising can build a Brand, so can the deliberate act of NOT advertising. With virtually no advertising, the only exception being very small, niche magazines, there was sufficient funding for local grass-root interaction with Consumers... where the advertised Brands cannot or are not willing to play.

⑪   Two Dollar Cash Money ... In Advance

Perhaps no Brand represents the Western brothels and their ruffled bodice fashion more authentically than this "maverick" marketer, Victoria's Secret. Beginning in the early 1980s, this fledging retail chain single-handedly redefined America's conception of lingerie.. The original San Franciscan lingerie store was designed with an inviting, male-friendly atmosphere, similar to that of a Victorian boudoir. At the time of acquisition by Limited Brands, the Company consisted of three San Francisco stores and a miniscule mail order catalog.

This "maverick" emerged when women's lingerie and undergarments were found only in two locations... in the back of the sixth floor at Lord & Taylor or in an adult bookstore. Roy Raymond, founder of Victoria's Secret, once said of a trip to a department store lingerie department, "I left empty-handed, wondering how a shy guy could buy a slip for his wife without feeling like a sexual deviant." Raymond had the epiphany that this was a major opportunity. He envisioned the public flocking to a store that made shopping for lingerie much more transparent... pun intended. Victoria's Secret discovered and exploited this wide gap between attitude and location. They successfully borrowed the best of the stuffy department store, where men would be horrified to shop, and the more exotic locales where they would not admit to shopping.

While the stores maintain a level of tastefulness designed not to offend the mainstream consumer, Victoria's Secret has also retained a certain level of sexual energy, particularly through special displays and attention grabbing windows. Victoria's Secret has positioned itself as an affordable and slightly naughty luxury, promoting a self-indulgence experience much like Starbucks. Originally positioned more as a 'gift-for-her,'" the Brand has successfully morphed into something women also buy for themselves, driving tremendous success in recent years. The ubiquitous stores are both sexy enough and respectable enough to welcome both men and women, increasingly of all ages, looking for "that special something." The romantic ambiance of the typical Victoria's Secret store, an environment specifically designed to make women feel both sexy and comfortable, is arguably just as important a selling point as the lingerie itself. For both men and women, shopping at Victoria's Secret is a complete change of pace from going to a mass merchant to buy a three-pack of cotton briefs.

Beyond the original foray out of the back room, Victoria's Secret has continued to behave like a true "maverick" marketer. Going against the grain of political correctness, it publishes a truly sexy catalog. It was a smashing marketing success which has blazed the trail for publications like Abercrombie & Fitch's racy "magalog." The Company touts Victoria's Secret as a total "lifestyle for someone who likes and wants to look and to feel sexy." The company's "maverick" strategy has brought lingerie to the average consumer by retaining more than just a bit of the naughtiness.

Aggressive "maverick" marketing has made Victoria's Secret the best-known lingerie brand and garnered greater attention to lingerie, practically creating an industry that previously did not exist. Victoria's Secret has positioned itself as a very aspirational brand. Sexy supermodels, top photographers, and bold sexy advertising allowed Victoria's Secret to penetrate the mass-market and to become an icon of pop culture. The supermodels are celebrities, featured in leading magazines and depicted in numerous tabloids, which furthers the aspirational sense of the Brand.

The Victoria's Secret fashion show, now broadcasted on CBS, has fueled much of Victoria's Secret's meteoric climb to success. The fashion show quickly became an exciting and over-the-top event, with the supermodels parading in some of the sexiest lingerie on the planet. But all that changed one February day when Victoria's Secret decided to broadcast the show on the Internet. To promote Valentine's Day spending and reach into the subconscious of men across the world as the ultimate present to get for one's significant other, Victoria's Secret would revolutionize the fashion world.

During the 1999 Super Bowl, the Company ran a commercial and a sneak preview for the Show, alerting viewers, many of them young to middle aged men, and directing them to VictoriasSecret.com. As a marketing "pioneer," it was the very first "dotcom" commercial ever in a Super Bowl. This was quite a bold move, considering it cost the Company $1.6 million. But it paid off in gold nuggets. The Company's website saw over one million hits within an hour of the commercial, during a time when everyone would generally be watching the game, hands full of pizza and beer.

The great surge of demand sparked technical problems, with servers crashing and many unable to access the website, but it was still an enormous coup. The Show was arguably the biggest event in the history of the Internet, with more than one million people logging on to watch an eighteen-minute Web segment. And this was only the beginning.

Today, the show has been broadcasted on CBS, garnering an average of 10 million viewers over the past three years. The Show was not broadcasted in 2004 due to the firestorm of political scrutiny following the Super Bowl halftime show indecency controversy.

The Show has become one big "advertisement" for the Brand. The goal of the show is to alert the viewer to all the new sexy lingerie choices, shapes, colors, and emotions that are available, with much less specific emphasis than on Victoria's Secret than one might imagine... indirect, but not subtle.

The show is a full-throttle party with hot music tracks, musical performances by top artists ranging from Sting, Mary J. Blige, and

Ricky Martin, and a slew of celebrity guests in attendance. The celebrities contribute to the slightly naughty, "maverick" Victoria's Secret brand by demonstrating the effect the supermodels and their lingerie have over them. From Denzel Washington raising his eyebrow on the side of the runway, to Sting kissing any model he can get his hands on, the celebrities sell the Victoria's Secret brand image.

Four billion dollars of hope, dreams, and lust were sold last year. With a 30% share of the intimate apparel market, this "maverick" marketer has saved many marriages...and also probably destroyed a few along the way.

Sheriff in Town

A brat, a beer, a few buddies, and *Monday Night Football*. For a lot of guys, this is a little slice of heaven and it is brought to you by Johnsonville Sausage. From a small town in Wisconsin, Johnsonville has blazed a trail through, over and around some of the giants of the food industry to become the Number One brand of sausage in America.

Like any true "maverick," innovation has spurred Johnsonville's ascent. But Innovation doesn't only apply to the Company's marketing techniques. It is the comprehensive culture at Johnsonville that permeates everything from product development to organizational structure. The "trailmaster" of Johnsonville for the past three decades, Ralph Stayer, is responsible for developing the Company's unique culture.

When I first met Ralph on one of our assignments, it was clear that, above all else, he is deeply passionate about his product. Like Jim Koch with his beer, Ralph Stayer is the ultimate authority on all aspects of sausage, from "hog to bun." Importantly, in addition, he also knows his business and ensures that his entire Company knows the retail customer and ultimate Consumer.

As with many charismatic corporate leaders, Ralph's depth of knowledge and passion allowed him to lead his Company through a period of significant growth. He has been the engine that drives Johnsonville and was personally responsible for creating the nurturing environment for the Company's successes and failures. But in 1980, with Johnsonville experiencing about 20% year-over-year growth and in good financial standing, Ralph Stayer showed his true "maverick" spirit. Rather than going the way of the "celebrity" CEO, Ralph decided to take a different trail.

Transforming Johnsonville's culture from one where employees just "punched the clock" to one in which everyone feels a sense of personal responsibility for the product quality and Company performance was not without its growing pains. Employees who were uneasy with Ralph's newfound "maverick" form of management and the responsibility imposed on them, either left or were eventually fired. And it took some time for Ralph himself to adjust to his new role of "coach," rather than "quarterback."

The outcome of this radical thinking has been the development of a Company filled with "self-starting, problem-solving, responsibility-grabbing, independent thinkers," who are now leading Johnsonville's continued growth.

One of Ralph's key operational tenets is understanding and addressing the needs and wants of the customers and the target audience. No horse apples! This is the goal of every other good marketer, but Ralph and Johnsonville take it to a new accentuated level. For their superlative bratwurst, Johnsonville goes straight to the hearts and minds of the heavy users... the macho men.

Cookout

Johnsonville's "maverick" ways extend well beyond the Company's corporate structure. The passion for bratwurst or just "brats" is reflected in its marketing communications. The most visible example, and it's certainly hard to miss, is the Johnsonville, "Big

Taste Grill." Imagine a 65-foot long, 27-ton oil tanker truck. Now cut the enormous oil tank in half horizontally, lift the top half of the tank up, and put a gigantic grill in the bottom half. What you get is a behemoth grill bigger than a wagon train that cooks 750 bratwursts at a time. Several "Big Taste Grills" crisscross the country appearing at football games, country fairs, NASCAR races, and other macho events. Want to open America's biggest truck stop? Call Johnsonville for the "Big Grill," as a kickoff event.

Johnsonville commercials take a similar tack of getting in synch with the core male "griller," and not necessarily the actual female purchaser. One such television execution implores the "griller" to use tongs or even a wrench and not a fork to tend the grill, lest one punctures the brat and let the manly flavor drain away. What red-blooded cowboy among us has not made use of our toolbox in cooking! I, for one, believe a hammer is the one required element of a successful lobster bake.

Johnsonville's media strategy is to utilize only very specific television shows, which not only "reach" its core target audience but also represents and "touches" the manly attribute. They advertise in such shows as *NASCAR, Bull Riding, Blue Collar TV,* and the Country Music version of *Idol.*

And the Company doesn't forget about those people who love to cook brats, but may not have a 65-foot long grill. Along with several marketing partners, Johnsonville runs an "Ugly Grill Contest," where customers submit pictures of their "ugly grills" in hopes of winning a shiny new one, and a year's supply of Johnsonville sausages. Conducted online (www.uglygrill.com), the contest certainly engages and involves the Consumer.

Johnsonville's advertising projects a similar "maverick" attitude. A recent television spot has its six-guns targeted squarely on the forehead of the "Bubba in all of us real men." The voice over challenges the viewer, "If you're having a bunch of guys over to watch synchronized swimming, forget it! Just serve 'em weenies. But if you're watching football, you better be grilling Johnsonville Brats." The spot goes on to mention that Johnsonville Brats are perfect with that other "home team" favorite… it comes in a can and you're not allowed to drink it until you're 21 years old.

To an extent that not many companies can claim, Johnsonville embraces its core customer… football-watching, beer-drinking males, who grill on the weekend for their buddies. By sticking to its six-guns and serving the needs of its core customers, Johnsonville joins the likes of Harley Davidson or Apple as an aspirational brand that stays true to its promise. In this case, the promise is great tasting sausage and an involving, "maverick" attitude. Even its website is pure fun for all.

If all of the discussion of bratwurst is making you hungry, Johnsonville has a great way to help you solve those stomach churnings. The Company is the title sponsor of the Johnsonville Brat-Eating World Championships. Flying in the face of the larger trend toward healthy eating, Johnsonville continues to bring a sense of excitement and lightheartedness to its promotional activities. They view the competition as a fun way to raise money for charity, not as an endorsement of overindulgent eating. Despite its critics, Johnsonville's decision to associate its name with an eating competition shows that they exhibit another core quality of "maverick" marketers, the willingness to take risks rather than conform to what its competition is doing or political correctness.

These entertaining promotions are not all for show, either. They drive word of mouth and ultimately drive sales. The Brat-Eating competition was nationally televised on ESPN, and the news of the record being broken by Takeru Kobayashi, who is also the world record holder in the Nathan's Famous Fourth of July International Hot Dog contest, received coverage in a number of major news outlets. To capture the record, Kobayashi ate 58 Johnsonville bratwursts in 10 minutes. The depth of positive press coverage that Johnsonville received for the Brat Eating contest could not have been afforded, and the success of the event serves as a prime example of how going against conventional wisdom can be a rewarding way to market a product or service.

Over the past 30 years, Johnsonville has faced off much bigger competitors with greater marketing resources at their disposal. However, through its innovative culture and "maverick" marketing tactics, Johnsonville has consistently proven that despite their size, they are the proverbial "sheriff in town" when it comes to sausage. And the "maverick" Ralph Stayer is the Trailmaster.

⑩ The General Store

Wyatt Earp and Miss Kitty never saw a general store like Costco.

Two of the "mavericks" of retailing, Wal-Mart and Costco, were successful because they diverged from the herd of competition, and from each other. While Wal-Mart was focused on EDLP, Everyday Low Prices, Jim Sinegal was leading Costco with a strategy we call BTH, or branded Treasure Hunt. So key to its long-term operations is the "Every Day Low Price" strategy, Wal-Mart has recently launched a thrust to trademark the "EDLP" acronym. This aggressive action has elicited a violent reaction from numerous competitors.

Admittedly, Costco has a powerful captive in the Kirkland private label brand, but the Consumer holds this store brand in the same regard as national brand. In fact, Kirkland accounts for only 17 % of Costco sales in representative categories. A recent study by The Hartman Group, a prominent market research group, probed over a thousand Consumers regarding their ratings of the Top Ten retail chains for marketing private labels. Wal-Mart led with 47% followed by Kroger (17%), Target (14%), and down to Publix at 5%. Costco and Kirkland were not even mentioned in association to private labels, indicating that the great majority of Consumers do not view Kirkland as a store brand but rather as a national brand.

The remaining herd of retail competitors continued to mill about waiting for a leader while being picked off by the hunter's Sharps .50.

Costco's BTH flies in the face of a traditional, generally accepted retailing precept that shoppers highly value the breadth and consistency of product offerings and location within the store. This is what we refer to as the "fast food" strategy of retailing. It is "idiot-proof" shopping.

Sinegal's BTH recognizes there is a germ of avarice in most of us. We all want to find a buried "treasure" that is not available to everyone. We all want a bargain and all want to feel "smart." This basic fact of human nature is the premise behind the "Branded Treasure Hunt" at Costco. The shopper knows that he or she will find some different and exciting "treasure" on every trip to Costco. It may be a box of Tide, Hanes Underwear, a fashionable sweater, a two-gallon jar of salad dressing, a giant bottle of One-a-Day Vitamins, a Perdue Chicken, or a large screen Sony TV. The treasures are almost always branded so the shopper has a fairly accurate perception of just how valuable their "treasure" is. It is likely to be something the shopper had no idea they really needed... and probably didn't. And when they get home, the shopper wants to share their good fortune of treasure hunting with the neighbors and relatives... almost 30 million prescriptions... 100,000 carats of diamonds... and a billion photos last year.

The treasures, big and small, change with each visit. The unexpected adds excitement to the Consumer's shopping experience. The merchandise is not remnant or seconds but rather first line products that may not be available anywhere other than Costco... or not exactly the same size or physical properties.

The sheer bulk of the treasure offering makes the special Costco "pack size" a conscious and very deliberate tactic of the Company. So what if you buy two-dozen tube socks at a time? If you only pay fifty cents a pair, the kids can wear them with no shoes on... just branded, disposable socks.

Starting out to service the needs of small business has fortunately accelerated Costco's impressive growth among Consumers. Thus the orientation is toward bulk purchases at an economical price, a relatively bare bones warehouse environment, and a wide variety of merchandise not constricted by an exclusive focus on food.

Small business continues in importance today, accounting for 60% of Costco sales. Don't tell the IRS! No one knows how many products for personal use are purchased at Costco, under corporate accounts. They come for the same BTH for their businesses: ... multi-gallon containers of Mazola cooking oil, some BOSE speakers for the office, and perhaps some Polo shirts as employee uniforms. The merchandise is well displayed, it is easy to shop, and the great savings to small businesses enable them to compete against larger competitors. About one third of the Costco members are small businesses.

Costco provides, in addition to merchandise, substantial added value to assist small businesses in conducting their operations. This includes services such as discounted health coverage for their employees, back office support, tax preparation, small business health and dental services, loans and lines of credit, business phone services, check printing, merchant credit card processing, online job posting, payroll services, and pre-paid overnight delivery.

The small business format and strategy has actually worked very well for Costco in targeting families. After all, the shopping and purchasing behavior of small business and families are very similar under the BTH overarching strategy.

Costco has employed many tactical executions to further distinguish itself from the herd of more traditional retailers, as well as the other successful retail "maverick," Wal-Mart.

Pricing	–	Restricts mark up to 15%
Selectively	–	Charges an annual fee and enforces limited admittance
Segmentation	–	Provides small business with designated hours
Customer Base	–	Targets both small businesses and Consumers
Payment	–	Accepts only cash, check, or American Express
Stocking Strategy	–	Not focused only on food
Merchandise	–	"In-out" rotation of products and brands
Sizing	–	Emphasis on super-sized bulk or banded multi-packs and pallet displays
Shopping Pattern	–	Encourages less frequent shopping trips with a much higher dollar ring
Promotion	–	No advertising and no public relations
Vendor Relationship	–	Demanding ... but fair

Costco is notoriously tough on its vendors to adhere to the BTH strategy. The Company demands "unique-to-Costco" products and pack-sizes even if the vendor must make a substantial investment merely to obtain the initial order. If the Consumer can find exactly the same product and size at Safeway, Costco probably doesn't want it. On the other hand, Costco is among the best of the major retailers in offering vendors an opportunity to "test" in a small number of retail locations. If successful, Costco will gradually expand the geographical footprint of the Brand and promotion.

Costco is not bashful in going toe-to-toe with its vendor partners. With an average of over ten million dollars per SKU, the Company deals from strength. Joel Benoliel, Senior Vice President of Marketing, is quoted as saying "If they, Procter & Gamble, wanted to keep doing business with us, they had to give us a unique formula." Its "in-and-out" product strategy permits Costco the ability to walk away from a brand like Tide... or Diet Coke... or Pierre Cardin... or Hanes... or "your Brand" in order to achieve its objectives. In contrast, Safeway's strategy does not allow it to be void of these "traffic generators." Procter & Gamble even developed a unique formula of Tide for Costco. This "maverick" Retailer has power.

We have worked with Wal-Mart as a Client, and with numerous other retailers and CPG and non-CPG companies. Costco is a very difficult "maverick" to corral. It has achieved sales of forty billion dollars and averages sales of three million dollars per store. That is a great deal of toasters, sweaters, and hamburger patties. In fact 20% more than the venerable Sam's Club. A "maverick" doesn't like any other horse out in front and runs fastest when challenged.

Even in advertising and promotion, Costco finds its own trail over the towering Sierras. The Company consciously and consistently limits marketing investments only to very specific and temporary tasks, including new openings and some direct mail for membership and selected merchandise.

The most recent mailing was targeted around Memorial Day and offered an unprecedented potential savings of $1,300 in manufacturers' coupons, for items as diverse as computers and cereals. The online savings were even greater and featured a $700 coupon on a grand piano. Certainly not how its competitors promote retail traffic.

In contrast, the "herd" of Costco's competitors are big spenders in annual media advertising.

$578 Million

$530 Million

$523 Million

$518 Million

$388 Million

$100 Million

We estimate Costco's annual advertising in measured media to be less than $20 million, while Sam's Club recently announced an increase in its advertising budget from $15 to $100 million

Ever the "maverick," Costco online does not have the same business model as their competitors, who carry many more SKUs in their portfolio.

Number of SKUs Online	
Amazaon.com	11,000,000
Wal-Mart.com	1,000,000+
Sears.com	200,000
Costco.com	3,500

Costco online operates as a virtual company, rarely taking physical possession and forcing its vendor suppliers to ship the product. It is accelerating the appeal of the website to the 36 million Costco's cardholder base.

Costco's Annual Report is another manifestation of the Company as a "maverick." While most annual reports are decorated with "pretty" pictures in four-color, lofty visions and slogans all intricately art-directed. Mount up! With 99.9% of corporations, including its competition headed one way, Costco bolts in another direction in the format of its Annual Report that represents its "no frills" approach to retailing:

- Black and white only

- No, no pictures

- Small, pedestrian typestyle

- Dense copy blocks flush right and left

- A single page of small charts

Overall, the Annual Report is about as plain as a pallet of toilet paper in one of their stores. Oops. Costco refers to its retail outlets as "warehouses."

Like a trip to one of the Costco "warehouses," reading the Annual Report is a treasure hunt, and there are a number of gold nuggets.

- Sales over $60 billion

- 7% same store sales growth

- Sales volume per outlet double that of Sam's Club

- 86% paid membership renewal rate

- e-Tailing venture up 42%

- Lowest employee turnover among "big" retailers

- Largest marketer of wine in the country

- An average sales of $10 million for every SKU

- $120 million in average sales per store

Whoa Nellie! Being a "maverick" means you get a lot of oats.

Ⓜ Bee Hive

Over the years, I have had the opportunity to work on a number of marketing and new product development assignments on skin care from Rx (Galderma) to OTC (Vaseline Intensive Care) to HBA (Pond's)... and from the brow (Olay) to the butt (A&D Ointment) and virtually every body part in between. When the project on Burt's Bees was initiated, I had never heard of Burt's Bees... and probably neither had the management of Procter, Unilever, Beiersdorf, or Kao.

Yippie ki-yay and Home on the Range! Did I learn something new about dermatological products and Burt's Bees, as soon as we began talking to Consumers! We were convinced this niche "maverick" Brand was just a fad, or as a cowboy and part-time gold miner would say, "a flash-in-the-pan."

Kemo Sabe, where did this "maverick" come from?

Even a Hollywood Western movie writer couldn't dream up this one. A woman with no job and no home is hitchhiking along a road in the wilds of Maine. A bearded bedraggled man, named Burt, stops and picks up the woman, Roxanne. They hit it off and live the "Woodstock Life" in Burt's log cabin, which has no running water and is several miles from the nearest road. Burt has a few beehives. The honey is eaten, and with little else to do, Roxanne begins to make candles. Burt and Roxanne have virtually no income and begin traveling to country and crafts fairs to sell candles. A good day was selling enough to cover the gas to get home. Roxanne honed her marketing skills first hand selling out of the trunk of her car.

The "Woodstock" experience certainly enhanced her natural independence as well as a "true love" for the Great Earth. Gradually, candles morphed into lip balm and skin care products made with the best natural ingredients possible. The Brand is also infused with a strong dose of anti-establishment attitude... natural ingredients, minimalist packaging, no animal testing, and ecological processes. And it sells!

We conducted five different comprehensive consumer research studies in four weeks of Marketing Due Diligence for AEA Capital, a major private equity firm. This research certainly proved us wrong. I have never seen such a strong "Top 2 Box" product concept scores or repeat rates or multiple SKU usage under a single brand banner. In our proprietary New England Consulting Group "SuperGroups," women gushed eloquently on this Brand, the products, and the entire gestalt. Consumers intuitively imagined the story of the Brand and it resonated strongly with them. Here is what a few Consumers made up without knowing the real story.

> "One day Burt was working in his Bee Farm – he brought into his house some honeycombs, placed it next to his wife's whale oil and got the idea to melt it in the kettle over the open hearth. The two melted together. When

he was done, he took a ladle full and poured it into a bowl. His wife came back along and sipped it – it tasted bad but she noticed her lips were much softer – and that was the birth of Burt's Bees Lip Balm."

– Cori (SuperGroup Participant)

"A guy named Burt had a bunch of bees that he inherited from his grandfather. Not knowing what to do with it, his wife suggested making a hand balm for his hard farmer hands. That's where it all started. Now there are many products that him and his wife developed and Burt's Bees are working hard for Burt."

– Jeannine (SuperGroup Participant)

Roxanne Quimby is a perfectionist with her products and creates a steady stream of new products and concoctions to entice trial. She utilized a drawing of "bearded, bedraggled Burt" on her bright yellow packaging. Just what a fancy New York cosmetic packaging house would do? Wrong. It was pure "maverick" marketing genius.

Consumer Perception

- "old-fashioned"
- "out-doors"
- "Grizzly Adams"
- "granola"
- "woodsy"
- "he looks kind of dirty"
- "fisherman"
- "natural"
- "roughing it"

This became "Tom's of Maine" on steroids. Distribution evolved on a viral basis from craft fairs, gift and card shops, into health food and natural channels. A breakthrough was the introduction into Cracker Barrel, which served as a major sampling conduit of an expansion of the geographic footprint. Some selected food and independent drug stores also obtained the Burt's Bees line.

When Roxanne and company found themselves with an exploding business, headquartered twenty-five miles from the nearest Fed Ex drop, it was time to move to a more modern campsite.

"Maverick" marketing also works brilliantly with Retail Trade. Burt's Bees represents a real alternative to the numerous "mass" skincare products they carry. It has restricted distribution, a high dollar ring, great margins, distinctive packaging, superior merchandising, and a strong impulse-buyer following. Recently, the manager at Carl's Pharmacy in Aspen told me, personally, very proudly, that they were the leading outlet for Burt's Bees products in the entire country. What is really interesting is the fact that at least five other retail outlets have told me the same thing.

Talk about a "maverick" marketer! Up until recently, Burt's Bees had never made, nor even had a "trade presentation." When chains like CVS called asking for the Brand, they were told "fine and the terms are the same as for everyone... cash upfront or C.O.D." For your Campbell's, L'Oréal, Glaxo companies out there, try that approach in Bentonville.

Like most westerners, this "maverick" story has a happy ending. For almost two hundred million dollars, Roxanne Quimby has entrusted 80% of her company to the secretive AEA private equity firm, their name is not even on their office door. This has permitted Roxanne to devote more time to her ecological pursuits and preserving large swaths of pristine Maine.

We were invited by AEA to the "lender's meeting" as a third-party marketing expert as a component of our Marketing Due Diligence assignment. The setting was the typical Park Avenue lenders meeting with numerous "I" bankers, normal bankers, and fund managers present and on the phone. Roxanne strode to the podium in a black J.C. Penny's pantsuit complete with an elementary school backpack. True to her indefatigable "maverick" spirit, she proclaimed to the puzzled bankers "John tells me about CAGR, Martin and James tell me about CAGR," referring to the AEA acquisition team of John Kenney, Martin Elhrich, and James Ho. "I don't know what CAGR is... but I sure can sell product."

The bankers could not get out their checkbooks fast enough and the deal was over-subscribed. Fast forward three years, in a bold strategic move, the Clorox Company purchased Burt's Bees for a staggering price of $961 million.

Ⓜ　Smoke Signals

Labeling Virgin Mobile a "maverick" marketer is analogous to calling John Wayne a cowboy. It is a badge they wear proudly. Virgin Mobile has clearly distanced itself from the much more staid "herd" of Sprint, Verizon, etc. in terms of demographic targeting, positioning, and unbridled "attitude." James Earl Jones they are not!

Even among the dysfunctional Virgin family members, Virgin Mobile stands apart. When you go to a major website and one of the headers is "STUFF" or "STASH," you know the wagon train is not in Kansas anymore. Virgin Mobile is intentionally irreverent, youthfully rebellious, and, in consultant's terms, funky and even weird. Virgin Mobile is blatantly commercial and very obvious and upfront in its intent to make money. The honesty is endearing to their specific target audience.

Even their altruistic programs under the theme, "STGG" or "Serving the Greater Good," are transparently linked to a commercial purpose. It is all a part of the blatant "maverick" attitude. Among Virgin's laundry list of causes is "Saving." This is implemented as a program to "save the trees," but look how Virgin provides the altruistic rationalization.

According to Virgin Mobile, other cell phone companies are turning our nation's trees into pulp in order to bind you to annual long-term contracts and gouge you with their monthly printed bills. Virgin Mobile cares about the environment. That's why they don't have long-term contracts or destroy trees to send you monthly bills. Download these informative materials. Spread the knowledge! Do it for generations to come! Together we can save the trees! Together we can serve the greater good!

Not sending a monthly bill becomes a "cause" and a competitive advantage. What is the master "maverick" tactic is reducing your operational cost by eliminating paper bills and converting it into an altruistic cause that appeals to your target audience.

Likewise, Virgin's "GIVING" is a tongue-in-cheek program to promote its offer of a text message for the cost of a penny. The banner is "Giving the Power back to the Penny." Abraham Lincoln must be very proud. Again "serving the greater good," the Company launched a campaign lobbying to protect the "penny" against pending legislation to eliminate the penny, despite the fact that the cost of producing a penny exceeds its actual value by 40%. This extensive, Virgin "Save the Penny" campaign includes advertising in major newspapers, a Times Square kickoff, and a petition drive. And who should know more about the economic impact of the penny than the spokesperson Virgin selected, Britney Spears' ex-husband, an unemployed back-up dancer. What? Just weird enough to be in-synch with its customer base. Nonsensical, but effective.

And of course, there is the "Befriend the Mime" cause and a Virgin Mobile rock concert, all under the banner of "STFF."

One of the few causes that are less commercial and more legitimate is Virgin's "The Re-Generation," which focuses on innovative," their word, non-profits, directed at youths. These include "Youth Noise" and "Stand up for Kids." Even here, the mechanism of donation is tied to Virgin's revenue.

Virgin Mobile has effectively targeted a specific age and attitudinal segment and designed the Company accordingly. With a member-base of five million, it has created a clear and distinguishing position as a "maverick."

"We dare to try," is Virgin's mantra.

2.7 Seconds on A Bull Named Fu Manchu

This is the refrain from a Country Western hit song called, "Live like you are dying."

I sauntered past a tethered burro into a thatched-roof bar with a packed dirt floor in the backwaters of the Galapagos Islands... about as far away from civilization as one can get. Yet, what did I see but a freestanding, cut-case display of Red Bull energy drink.

No bull, Red Bull. This is a true "maverick" marketer of the highest order exhibiting pure genius in capturing the mass market, without a mass market approach.

First launched in 1987, Red Bull has emerged as a powerful global force in the beverage industry, essentially creating its own fast growing "energy drink" market, while regular soft drinks experience substantial sales declines. In the U.S., the energy drink market, fueled by the caffeine high of Red Bull continues to grow, expanding at a compounded annual growth rate of 80%+ based on our projected numbers.

U.S. Energy Drink Market

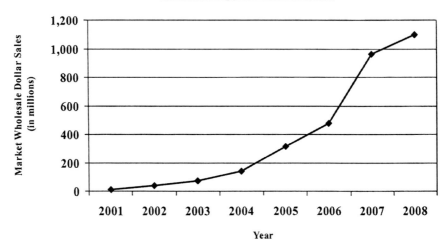

And Red Bull fuels the "ride" experiencing strong sales growth, with a compound annual growth rate of 20%+, after selling 1.9 billion cans and generating $2 billion in revenue.

Red Bull GmbH is the world's leading energy drinks producer and yet, markets only two products, Red Bull Energy Drink and Red Bull Sugar free in over 100 countries. Both drinks are described as functional drinks developed especially for periods of increased mental and physical exertion, claiming its ability to

- Improve performance

- Improve concentration and reaction speed

- Improve vigilance

- Improve emotional status

- Improve metabolism

and virtually any situation such as sports, work, study, driving, and, perhaps most importantly, socializing.

Although viewed by many as being loaded with caffeine, Red Bull's 80 mg of caffeine is comparable to just one mug of coffee. The reaction between caffeine and its other main ingredients, such as non-essential amino acids, taurine, and glucuronolacctone, is actually the synergistic elixir that gives the user a lift.

Red Bull's rip-roaring success has several key components:

- Single product evangelism

- Unique physical and emotional positioning

- "Maverick" marketing approach

- Heavy grassroots marketing investment

- Ubiquitous distribution, including the Galapagos and beyond.

And perhaps most importantly, a true "maverick" founder.

And what are some of the obstacles and fences jumped by Red Bull?

- Taste – Red Bull was given a D+ in taste on BevNet, with consumers claiming Red Bull's taste to be "medicinal" and "tinny."

- Pricing – At $2 for an 8.3-ounce can, Red Bull's retail price is at least double the price of a 12-ounce can of Coke.

- Government Intervention – Norway, Denmark, and France have banned the sale of Red Bull as a normal soft drink, due to serious health concerns.

- Name Calling – Red Bull has been accused of encouraging underage drinking while promoting a drink that has been called "legal cocaine," "crack in a can," and "over-the-counter amphetamine."

But the Bull just keeps charging!

From the start, Red Bull targeted mostly trend-setting male teenagers and twenty-somethings who were looking for value-added beverages to improve their intensity of life, specially their social life.

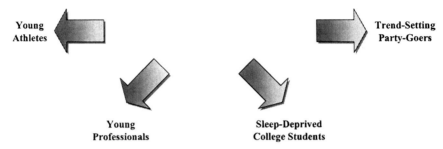

| Young Athletes | | Trend-Setting Party-Goers |

Young Professionals   Sleep-Deprived College Students

The Brand was conceived and nurtured as a lifestyle product for those who enjoyed the thrill of danger. Red Bull like "Maverick," the appropriate call sign for Tom Cruise in *Top Gun*, postured, "I feel the need for speed." Competition and the social environment are key components of the Brand's gestalt.

Red Bull developed a brand positioning as a personality its target consumer desires to emulate: exciting, eccentric and extreme.

Target Market	• Primarily men (but also women), 16-19 years old • Those looking for value-added beverages, willing to experiment and pay a premium price
Rational Benefits	• Instant energy boost

Reason Why/ Permission to Believe	• Aspirational desire to
	   – Improve performance
	   – Improve concentration and reaction speed
	   – Improve vigilance
	   – Improve an emotional status
	   – Stimulate metabolism

Emotional Reward	• Improve your quality of life
Competitive Frame	• Primarily all other energy drinks • Caffeinated soft-drinks and coffee
Brand Character	• Irreverent, anti-establishment, different from your parents
Focus of Sale	• Red Bull Gives You Wings to do anything that you want to do

Following the personality of the founder, Red Bull utilizes a "maverick" marketing strategy with non-conventional tactics, over the typical and traditional methodologies to generate brand awareness and to project the Brand's personality. You may have witnessed some of Red Bull's tactics:

- Using pick-up trucks or VW bugs as mobile displays, painted blue and silver with a giant can on top

- Giving cans for free to people on the street who looked as though they needed energy

- Providing club DJs drinks for free

- Leaving empty cans on tables at trendy bars, clubs, and pubs

Additionally, Red Bull created a unique marketing force that was powerful, efficient, and cheap by hiring "Student Brand Managers" at colleges worldwide. This gave Red Bull instant credibility among these historically cynical and fickle consumers. Student Brand Managers are ambassadors of the products who vie to integrate the product into college life. They are often provided with free cases of Red Bull as a sampling mechanism.

These frontline troops in Red Bull's continuing charge are the Campus Managers, themselves students, and are assigned to coordinate and promote activities at a specific college. I had a long conversation with Scott Hong, Student Brand Manager for the University of Pennsylvania, which is a virtual city of 30,000. Scott related how he found the position advertised in *The Daily Pennsylvanian* student newspaper.

His assigned objectives were "sampling" and "image building" for the Red Bull Brand. I was somewhat surprised at Scott's astute observations. For example, I had no idea that college staff and faculty were targets, along with students. Furthermore, the

Company's specific directions were to focus almost exclusively on its functionality of enhancing performance, and not as a social drink or alcohol amplifier. He did not focus on bar accounts and "party time" situations. The key was to find unique venues, such as near the library late at night around exam time, for one-to-one sampling and consumer engagement.

Scott and I discussed the marketing support available to him as the Campus Manager. In typical Red Bull aggressiveness, the grassroots resources provided are impressive. This includes a "Mobile Energy Team" of two to three people who could be called in for larger campus events, flyers, free DVDs, email sports updates, a Red Bull "loaner" fridge, and, of course, product for sampling. Scott clearly enjoyed his stint with Red Bull as Campus Manager and he parlayed this student experience into a full-time marketing position at MTV.

This all adds to making Red Bull a "popular drink among popular people" on campus, a technique expanded to more traditional social venues. Red Bull has now begun to sample in-office, with small- and medium-size businesses, to pep up the energy level.

Although Red Bull relies on cheaper sales talent and low-cost marketing to generate brand awareness, it spends over $600 million on marketing annually, approximately 30% of its revenue. But it has virtually no advertising!

The Company utilizes very little traditional media and places its bet on experiential marketing, where they can relate "one-on-one," in event situations. This approach is as complex and expensive as it is effective. Red Bull, more than many marketers, understands that its true product as enjoyed by the Consumer, extends far beyond the "can" or the actual taste. It is a lifestyle... a fast-paced lifestyle. We estimate that about 40% of the marketing dollars go into sports marketing, dwarfing that of other sports marketing aficionados like Anheuser-Busch.

To further endorse its edgy branding and "Red Bull Gives You Wings" slogan, Red Bull sponsors extreme sporting events worldwide, including motor sports, winter sports, base jumping, and mountain biking — in addition to sponsoring more than 500 athletes worldwide.

But even in sports and social marketing, Red Bull is ever the "maverick" and "zigging" where the herd "zagged." Red Bull goes well beyond mere sponsorship to actually own events, teams, cars, boats, and planes. Who else would buy a little known soccer team and rename them the New York Red Bulls? Who else would invest $100 million in major league soccer in the U.S.? Who else would be the first to get their logo on the jersey of a major league sport... but a "maverick?"

From NASCAR to skateboards, Red Bull controls the entire marketing environment, the physical assets, and the "players." Its logo adorns planes, parachutes, and Formula One racing cars. These events encapsulate Red Bull as a "found experience," fast, rebellious and on the edge of danger.

You can measure the success of a "pioneer" like Red Bull by the competition it attracts.

More than 1,000 competitors have entered the market, approaching Red Bull's dominant market share in strategically different directions ranging from attacking Red Bull head on, differentiating its product to add value, or building loyalty in a niche market. Everyone from Coke, Pepsi, SoBe, and numerous start-ups have shot at Red Bull from every angle of the marketing compass.

Yet Red Bull remains ranked as the #1 energy drink and "maverick" in the bullring, with increasing double-digit sales. Its market share in the U.S. has been gradually falling, dropping from 75% in 1998 to 47% in 2005 in the greatly expanded market it created.

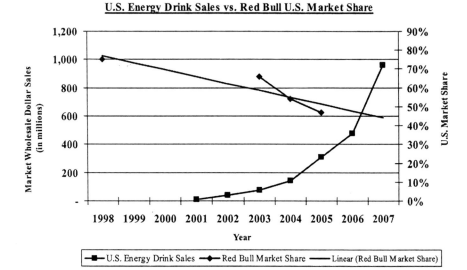

U.S. Energy Drink Sales vs. Red Bull U.S. Market Share

As a "maverick" marketer, Red Bull must be very proud of the hippest, coolest corral of competitors I have even witnessed:

Coolest Corral of Competitors

– 180 Energy Drink	– Adrenaline Rush
– Amp	– Bawls Guarana
– Bong Water	– Crunk
– DefCon3	– Gay Fuel
– Go Fast!	– Hip-Hop
– KMX	– Monster
– No Fear	– Omega
– Pimp Juice	– Rockstar

Tired of being shot at by everyone north of the Pecos, Red Bull is turning over the poker table and launching into the cola market. Red Bull is riding directly at Coca-cola and Pepsi-Cola with a premium-priced cola, even as the segment declined 4%.

Ⓜ Doc Holliday

"Doc, you won't believe where I got shot." Medicine has come a long way since the cowboy era of the late 1800's, when the only anesthetic was a bottle of rotgut whisky.

The Proctoids and many CPG marketers claiming ownership of the most sophisticated marketing prowess and techniques would not necessarily agree, but we have found some of the pharmaceutical companies to be among the most innovative marketers by necessity. This is particularly true given the regulatory environment in which they operate. Pharmaceutical marketers must negotiate a narrow trail between the regulatory chasms and political mountains. Virtually no one, including the Government, FDA, physicians, hospitals, state governments, Medicare, Medicaid, and other interested parties want pharmaceutical companies to actively market their products. Their foes are numerous and powerful. Only the Consumer wants this access to knowledge of disease states and treatments, as they take more control over their own healthcare.

Pharmaceuticals marketers are criticized and vilified at every turn. They must market in an environment of negativity and overwhelming scrutinization. Subject to massive fines in the hundreds of million dollars for the slightest transgression of amorphous regulations, they must submit all, and we mean "all," marketing materials in advance to the Department of Drug Marketing, Advertising, and Communication, affectionately known as "DDMAC." These submissions are not reviewed until months or years after the fact, but the Marketer remains liable. Advertisers must spend a major portion of their commercial time on what is euphemistically referred to as "fair balance," or why the Consumer should not even bother to ask their doctor. Risks, even at a very low level of incidence, must be explained in frightening detail even though the only means to get the prescription is through a physician and a pharmacist, who are much more informed regarding the risks. At least an additional page of Patient Information or P.I. is required for every "selling" page of print media. So the pharma Marketers have to purchase two pages in order to advertise on one, increasing the print advertising costs by at least 50%.

Warnings such as incontinence, diarrhea, dizziness, weight gain, flushing, loss of vision, and, of course, the notorious "more than a four-hour erection," must be included in their television commercials.

Boot Hill

Until about 1983, there were no specific laws or regulations prohibiting the advertising of pharmaceutical drugs. That concept was so foreign and outrageous no one even considered the possibilities... until a "maverick" in Boots Pharmaceuticals and the President, John Bryer.

This television commercial featuring John, focuses on Boots and how it developed and patented prescription ibuprofen. John diagrams that the two prescriptions, Motrin and Rufen... are exactly the same except for cost. He even includes some of the negative side effects. This 1983 commercial sounds eerily familiar with the phrase: "Ask your physician or pharmacist or call 800-22-Rufen."

We hold this commercial for the prescription Rufen brand to be the very first Direct-to-Consumer commercial ever, the pioneer. The ex-head of the FDA told me this was the advertising campaign that forced them to institute the restrictive regulations, which were not changed for a decade. Boots Pharmaceuticals and John Bryer were true "mavericks," who changed the landscape of The Great Prairie of Medical Marketing and the entire healthcare system.

The First Television Commercial for a Prescription Drug

The Federal Drug Administration was so terrified at what could transpire if others followed Boots, it garnered from Congress the authority to prevent such Consumer advertising for prescription drugs. Not until almost ten years later did the FDA finally relent and provide for Direct-to-Consumer or DTC marketing, but only under a thick horse blanket of rules and restrictions. Permitting DTC was seen as a Consumerism movement to provide information and more control over a person's own healthcare. There was also the very important strategic recognition that the most severe health issues was, and continuous to be, undiagnosed diseases Many are not even discussed between the physician and the patient and went untreated. Undiagnosed and under-treatment remain one of the greatest shortcomings of our current health system. For example, 25% of all people with diabetes remain undiagnosed and, therefore, untreated despite the catastrophic consequences. "Don't ask" by physicians and "don't tell" by patients, leads to major health issues. DTC addresses this directly, despite the political climate.

Direct-to-Consumer advertising began as a trickle but quickly became a torrent of dollars. As a Brand, even with a limited life of only 6 to 12 years, pharmaceutical drugs dwarf CPG brands in terms of size. For example, Lipitor's sales of $12 billion are roughly equivalent to an entire herd of well-known consumer brands... Folgers, Oreo, Maxwell House, Tylenol, Pedigree, Duracell, Huggies, Lays Potato Chips, and Pantene... combined!

The Lipitor brand alone is about half the revenue of the entire Coca-Cola Company.

As a result, pharmaceutical marketers have enormous marketing and advertising budgets. A $100 million annual investment is not at all unusual. In fact, in just the first quarter of the launch year, one prescription drug, Lunesta, racked up $109 million in measured media. Another ten drugs are on track for a hundred million dollars in advertising for the year.

In the first phrase of DTC, the incumbent healthcare advertising agencies were dominant, since the Clients lacked virtually any marketing and advertising talent. These medical specialist agencies have been gradually replaced by the "who's who" of consumer advertising agencies, with their greater creative and Consumer skills. Currently, after ten plus years of experience, the pharmaceutical industry has developed and educated its own cadre of internal marketing talent.

In our experience, the pharmaceutical marketers have available more granular data in greater volume and more linked to actual purchase and use behavior than does the typical CPG marketer. While debatable, the drug companies seem to have a better reading on their ROI of marketing dollars.

What may be standard techniques in the CPG world can be truly a "maverick" application in the heavily regulated and political world of pharmaceuticals. Drug makers are currently a sophisticated user of rebates, coupons, and co-pay coverage because the lifetime value of a customer can be ten thousand dollars for an ordinary chronic drug. Such "discounts" are a boon to the Consumer and lowers the out-of-pocket costs. Pfizer uses a loyalty card for Viagra that provides a seventh prescription ($100 value) free. A single drug wholesaler has run over 10 million free trial vouchers, executed through physicians and pharmacists, since DTC was renewed.

Reducing the Consumer's cost of a prescription issued by a physician and through a pharmacist... sounds like a win-win for everyone. Yet look at the very public critical cow pies heaped upon pharmaceutical marketers:

> *"Prescription drugs promoted with coupons or free trial offers may be seen as more widely indicated, more appropriate and less risky than they really are."*
>
> – FDA

"The ascendancy of marketing over science... preoccupied with marketing."

– Harvard Professor

"Coupons can increase the patient's desire to take a drug."

– Spokesperson soliciting the FDA to ban coupons

There are many pharmaceutical constituencies and critics who are allergic to any marketing activity. To advance virtually any new consumer approach takes a stalwart "maverick," willing to be surrounded and hit by arrows from every direction. Attention CPG marketers. When was the last time a standing Governor called on Congress to institute a two-year moratorium on all your Consumer marketing activities?

The prescription marketers have become astute users of digital media, given that their target audiences are often relatively small and informationally driven. However, pharmaceutical companies are subject to the same FDA restrictions on the commercial messaging in the digital world as in traditional media. The requirement for complete control and responsibility for what is "published" renders some techniques, such as using blogs, a dangerous and potentially fatal practice. In the first half of the year, Internet advertising slipped four percent under such regulatory and control issues. Nevertheless, the Internet ranks equally alongside (33%) "family and friends" and the television medium as the source or catalyst for asking their physician for a specific brand of drug. And about 90% of physician honor that request.

As an example, Glaxo, the second largest pharmaceutical firm, switched a prescription weight-loss drug previously called Xenical. We know from our own extensive experience with numerous weight-loss Clients including Weight Watchers, Jenny Craig, NutriSystem,

Meridia Rx, another prescription drug and even Xenical, just how difficult is this arena to actually change human behavior.

As an over-the-counter drug, Xenical is now called Alli. Well in advance of the actual launch, Glaxo set up a very interesting unbranded website called "Questioneverything.com," to establish itself as the expert in overall weight management. The title is deliberate in taking a position negotiated with the FDA as a condition of approving the OTC switch to dispel the myth that weight-loss is easy and pain-free. The site as the expert, conveys a wide array of topics and peer advice. The tonality is deliberately candid and places the task of weight management in proper perspective, with a large dose of personal control.

Glaxo smartly utilized this unbranded website as marketing research of the issues and language of the Consumer involved with weight management well in advance of the actual launch. Furthermore, it built a preparatory database in anticipation of final approval to launch in the non-prescription market.

An unintended but highly beneficial impact of Net marketing for pharmaceutical companies and Brands is the use of search activities by healthcare professionals. While most Brand sites are intended for Consumers, they are very appealing for physicians and nurses. Nine out of ten healthcare professionals believe the Net is the critical source for information. And 70% plus indicate that it influences their script patterns. It is a "real time" source.

Healthcare professionals particularly look to branded websites regarding new products or new indications. Furthermore, products with a well-funded DTC advertising program tend to generate healthcare professional traffic to their website. We tend to forget that physicians are just people with an advanced degree and that they kick off their boots and watch *CSI* and *Law and Order* also just like the rest of us.

Top 10 Product Websites Among Physicians

Rank	Brand
1	Lipitor
2	Fosamax
3	Adderall XR
4	Advair
5	Plavix
6	Concerta
7	Singulair
8	Lexapro
9	Crestor
10	Zetia

Source: Manhattan Research

We concur with industry experts that the shift from targeting "Consumers" to focusing on "Patients" will result in additional Net marketing investments to bolster an exciting relationship.

High Noon

Cholesterol was never a problem in the Wild West. Despite the ready availability of beef, the cowboys got plenty of exercise and, due to gunfights, Indian wars, and occupational hazards, they did not tend to live long enough to clog their arteries. However, the marketing of products to reduce bad cholesterol illustrates why many pharmaceutical Marketers are awarded our accolade of being "mavericks."

Let's compare Pfizer's Lipitor, the largest drug in the world with an established medical efficacy based on 400 clinical studies and the experience with 100 million patients to its competition Quaker

Oats Cereal. The competitive claims permitted are instructive of the difficulties of pharma marketing versus traditional marketing.

Lipitor	Quaker Oats
• Lowers cholesterol	• Removes cholesterol
• Lowers "bad" (LDL) cholesterol	• Soaks up excess cholesterol
• Reduces risk for heart attack and strokes	• Actively finds and binds with cholesterol
	• "Your should see a drop in your overall (cholesterol) number"
Cost $80 - $100 per month	Cost $12 per month
Warnings: Pregnancy warnings, liver dysfunction, renal failure, muscle weakness, gastric complications, toxicity, infertility, etc	Warnings: None
FDA-governed	FTC-governed

In the duel of playing "music' for the Consumer's attention and mindset regarding a vitally important medial issue like cholesterol, Quaker may very well win over Lipitor.

Bull's-eye

There are few trails that marketers will not take in order to gain that extra fraction of retail exposure from Retailers. This includes utilizing slotting fees, advertising allowances, buy-backs, consignment sales, free goods, co-op advertising, new product fees, re-set costs, and trips to Las Vegas. And "what happens in Vegas, stays in Vegas." With a grip on distribution and the access to the Consumer, many Retailers make more profit from charging manufacturers "rent," in the form of slotting fees, than from actually selling merchandise.

The Big Box retailers are most desirable since they provide instant and massive exposure to the Consumer. Wal-Mart alone accounts for 20–35% of All Commodity Volume depending on the category.

Big Boxes provide not only the opportunity for substantial sales and share gains, but also the credibility from the retail partner's Brand and environment.

In construction materials, hardware, and power tools, two chains... Lowe's with 1,275 stores and Home Depot with 2,080 outlets are truly dominant. Manufacturers go to great lengths in their pitch to these twin players. Lowe's is slightly more feminine and emphasizes home decoration and Home Depot, more macho and home construction. Manufacturers will lower their price, provide special warranties, create special product offerings, execute co-op advertising, issue coupons, proudly proclaim their distribution, and basically "bet the ranch" on distribution in the Big Boxes.

Texas Hold'em

While the other manufacturers of power tools are executing everything they can to gain and maintain distribution in Home Depot and Lowe's, one "maverick" marketer not only refuses to sell to the Big Boxes, they widely advertise that their products are not available in these stores.

Stihl, a German-based company with extensive manufacturing at its Virginia-based facilities, manufactures an upper-end line of chainsaws, trimmers, and tools and distributes only through some 8,000 independent, smaller dealers.

Its products are a trademarked phosphorescent orange so guys like me cannot lose them out on the "North 40," ... but the Big Box chains must be seeing red. Stihl's ads proclaim and document, that they are "not sold at Lowe's or The Home Depot." The strong statement and positioning is that Stihl's products are too professional in nature to be distributed in such outlets.

This is a risky, but, in our opinion, a smart, well calculated, and "maverick" move on Stihl's part. The advertising not only cuts through the general clutter of competing messages but also, what a rallying call to its independent dealers who are getting their donkeys kicked by this Big Box duo.

This provocative message is as valuable to the Retail channel as it is to the Consumer. When the next Consumer walks into one of these 8,000 smaller dealers asking for a recommendation, Stihl's products will be in the top slot. Stihl's actions and advertisings are a manifestation of a conscious two-prong marketing strategy.

Where Stihl is <u>not</u> ... in terms of distribution

Where Stihl <u>is</u> ... in terms of product superiority

The following is a conversation between Peter Burton, Executive Vice President of Stihl, and me.

Tom: "Maybe you could just tell me how this strategy of telling people where you're 'not distributed' began?"

Peter: "The commencement was two and half years ago. Anybody that's worked with Stihl and travels with the company logo on our shirts knows that inevitably people want to talk to us about our Brand, which I often find is very rewarding. 'Hey, I love your product... where do I buy it, Home Depot or Lowe's'? is a typical question. Our consumer research was supporting that as well with nearly 60% of Consumers, saying that they were convinced that we were either in Lowe's or Home Depot. In fact, we have never distributed in the mass merchant channel in the history of the Company. We have always been servicing only independent dealers."

"So, it was a very real need to address the belief that exists with the Consumer or the potential consumer. We have a great Brand... we have great Brand equity... we have a reputation for quality and durability but the biggest stumbling block or problem for potential Consumers was, where do I get it?"

Tom: "Well, it is a very enviable position to be where people are proactively looking for your product."

Peter: "And, this has a number of dimensions to it, which intertwine. Now, many of the dealers see a manufacturer who is completely invested in the channel with them. That reinforces our relationship and so they're more encouraged to support our Brand accordingly."

Tom: "I would think, particularly now, as the mass channels have grown so rapidly, that that's even more important than even four or five years ago."

Peter: "Tom, you're right. There are competitors who have benefited as a result of the growth of the mass merchant. They're all in there, or most of them. Most of them are in there so they're getting something out of this. From a strategic point of view, the right thing to do was to address that issue."

Tom: "Has there been any specific reaction to this "maverick" strategy? I mean your dealers must be rooting you on, because it's the old enemy of my enemy situation."

Peter: "There have been many instances where we have received correspondence here from our dealers wanting to talk to their other suppliers about a similar program. We recently had one from a very, very successful multi-location dealer who wanted permission to run this up the flagpole with the major lawn care brand that he carries."

"We've had correspondence from people outside of the industry... people from the electronic games, roofing, and DVD industries who leave a message along the lines of 'I wish more manufacturers where thinking in this direction.'"

Tom: "We were discussing with a Client the other day and he said, 'Well, I've got good news and I've got bad news,' and the answer to both was that he got a big order at Home Depot. It's definitely a double-edged sword."

"From a Consumer point of view, what has been the feedback? Does that dovetail with what they would think about it or does it come as news that you would not be in those outlets?"

Peter: "I think the answer to that is, from the research, 60% of people believed that's where we are. In newspapers such as *USA Today, Wall Street Journal, The New York Times*, and so on, we run those ads where we say clearly that we're <u>not</u> in the Depot and Lowe's."

"In conjunction with that, across the country and all the major media from coast to coast, we have what I will refer to as reach-out advertising, which doesn't talk to this issue. But it talks to Stihl, as a formidable and quality Brand, as well as the specific dealer locations. On the one hand you can't buy it at the mass merchant, but the answer is, this is where you can buy it."

Tom: "That's very smart. That really is. What metrics do you utilize to evaluate this strategy?"

Peter: "The way we are monitoring it at the moment is just to monitor the sales results. This has really been excellent for the first half of this year and we are looking at sales results in various categories and various locations around the country."

"I think what encourages us as we're going to next year's sell-in now, is that dealers are extremely positive regarding supporting this campaign... which they support financially, contributing their own money, and they get tagged on the retail ads. And, we're extremely encouraged with their attitude towards what is being done here. I suppose this is a form of attitudinal response, in that we're seeing increasing commitment from our dealer network to participate."

Tom: "That's interesting. Your dealers are investing some money into this program, then."

Peter: "Absolutely, they put their own advertising money into it. The more they put into it the better that they get on the retail end, and we're seeing an increasing desire to participate. So, they're voting with their own checkbooks."

"SERVICE DEALER" (Advice) :25/:05
2004 Stihl Television

STIHL ®

VIDEO | SOUND

VIDEO: Open inside a STIHL shop. A middle-aged STIHL dealer is courteously explaining how to start a 2-cycle engine to a man who is in his early twenties. The young man is holding a pencil and small notepad, checking his notes as the dealer speaks. He has a piece of blue fabric hanging out of his back pocket.

SOUND: DEALER: ...So, for most 2-cycle engines, you set the switch to "on"... set the choke ... prime it ... and then pull the cord.

MAN: Cool. Thanks.

The customer suddenly runs out the door, and down the sidewalk, pulling a blue apron from his back pocket.

Cut to the outdoor power equipment aisle in a home center. The young man, runs up to a visibly annoyed customer.

MAN: Okay, I figured it out.

Cut to reaction shot of the customer.

AVO: When you're ready for outdoor power equipment, assembled, sold and serviced by real experts, you're ready for a STIHL.

Cut to the same customer, who is now happy and interacting with the STIHL dealer in the STIHL shop.

SUPER: Are you ready for a STIHL?

1-800-GO-STIHL
www.stihlusa.com

To order this TV spot, call Red Letter Communications @ 1-800-732-0054 and ask for Part # 0463-901-0319 for a 3/4" or Beta SP tape for broadcast use and Part # 0463-901-0320 for a VHS tape for viewing purposes.

Tom: "Is it ever in the cards that you would have a different Brand name or is the conscious corporate strategy to stay with the single Brand name?"

Peter: "We're not a publicly listed company. This is family-owned and they are still active in the Company. And, it's no longer about money. It's about legacy, building a Brand that's got a reputation worldwide. It's not about shareholders and the immediate demands of your shareholder and the increasing productivity beyond capabilities. We are a very, very successful company. This whole campaign is driven to increase our market share. Accordingly in the categories that we play in, we've been able to do that."

"The market is already there. If the Box has done anything, it has expanded markets in most categories … whether it is paint, nuts and bolts, and certainly in the hand-held outdoors power equipment industry. We're saying that we don't want to grow the market any bigger... we just want more of our share. That's what this strategy is designed to do."

"And, we're focused exclusively on the Stihl brand. That's all our distributors' carry. And, so the idea of building bigger plants and more plants and more investment to get other brand names launched is not a consideration for us. Great potential still exists for the Stihl Brand."

Tom: "You know, when your name's on the door, it suddenly changes a number of the decisions and how you approach the market. Nevertheless, you are a very successful 'maverick' relative to your competition."

Peter "It's interesting that you used the word 'maverick' for this. We haven't changed our philosophy toward the servicing dealer in 80 years. It's always been supporting our dealer. I suppose what this campaign has done, is raise the profile as to where our tradition has always been. Nothing has changed. That's the unique thing about this advertising. We've always been there. Now we're just singing a little louder than perhaps we had in the past."

Stihl clearly has distinguished themselves from the herd of longhorn competitors.

Louisiana Purchase

"Mavericks" discover and occupy empty geography or "white space."

These companies harness the power of "maverick" thinking and acting in a highly strategic manner. It has been inculcated into the DNA of the organization and is viewed as an advantage against their own unique set of larger, more traditional competitors.

In working alongside many of these "maverick" companies, we have observed several common tendencies or characteristics that other companies can emulate, on a strategic or tactical level.

- Product or Service Focus

- "Outside-In" Thinking

- Consistent Application

- Long-Term Strategy

- Managed Controversy

And finally, all have a "Lone Ranger in a white hat" or trail boss that truly "believes" and leads his or her herd in a definingly different direction.

Campfire Coffee

> *"Our primary objective with Toleratemornings.com was to experiment and learn about new ways to interact with consumers."*
>
> *"It's a different way and place to engage with consumers."*
>
> *"In this new media environment, you have to be willing as a marketer to give up a little bit of control, really respecting consumer to be the boss, to decide what content to engage with them."*
>
> Tami Yamashita
> Director of Marketing

Folgers' innovative "Toleretemornings.com" exhibits the Coffee Marketing Group's willingness to step out of Procter's comfort zone, in order to engage the Consumer as a "maverick." While the Procter & Gamble Company is not a "maverick" marketer, key Divisions and brands can act like one to achieve specific objectives.

Trail Markers

 Turn being a "maverick" into a competitive advantage against less agile peers.

 Ensure that the internal policies, procedures and philosophy are in alignment and contribute to your external marketing program.

 Experiment with a CPG brand or business without any advertising… forcing your organization to find productive brand-building alternatives.

 Push the envelope yourself and elicit that riskier attitude and approach.

 Be maniacal in embracing, enveloping, and engaging your core user base. They have come to your Brand for a reason.

 Challenge conventional wisdom regarding your distribution strategy, specifically for new products.

 Remember and harness the fact that what people want most is often what they cannot have.

CHAPTER SEVEN

NEW FRONTIERS

Perhaps in no arena have the traditional marketers been forced to emulate the "mavericks" as on the "new frontier" of Innovation and New Products. It is a lonely and scary experience venturing off the beaten path into truly unexplored territory. Many in the competitive world of consumer package goods marketing believe that an innovation or new product assignment is as dangerous and potentially fatal as a buffalo charge. And there is some truth to that assessment. The failure rate is high and compounded by an equal degree of visibility, both inside and outside the company.

Yet, Innovation is the oxygen for any company as it multiplies, expands, and attempts to adapt to a rapidly changing environment. And the required "speed" of Innovation has warped into the "acceleration" of Innovation in today's marketing arena. Forcing a major change in managerial behavior, every aspect of corporate growth and adaptation is transformed even more quickly, including the tenure of C-level executives.

Mountain Crossing

Tom Hayes

The westward-ho wagon trains snaking across The Great Plains would come to an abrupt halt when faced with major geographic obstacles. The heavily loaded Conestoga wagons could make a steady pace of eight miles a day on the level plains. But a river crossing or mountain range was both dangerous and diverting.

Too many traditional companies unintentionally build those obstacles into their Innovation and New Product Development. They institutionalize roadblocks and create diversions.

With NECG's company perspective, founded in 1981, and the "experience-advantage" of our Principals, each a battle-harden CEO or CMO themselves, we have observed and been integrally linked in the "great, the mediocre, and the atrocious" of corporate Innovation from business models to New Product Development, marketing and sales practices to organizational change, and restaurant menus to strategic change points.

Over the years... across an array of categories... with hundreds of diverse Clients, we have identified five key and fatal company impediments to a high ROI... Return on Innovation.

These five fatal impediments or mountain crossings revolve around the:

- Lack of corporate commitment (A commitment to Innovation is often erratic and easily diverted by the problems of going business sectors.)

- Lack of experienced personnel skilled in Innovation (The Innovation Team is often a "training" or developmental position.)

- Lack of continuity of organizational process and personnel (We recently conducted a global Innovation assignment that involved three changes in management during the life of the project.)

- Lack of seamless interface (At each sequential organizational interface, there is a substantial loss of energy and direction.)

- Lack of consistent vested interest (Too often, the internal Company personnel have their own unique agenda focused on the going, and more visible revenue business sectors... and, more importantly, their next career move.)

The wagon wheels of Innovation can become mired in the mud of today's problems rather focused on tomorrow's opportunities.

Cattle Wanderings

One of the main issues is the corporate or traditional approach to Innovation and New Product Development which tends to be militarily linear as if in a march. "Mavericks" are better represented as a Calvary change. Like hunters on The Great Plains, "maverick" marketers rarely move in a straight line. Number one, it is dangerous. Secondly, moving in a straight line traps you into the same perspective throughout the process.

One of the very best "maverick" marketers in new products, Creative Director and member of the prestigious Advertising Hall of Fame, Janet Wolff, explained "Tom, traditional marketers want to believe that we develop new products like this."

"And in reality, this is the path we take."

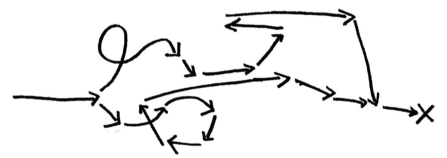

Yup! A "maverick's" wanderings find the gold mine.

Open Range

Before the barbed wire innovation and the advent of the "Iron Horse," the entire Great Plains was open range. Did you know there were almost 600 patents issued on barbed wire in the mid-1800s? The "mavericks" could meander wherever they wanted, unimpeded by fences and with a free interchange of gossip and ideas.

Talking to others outside your own teepee is often a catalyst to simulating learning and new ideas.

Alas, the more traditional and established marketers have been forced to follow their "maverick" counterparts out onto the open range. These larger companies have obliterated many of the organizational silos and legal handcuffs that restricted their Innovation and New Product Development progress.

The new "open range" has become "open innovation," the hottest new approach on The Plains since the repeating Winchester rifle. The "who's who" of Marketing have recognized that they must go outside their own organization and comfort zone to increase both the rate and magnitude of new product development. This is a dose of cold water for many frustrated Marketers as they learn, begrudgingly, how to become more "maverick" in their behavior. It can be extremely difficult to train an old horse into new activities and tricks.

The Cavalry charge into "open range innovation" includes many of the higher tech companies such as Philips (with consumer insight generating locations around the world), HP (focused on describing and validating unmet needs), and Xerox (concentrating on deep observation to "watching behavior" rather than "asking attitudes.")

Also CPG marketers with "maverick" tendencies are companies like Wrigley, with a segment-based platform Innovation team that led the Company into viewing chewing gum in a totally new way... as a delivery system of health benefits. Pepsi is another major player in Innovation and placing greater emphasis on outsourcing ideation, concept scripting, and even product positioning.

Circle The Wagons

When any outside threat appeared on the horizon, the pioneers would circle the wagons into a moveable fort to repel any intruders.

Similarly for generations, corporations built a legal fort to keep outside ideas or technologies from breaching their sacrosanct walls. Many companies, fearing legal action, even dismantled the quaint Suggestion Box, and forwarded any vendor or Consumer ideas directly to the legal staff for return – unopened, if possible.

Observing that more successful "maverick" innovators welcomed such outside ideation and in-and-out licensing of technologies, these same companies began to find an appropriate and legally manageable means to import Innovation.

A case in point is Procter & Gamble, who at one time had among the more draconian and deliberate set of exclusionary and isolationist policies. Although a degree of proprietary paranoia was justified, as competitors specifically targeted the Company for its technology and marketing best practices. Durk Jager, President and CEO in the '90s began the "open range" policy, but with solely an internal focus by dismantling some of the silo barriers among Procter's various business sectors. He created cross-functional Innovation teams and held Company-wide Innovation "fairs," for internal fertilization and sharing.

Later, in a push toward technological Innovation, the gates to Procter & Gamble's insular fortress were flung open, to the outside barbarians by A.G. Lafley, the current CEO in a push toward technological open Innovation. The main purpose was to primarily focus on gaining access to new technologies. Furthermore, Lafley began to out-license under-utilized P&G technologies after substantial internal vetting. To long term Procter watchers, this is extreme "maverick" behavior... like Custer and Geronimo sitting down to share a meal and the best practices of hunting buffalo.

This new "open range" attitude is manifested in the Company's "connect and develop," Open Innovation program, which proactively solicits outside technologies to supplement its own. The emphasis is on targeted technologies under issued "open briefs," rather than general Innovation. This is a substantial endeavor, with almost ninety internal R&D personnel designated as "tech scouts" as well as the utilization of several third-party open networks. Beginning with the first such new product, Mr. Clean Magic Eraser, the results have been very encouraging... increasing the new product success rate... with nearly half of new products based on or magnified by outside technologies... and a reduced expenditure on internal R&D.

Plumb loco! Plumb "maverick"!

In a further opening of the corporate tent, Procter is harnessing the Net to solicit consumer input on controversial issues, such as in what TV shows they should or should not advertise. This is an arena where very few P&G Brand Managers get the opportunity to weigh-in.

Another previously staid and traditionalist company that was forced to change its approach to Innovation is the venerable Kraft organization. The Company has implemented on the Net the "Innovate with Kraft" program. In contrast to Procter, Kraft "open range" sourcing is more focused on new product ideas rather than technologies and has more appeal to Consumers and customers. The process for submitting to "Innovate with Kraft" is legally complex and includes a recommendation that you should get a patent as the first step.

But "Innovate with Kraft" is a positive but short venture onto the open Plains. The first product initiated under this approach was a block of parmesan cheese encased in a disposable plastic cheese grater. The idea was generated from a store in Italy.

John Wayne

Never underestimate the power of a single "John Wayne" or select group of scouts to rally the troops in New Products Development. Someone has to believe, defend, guard, shepherd, and feed both the process as well as the idea itself in order to move through to commercialization.

The John Waynes are much more decisive than traditionalists... noisier and more visible. And whether within a large or small company, "maverick" marketers have a vested interest in and live with their successes and failures. "Mavericks" tend to be more tenacious and are not typically bounced to the next corporate job in six months.

Who are some of the "mavericks" developing and launching truly new-to-the-world products? I would nominate:

- Birds Eye Steamfresh Vegetables

- Dibs Ice Cream

- Johnson & Johnson's drug delivery system though contact lenses

- U.S. Army's robotic exoskeleton

- LeapFrog kids' products

- Roomba Vacuum Cleaner

- Dippin' Dots Ice Cream

- DanActive Yogurt

And a high tech Innovation called "QR." "QRs" are two-dimensional bar codes engraved on tombstones in Japan. Take a picture with your cell phone and you linked to a Web site or digital obituary for that person. Only a "maverick" would or could conjure up "QRs."

The latest technique being utilized to spark creativity and Innovation is hypnotism. The theory is that a hypnotic state overcomes inhibitions and straight-line thinking. This is intended to permit a deeper intrusion into the subconscious for more original and child-like concepts. A "maverick" will try and experiment with any new tool or approach. Hypnotism in the New Product Development process might very well frighten the legal staff of any Fortune 1000 company, but it won't scare a "maverick" founder.

Iron Horse

Is appropriately stuffy, conservative, and preppy Callaway Golf a "maverick" marketer and Innovator? You bet your saddle.

Virtually every Marketer from CPG to Retailing is creating a hybrid channel of distribution with a direct-to-the-customer option via the Net being the new component. This obviously diverts revenue from traditional channels. The airlines have the pure unadulterated cowboy bravado to inform the Consumer and their travel agents that, "Airfares may be cheaper on our website and you do not incur a fee."

Very wisely, Callaway has bolted from the sameness of the marketing "herd" and developed differentiating Innovation in distribution. Instead of alienating its impressive dealer network, Callaway has harnessed the Net to promote and funnel revenue to its retail distribution partners, rather than going "direct." Callaway is ingenious in basing this dealer revenue allocation on factors such as physical proximity to the Consumer, which Retailer is stocking the particular item, and other proprietary factors. This dealer revenue sharing technique strengthens Callaway's relationship to its valuable dealer network, while capitalizing on the power of the Net.

Innovation in distribution is often overlooked.

The Cattlemen's Club

Well, partner, to join the Cattlemen's Club, you have to actually be an active cattleman. It's exclusive down in Texas where "all hat and no cattle" is not a complimentary description.

With virtually all Marketers in an intense pursuit of the broadest possible geographical and distribution footprint, there are some "mavericks" leaving the herd. The intense competition for maximizing distribution has become draining and counterproductive. It's time to find new grazing land!

The new business model for some "maverick" marketers is focused on granting exclusive distribution. By striking an arrangement with a single or limited number of Retailers, a Brand or Company can gain many competitive advantages:

- Eliminates or reduces the excessive costs of competing for distribution.

- Greater control of Brand imagery, enhanced by more exclusive distribution.

- Higher margins.

- Greater ability to synchronize manufacturing and marketing.

- Greater focus and cooperation from the more limited channel.

The select Retailer must, in turn, provide a more favorable sales environment and commitment to the Brand. In the frantic battle by retailers to be "different," having an exclusive or restricted distribution Brand can be a great advantage.

We work with Clients across a wide array of categories in analyzing the opportunities for exclusive distribution. From our experience, there are two key criteria. The first is finding a retail channel that can become committed to the Brand's objectives. The equation must be additive to both parties. The Brand equity of both the Manufacturer and the Retailer should be enhanced by the combination. We find it is well worth the time to create a dialogue with other Manufacturers who may have or were in a similar arrangement with the same Retail channel. There must be some concrete benefit to the exclusive channel members, be it combating the Big Box stores, an increased dollar ring, higher margins, or attracting desirable shoppers.

The second key factor in determining the exclusive distribution opportunity is assessing the match-up of the Retailer's capability to move your product in relationship to your own manufacturing capabilities. Can a reasonable performance by the restricted distribution channel provide a steady and appropriate demand level? If the retail channel is wildly successful with your Brand, can you ramp up the manufacturing rate sufficiently? There must be an alignment of manufacturing capabilities and marketing performance... and the flexibility to adapt to a changing environment.

Here are a few of the "mavericks" who have chosen another trail, into an exclusive or restricted distribution channel.

Brand	Exclusive Distribution
Snapper (lawnmowers)	– Professional, independent dealers (pulled out of Wal-Mart)
Disney Magic Selections ($100M SKU line of kids food and health and beauty products)	– Kroger
Candies (teen fashion line)	– Kohl's
Garth Brooks (Country & Western albums)	– Wal-Mart
Joe Boxer (sportswear)	– Sears
Cherokee (jeans, sportswear)	– Target
Rolling Stones (DVD)	– Best Buy
Playskool (diapers, baby items)	– CVS
Nuprin (analgesics, cold & cough)	– CVS

The venerable CVS drug chain is particularly cooperative in being open to exclusive distribution agreements. CVS has an aggressive strategy of having exclusive Brands... many of which have been successful in Europe.

⋀ Boots Cosmetics

⋀ Lumene (French Skin Care)

⋀ XCD Men's Grooming Line

⋀ Christophe Hair Care

⋀ Life Fitness VSM

⋀ Playskool Baby Care

⋀ Nuprin

Hungry Grizzly

Individual traditionalists tend to develop an engrained attitude of "not invented here" that severely constricts Innovation and slows the flow of new products. After all, why have massive R&D centers, thousands of researchers, and spend two to five percent of your topline revenue if you must ultimately turn to three people in a garage with a souped-up Apple.

We have observed and had to assist in redirecting these tremendous force vectors within many Companies that are actually inhibitors to growth. It is not only the inbred policies and procedures but also the reward structures that encourage utilization of exclusively existing internal assets... at the high price of failure.

In contrast, the "maverick" spirits are like a hungry grizzly in springtime marauding across the landscape. They actively seek and network with outside stimulus for Innovation. "Mavericks" are inclined to "beg, steal, or borrow" superlative ideas, techniques, or technologies from any source. There is no implied shame in having to import intelligence or ideation skills. A "maverick" neither is punished nor does she punish other "mavericks" in her organization for looking off their ranch for magnifying ideas.

"Maverick" marketers are less focused or preoccupied with a process and likely see ADHD as a competitive advantage. They rely on a heavy dose of judgment. In New Product Development and Innovation, "mavericks" rarely think in a straight line, but meander in discovery like a Lewis and Clark expedition.

Stagecoach

Not stagecoach, StageGate. StageGate is the new product process utilized by most traditional marketers and consultancies.

In the zero-sum game of consumer package goods, the generation of organic growth through New Products is vital. There is currently an enormous "reservoir of cash" and pent-up demand rendering the acquisition of viable brands to be an expensive undertaking. Yet, development of New Products remains one of the most difficult and thankless functions within many organizations of many excellent marketers.

The science within most CPG categories is asymptotically approaching the point of diminishing returns. The science or technology of hand lotion, eye drops, pizza, spaghetti sauce, or many packaged goods is fairly well exhausted. Further improvements are difficult and may be cost or price-point prohibitive. The so-called mass market is becoming more segmented into smaller niches... and the supporting mass medium has difficulty in reaching the targeted Consumer in a meaningful manner.

Being buried by a torrent of 35,000+ new CPG product introductions in the past year, the Food/Drug/Mass/Club channel resists or barely tolerates new products. The Retailer may passively receive your new product sales presentation... collect his slotting toll... and wait for your "baby" to stumble. As a result, fewer and fewer new products become profitable on a sustained basis.

Many products are doomed from the beginning due to the rigid progression of discovering and testing attributes. For non-"mavericks," failure lies in more than just thinking; it begins with their process. There is a serious question if the traditional and sequential StageGate New Product Development processes are up to the task in the current environment of New Marketing.

Sequential StageGate

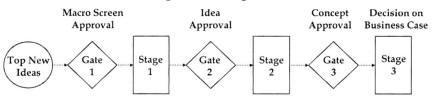

As evidenced by the costly high failure rate of 90%, the traditional StageGate process, as it is practiced by so many companies, agencies, and consultants, has many disadvantages.

StageGate worked in a different market, in a different time. The process divides the product development effort into distinct time-sequenced stages, separated by managerial decision gates. StageGate'ing breaks up the process to ensure that a prescribed set of tasks where completed before moving to the next stage.

This organized process is within the comfort zone of many marketers, but should actually make them very uncomfortable with the current output and failure rate. The traditional StageGate is normally a closed system, once the process has been initiated.

But what happens when new products do fail? Who plays the role of the fall guy? In most traditional organizations, someone has to be hanged. With an average cost of double-digit millions, invested just in development, many astute executives do not want to put their jobs on the line. For many players, taking charge of a New Product Development provides little job security and can blemish an executive's advancement.

In today's dynamic market, the traditional StageGate process is inherently inferior because it is:

- Highly linear and one-directional

- Comprised of a sequential process accepting a theoretical "win" at each decision point

- Totally reliant on the Consumer… with no input from the Channel or trade

- Completely dependent on the initial input ("garbage in… garbage out")

The traditional StageGate New Product Development process has been eclipsed by the complexities of today's marketing environment. It is not yet planted on Boot Hill, but is wounded and compromised.

Ear To The Ground

An ancient Indian ingenuity of finding buffalo was cupping an ear to the ground in order to sense the vibrations of the thundering herd. You can learn a great deal by listening.

Over the years working closely with literally hundreds of Innovation and New Product Development engagements, we have observed both the best and the worst practices. Working with the "mavericks," we have moved and evolved away from the traditional StageGate process to a less rigid and more fluid approach, with a proven success rate. Our proprietary "better mousetrap" process is more complex and open to additional inputs, as the concepts and ideas progress.

Over many years of many successful… and a few not so successful… New Product Development projects, we have improved on the process utilized by so many.

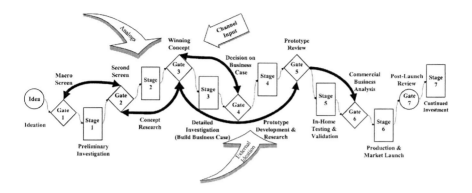

This model researches the key constituencies of the Consumer and the Channel simultaneously. Doing so taps into the knowledge, attitudes, and beliefs of both the Consumer and the Channel at a very early stage.

Different of the StageGate method, our approach utilizes both a convergent and divergent process to yield results… often making the results both superior and with greater sustainability. By addressing the Channel's issues throughout the process, there is a tendency to eliminate costly launches requiring massive support.

The advantages of our process over the traditional StageGate'ing are many:

- Enhances the size of the ultimate business opportunity

- Relies on parallel inputs from both the Consumer and the Channel… simultaneously

- Provides tested concepts with greater sustainability and longevity

- Enables more stringent and strategic screening

- Can result in multiple opportunities

Of course, once an opportunity has been realized, a "maverick" understands that games are often won over the course of several poker hands, not just limiting themselves to going "all-in" on several large pots. Due to their lower threshold of success, a "maverick" is able to seize the opportunity others look past.

Like the "maverick," this is not a closed system but rather brings in external ideation, from many sources and at many junctures. It is less sequential and emphasizes "improving" rather than "killing" an idea... more emprical.

Know When To Hold'Em

While traveling in Asia as part of his work for Unilever, an Austrian entrepreneur, Dietrich Mateschitz, came across popular syrupy drinks Asian business executives were drinking for energy... including late at night and in the sake bars. Seeing the potential of these drinks in other markets, he refined the recipe for Western tastes and named it "Red Bull Krateng Dang." ¨Krateng Dang" is a Thai herbal. Before launching the product in Austria, he hired a market research firm to test its acceptance. The results were terrible! Consumers didn't believe in the product and also disliked the taste. Like so many "mavericks," Mateschitz ignored the research, and upon approval of the Ministries of Health, he launched the product in 1987. Red Bull sold one million cans its first year. Mateschitz has proceeded to expand globally, doubling the number of cans sold the second year and then tripling the cans sold the following year.

What are some true "maverick" innovations? How about special contact lenses that, depending on the sport you are playing, block certain wavelengths of light? Or how about plastic food containers that contain antimicrobial silver nanoparticles, which keep food fresher longer? Or a portable pen of WD-40? How about the 3-D television from Hyundai?

In the CPG arena, two "mavericks" outgunned by larger rivals have taken their Innovation in a common theme, spanning from marketing strategy to advertising to in-store. And speaking of Western pioneers, Coors Brewing Company came out with their blazing six-guns and a never-addressed umbrella marketing strategy of "cold." It is very difficult to discover a fresh approach in beer marketing, but this is an original. Coors has been brilliant in integrating the "cold" superiority throughout the advertising (Coors Cold Express), packaging (thermocromatic ink enables the label to change color at 42 degrees) and even in-store (a special bar-top dispenser that pours out Coors draft about 8 degrees less than other beers). How could you "borrow" this thermochromatic ink for your Innovation?

A good friend ran straight into another Innovation when he happened to order a "Whopper" at Burger King when this "maverick" staged its "Whopper Freakout." As if the "King" character is not freaky enough, the challenged food chain actually had selected locations deliberately not serve the ubiquitous Whopper. My friend's reaction was exactly what they intended. He freaked out! With the herd of every other food chain spending millions in advertising, virtually begging the Consumer to buy, this "maverick" actually advertises what you couldn't have.

Burger King struck gold! This candid camera, "Whopper Freakout" advertising became the best remembered string of commercials in five years and spawned a number of consumer-generated videos.

This fight at the OK Corral, was won by Burger King with sales gains twice that of McDonald's. The chain's CEO proclaimed, "The Whopper line posted double-digit sales over the prior-year period."

Predator

The Western cougar is an opportunistic predator who hunts with stealth and ambush. It eats virtually any meat source, from moose to mice. It appears suddenly like an angry ghost.

"Maverick" marketers are themselves hostile predators and more aggressive than the traditionalists in pursuing New Products. They are aroused by the smell of blood and follow any lead with a genetic programming. "Maverick" marketers are hungry beasts and are not easily diverted from the "kill." They are not distracted by consideration of the next job move, the latest corporate fad-of-the-month, or internal corporate politics. As a result, "maverick" marketers tend to have a maniacal focus.

"Mavericks" are omnivorous marketers less chained to process, and agnostic regarding technologies and sourcing of ideas. Their slate of options is more open and normally involves less well-established business situations. This means that "mavericks" often have a lower "threshold of success" which becomes a substantial advantage in true Innovation.

When we were working for the CEO of Procter & Gamble on an assignment to develop new products, the minimum Year One sales objective was $100 million. We made the goal, but not without a struggle. Many publicly traded companies simply will not entertain Innovations or New Products, unless they are of sufficient size to be meaningful for their top or bottom lines. Such high thresholds have the impact of impeding productive change and innovation. There are far fewer truly new ideas at a $100 million than at $10 million sales objectives. Philosophically, "maverick" marketers enjoy roulette over playing blackjack. They prefer to bet on more options and then muscle and nurture those ideas into greater successes. Traditional marketers make fewer, larger bets, which increases the risk of failure.

Hang 'Em High

Another extremely detrimental attribute held by traditional herds is the mentality of a "national launch" or "kill it," that results from the StageGate process. It is often forgotten that a large gray area ... or even white space... lies in between. Names, tastes, habits, and emotional benefits of Consumers vary by region, and so should the products. Be it economical, political, or cultural, people tend to group and develop common tastes and habits. Sometimes a New Product must actually consist of several new products to be national. As in politics, there are "red" states and "blue" states or even "square" states.

Nestlé Waters has been very successful as a business model. By developing their product as "bottled water" instead of as a new national Brand, they have been able to produce successful, differing regional brands as a single product. Even though each Brand differs only slightly per region, this model allows for the personalization needed for marketing to Consumer response. The needed national infrastructure for production and distribution size is executed through a regional system. Understanding whether a New Product or Brand has the potential to expand nationally or is limited regionally is best determined through test markets. However effective, this method has slowly fallen out of favor in recent times, due to costs.

Campfire Ashes

From the ashes of many campfires and New Product failures, "mavericks" press onward across the desert on a horse with no name. New Products often lead into dead-end canyons and failures along the developmental trail. The traditional StageGate process simply kills off and discards ideas, without the needed forensics and re-inspection applied by "mavericks." "Mavericks," either on their own or within a large organization, are superior at learning from their mistakes. And so-called mistakes are a powerful learning mechanism. You don't always hit the original target. Sometimes a new product success is actually a ricochet.

Mavericks, due to their persistency and commitment, are acclimated to being bucked off by mistakes... but get right back up on the horse. Rather than killing an idea at the first stumble, as do traditional

StageGate enthusiasts, the entrepreneurial "mavericks" learn and capitalize on their mistakes. Going back to the discovery of penicillin, there is a strong element of serendipity in true Innovation. Here are a few more success stories rising out of the campfire ashes:

Failed as		Ultimage but Different Successes
Cough Syrup	→	Coca Cola
Panty Hose	→	Kevlar
Extra Strength Adhesive Tape	→	Post-it
Birth Control	→	Evista (Osteoporosis)
Niche hand cream for African Americans	→	Vaseline Intensive Care Lotion
Cardiovascular Drug	→	Viagra (Erectile Dysfunction)

Fort Apache

The predecessor to a Western town was often a fort built for protection and as a gathering place for trade and the exchange of ideas. The mere act of building such a structure created the need for advanced planning and a high degree of commitment.

And the same is true for many companies when they make a strategic and financial investment in a physical plant specifically dedicated to Innovation.

Hen House

Tyson Foods, the $27 billion company focused mainly on chicken, is not where one would expect to go searching for Innovation and new approaches. The meat processing business is one of the most difficult and complex feats in business today. And having managed a meat packing operation, I can attest to the difficulty from personal experience. Whereas GM "assembles" a car, Tyson "disassembles" a chicken or cow, and then must be able to sell every single ounce and piece... even down to the cartilage and the beaks in order to make any money. The margins in the industry are razor-thin. Tyson's management came to the very astute conclusion that they must break out of the traditional meat processing business model harnessing with Innovation in an ancient business sector.

This "maverick" approach by Tyson was manifested in the opening of its state-of-the-art Discovery Center. This "hen house" is a hundred thousand square foot R&D center, adjacent to a 40,000 square foot pilot plant and involves nineteen kitchens and over a hundred culinary researchers. The Tyson "Discover Center" has become the key catalyst for a major business model change beyond the bricks-and-mortar... to refocus on the Customer with significant strategic relevance to the entire company.

Strategic Relevance

Innovative Product Development	Customer Focus
• Speed innovation with dedicated R&D center	• Focus on large global Customers
• Drive for value-added solutions for Customers	• Utilize the new R&D center as a "showcase" selling tool
• Search for Customer cost reduction	• Sell Tyson outputs (i.e., beaks) which have low demand through new applications
• Understand Consumers and Customers and answer their issues with innovative products	• Partner with national accounts

In a conversation with Hal Carper, head of Corporate Research and Development at Tyson Foods, he explained that the Discovery Center has assisted the company in moving from a silo philosophy to one of shared technology. While many Innovation centers are top secret, "No Visitors Allowed" facilities, Tyson's is quite transparent and provides a substantial means to "partner" and share with Customers. The customer visit is designed as a targeted interactive experience. According to Hal, "Last year, more key customers visited with us than in the past five years." And Wendy Davidson, Senior Vice President of National Accounts is quoted in agreement "We call this our 'National Account Playplace' because we now can go from ideation to bench top and into a pilot plant within just a matter of days."

Winchester 57

The Winchester 57 was a superlative rifle but we want to talk about another 57... Heinz, the "57" Company, and their very impressive and productive Innovation and Quality Center.

Bill Johnson, a long-term Client of NECG and Chief Executive Officer of Heinz, blazed his mark high on the tree when he dedicated the Annual Report, "To the talented men and women at the Heinz Innovation and Quality Center and our other global development centers."

The name itself is indicative of the vital mission in combining, rather than segregating, Innovation and quality, as do too many companies. More than 100 chefs, food technicians, packaging engineers, and researchers are concentrated in this one facility with dynamic links to the other global Heinz centers. Even the design and layout of the building was harnessed to promote Innovation and a hands-on experience by locating many of common rooms and labs along the perimeter, as a greater attraction.

The Center also provides a common venue for the interaction and exchange of ideas between the Retail and Foodservice sectors, whether the subject is sensory analysis, organoleptic reviews, or even packaging. An example of the highly successful innovations emerging from the Innovation and Quality Center is the "Fridge Door Fit" package, for its flagship tomato ketchup. The new pack can be stored in any of three dimensions… horizontal, vertical or upside down. This 64-ounce pack is designed for heavy users and fits inside the refrigerator door. Just being omnipresent in the refrigerator has increased consumption by 68%.

Heinz Innovation and Quality Center

This $20 million investment in the future of Heinz also has the responsibility for appropriate cost reduction, which are so vital in a time of rising commodity prices on the global landscape. Pressured by private label, consumer spending constriction, and rising commodity costs, great companies such as Heinz must continue to seek innovations in controlling costs without sacrificing Consumer and Customer satisfaction.

Talk about results! Heinz revenues are up 14% and crossed the magical $10 billion milepost for the first time. Heinz recently indicated to the *Street* that the Company has 400 new products in the two-year pipeline, many of which have emerged from the Innovation and Quality Center.

Town Hall

More and more companies are taking the not unsubstantial legal risk of opening their own "Town Halls," to proactively solicit ideas from the general public. Faced with stagnate same-store sales, Starbucks set up a designated Web site, mystarbucks.com, for just such a purpose. We have labeled this as Consumer Generated Ideas or CGI. Hundreds of thousands of ideas have been shared regarding major and minor changes in the Starbucks experience, and a few have actually been implemented. A corporate openness to Innovation has the added benefit of inculcating the customer and her ideas into a closer relationship to the Company.

Pow Wow

How about a pow wow or gathering of outside experts around your village to exchange ideas and vet your latest new products ideas?

Apple, always the "maverick" and Innovator, has successfully utilized such an annual event with the ongoing "Apple Worldwide Developers Conference." The most recent annual Conference drew over 5,000 developers from around the World. This weeklong event enables developers and Apple aficionados to interact and bond directly with the Company's engineers, and even Steve himself. New software and hardware are presented to some of the brightest developers who provide a perspective and invaluable input impossible to generate from within the Company itself... while continuing to sell key opinion leaders.

New Fangled

Innovation is a common "maverick" characteristic, where one diverges from traditional marketing and their competition. The fact that it is fresh and new makes "maverick" marketing more appealing and acceptable to the desired target audience. It is not necessary to be new-to-the-world, only new-to-the-category. This is one major reason we place such an emphasis on analog marketing, a transferring of ideas, learning, and insight from one category to another.

We find it very productive to step back and pose to our CEO clients, questions like: How would Pfizer participate in your CPG category? What would Bill Gates do with your telecom company? How would the management metrics change if GE acquired your company? Time after time and across many categories and businesses, we have found with our Clients that generating pathways of growth and solving fundamental business problems are greatly enhanced by studying similar issues and how they were, successfully or unsuccessfully, addressed by companies outside your own space. True innovation is often ignited by the "pioneers" who have traveled a similar trail. This often requires "outside-in" perspective.

The degree of innovation may need to be extreme in order to be most effective. This is not the arena in which to be faint of heart or conservative in action. "Maverick" marketing is where a marketer might be willing to "stretch" her Brand, even uncomfortably so, in order to be truly different.

Indian Curse

The rich culture of many Indian tribes included a substantial component of mysticism with the Earth and the Spirit worlds being an uninterrupted continuum. Animals and humans inter-twined. And ancient curses were both common and powerful tools.

Gaurav Kapoor, my Partner and one of the smartest people on the planet, describes a curse that haunts many companies in their quest for Innovation… the Curse of Convergence:

> "The 'curse of convergence' forces the operation of
> a category, and sometimes even an entire industry,
> down to a state of No-Innovation. It is a one of the

worst situations to affect a category, and can often take years, if not decades to correct.

The curse of convergence is not just another fancy term for market differentiation. Categories that have been "cursed" converge not just on products and positioning in the market, but essentially across the entire business chain, including the following:

- the way companies are organized

- where companies source product and ideas

- people working at these companies

- market research techniques used

- types of consumers researched

- the go-to-market model

and literally every aspect of the business."

When the <u>same people</u> use the <u>same techniques</u> to come up with the <u>same ideas</u> on doing business essentially the <u>same way</u>, the result is the curse of convergence. Innovation requires a fundamentally different approach.

The good news is that when the current players in a category have converged, this leaves empty grasslands or "white space" for the "mavericks" to exploit.

Campfire Coffee

"The Folgers manhole covers were an installation in New York City that was an experiment in alternative media as a new unexpected and somewhat surprising way to engage with consumers. It was created by Saatchi & Saatchi, our agency of record on Folgers and it developed as another way to remind folks that Folgers is the best part of waking up. "Best part of waking up" has been our equity and our heritage for many, many years. But certainly, the manhole covers are a unique way to interact with consumers with that message."

Tami Yamashita
Director of Marketing

Trail Markers

The following are ten precepts or trail markers of "maverick" Innovation.

 Celebrate Innovation as a continuing, on-going process or journey... not as a management event.

 Harness the "creativity of bi-association," forming relationships among seemingly unrelated events, products, companies and industries.

 Employ continuous oscillation between Convergent and Divergent thinking throughout all phases of the Innovation process.

Create and analyze in terms of patterns, sets, and analogs to stimulate and to guide Innovation.

 Intersect with future time zones based on current and developing trends as the basis of Innovation.

 Transform the reservoir of historical individual and collective experiences into actionable Innovation.

 Play Innovation as a contact, "team" sport, that is challenging, probing, and builds on the ideas of others with each serving as a catalyst to the Team.

 Attack along multiple dimensions simultaneously... reapplying, rearranging, re-engineering all components of the situation.

 Engage all available idea-generation processes and metric evaluators, and tailor their application to the category or issue at hand.

 Deep probe the edges of Innovation, along the boundaries of different thought and across the frontiers of technology.

CHAPTER EIGHT

THE LAST ROUNDUP

Tom Hayes

It is time to hang our trophies on the teepee, gather around the campfire, pour two fingers of rotgut whiskey, and ruminate on the concept of "maverick" marketing. A key factor is how to ride this horse without hobbling the very characteristics that make it so powerful and dynamic.

"Maverick" today, mundane tomorrow. Whatever new technique, Innovation, or business model that seems out-of-the-box today is likely to be "old hat" and yesterday's news in the future. Back in the day, the Camel cigarette billboard that blew giant smoke rings over Time Square was considered to be quite the "maverick." This book and even the topic itself has a half-life of short duration, which is one of the reasons I have chosen print-on-demand publishing as a means to keep it current. The copy ordered and printed today can be efficiently updated for the next day's printing. A "maverick" must keep the pace with changing conditions and take advantage of available technologies.

Pocket Watch

Corporate tachypsychia, distorting the perception of time, is a major impact of the rate of change in today's marketing and business environment. Some companies are overestimating the speed of change, stampeding across The Great Plains. Procter & Gamble, arguably the best global marketer, is one that has over course-corrected… perhaps out of corporate guilt of having been so traditional regarding the Consumer in decades past. The current leadership at Procter is extorting their own marketers, as well as the rest of us, to "let go of control" and build a relationship with the Consumer. While directionally correct, I do not want a "buddy," I want a Customer. As marketers, we should never actually cede control, but only give that impression. In today's Wild West of New Marketing, we need to loosen the reins a bit as the horse picks up speed, but "letting go" is a dangerous attitude and can lead to chaos.

Advertising Age posed the query to its online subscribers if "marketer's embrace of new media was premature," given the low incidence of Consumer use of the more sophisticated Net technologies. When I last checked the results online, the poll was a clarifying vote of 48% "yes" and 52% "no," indicating the polarity of opinions. Another research poll of at-work Internet users was quite sobering regarding the focus and buzz on the more advanced digital technologies and techniques:

> … only 8% even listen to podcasts

> … only 22% read blogs

and … 88% had no recognition or knowledge of RSS.

Other companies, at the other end of "maverick" spectrum, continue to stick their head in the proverbial gopher hole and pretend the New World of Marketing does not exist. They may make a foray into new media, but the traditionalist marketing attitude remains dominant and counter-productive.

Town Bank

The flotsam from the wagon trains gradually coalesced into small towns and settlements. Each isolated center of population hovered around the nucleus of a bank, which was usually co-operative in nature. The bank was key to the town's survival and was well defended by the entire population.

My conversation with Jim Garrity, Chief Marketing Officer at Wachovia, touches on a number of key issues in the Wild West of New Marketing today. Jim's comments are highly reflective of the many issues facing CMOs in the current dynamic environment.

Jim: "Things have changed with technology influencing and impacting the way we communicate with each other, the way we communicate with individuals and groups or the way we obtain information and stay on top of the latest developments. However, nothing is more important for us than a face-to-face contact with the customer or prospect. Ten years ago there was a belief, not in our company, but in many financial institutions, that the changes in technology would drive very different ways of doing business. The technology tools would change people's behavior and alleviating the need for actual bricks and mortar and the personal relationships and intimate contacts with real people."

"No matter how people do business with us, the financial center and the people in it seem to be the anchor of all relationships, even if the multitude of transactions are happening through other channels."

Tom: "Do you think this behavior is because we are so swamped with electronic and voice triages that it has made that personal contact even more valuable?"

Jim: "Maybe. I also think, frankly, it just speaks to the intimate nature of our relationship with financial information, our financial well-being, and there's something reassuring about being able to sit down with someone and talk to them and look them in the eye when you talk about something this important to you and something this important for you to fully understand. So we are not just doing a Google search on a part number for a consumer electronics device and then looking for the lowest price."

Tom: "Right. When you get into those issues of health and wealth that the same dynamic has transpired with some of our pharmaceutical and healthcare Clients. Along with technology the personal touch and reassurance is absolutely vital."

Jim: "With all that said, doesn't mean we're not also very interested in understanding the changes in communication, techniques, technology and experimenting with some of the emerging techniques... particularly, as we watch what's happening in the world of television and broadcast advertising and we are significantly shifting our marketing investment mix as a result of some of that."

Tom: "Towards specific programming or less television?"

Jim:　"We tend to, overtime, skew much more towards cable. Partly because of demographics, we can target through cable and partly in the world of everybody having a DVR, much of the programming on cable are for those people tend to watch 'real time' news and sports, in particular."

　　　"We are also looking at this whole phenomenon of user-generated content. How can we leverage that in a positive way for our Brand for communication? How can we potentially capitalize on some of these more viral tactics leveraging into brand messaging and a good brand vibe about Wachovia in this connected world?"

Tom:　"Are you tending to use blogs and similar advanced tools as a source of consumer research or feedback?"

Jim:　"We certainly do a great deal in terms of online research to understand trends. We also do want to know what people are saying about our Brand, so we very much track that. We don't do anything proactively with blogs. We stay on top of that world, as well as podcasts. We've done some work with video-on-demand and creating highly tailored deliveries of TV commercials. This is for a household demographic where the cable delivery system allows that level of business."

Tom:　"It seems to me that just looking at some of these things that, on one hand, people are avoiding commercials and yet on the other have to see events, Super Bowl, Oscar, you name it, that the commercials have become more and more important relative to the program. It's interesting the polarization of how Consumers are willing to treat or look at the advertising itself."

Jim:　"I think a lot of that has to do with getting the right content in the right place at the right time. If you look at some of the high volume, frequently viewed videos on a website like YouTube, a good percentage of those are TV commercials that somebody chose to put up there. They are going to, on their own time, and finding them so they can view them. I'm not running away saying I'm going to be TiVoed to death and nobody ever is going to get my messaging. I'm going to find a way to get the right message to the right audience in the way they want to consume it when they want to consume it. Not the raw tonnage, broad distribution paradigm of the past."

Tom: "Right. Do you find that you shifted your efforts into customer retention versus generating new leads, or is there a different change in mix maybe over the last five years?"

Jim: "We found through a marketing mix modeling approach that we can differentiate the impact the marketing investment has on loyalty versus acquisition. Frankly, we announced after the Wachovia-First Union merger that "job one, day one" was to be the leader in customer satisfaction. We've been very successful and have, I think, among large financial institutions, the lowest attrition rate in the industry. And according the University of Michigan ACSI survey, we were just named leader in customer satisfaction six years in a row. So frankly, our infrastructure and our culture is driving our loyalty."

Tom: "In consumer-generated content, there is certainly a risk factor there. I'm sure that certainly has figured into your thinking."

Jim: "That's one of the reason why we haven't done anything publicly yet. We are in discussion, though, with online companies to potentially dabble in that area where the online company, and us, in partnership with them, would have complete control about what user-generated content might be posted."

"You won't see us encouraging people to put their Wachovia stories on YouTube. If you search YouTube for Wachovia, there is an astounding number of things you will find. There are three categories… building implosions, kids skateboarding in Wachovia buildings and parking lots and, far and away, the most is probably illegal footage that people took during concerts at the Wachovia Center... hundreds of those."

Tom: "It is interesting in working with a number of our Clients a company has to accept a certain amount of risk and deal with that particular corporation's tolerability of risk. Virgin Mobile would certainly have a higher tolerance level than would Wachovia for sure for good reasons."

Jim: "Yeah because of the business we're in, we will be taking risks and trying to take more as we become innovative, but we'll take that type of risk."

Tom: "As you look forward, what are some of the changes in marketing that you might have to address?"

Jim: "I can tell you right off the top, it's shifting our emphasis as a corporation, from growth by acquiring companies that have additional customer relationships, to growing organically. That's going to happen in our case, through innovation. We are going to have to broaden our definition on what is marketing and how does marketing drive innovation and our organic growth."

Tom: "We're finding that with a number of our Clients that despite the interest rates, the acquisition pace may have reached an inflection point where every company is going to have to find a way to grow organically. We are seeing that across a broad array of industries."

Given the crucible of the Wild West of New Marketing, true innovators will disrupt and forever alter the terrain and competitive landscape. The catalyst can have humble beginnings.

Loveable Lizards

While the *heloderma suspectum* or Gila monster lizard is not particularly appetizing, many of the wagon trains supplemented their diet with the edible species of chuckwalla lizard. Sort of sounds like "chuckwagon."

However, the particular reptile genus we want to label as a "maverick" is GEICO. This Company not only left the common herd of its competitors, but in becoming so different and successful, they forced competitors to mimic GEICO's business model. This "maverick" changed an entire industry.

... and broke every rule in The Good Book.

Auto insurance is truly one of the toughest categories in which to compete, especially since the competitors are large, entrenched, and have very deep pockets. And GEICO is not nearly as large or dominant as an outside observer would imagine, from its advertising presence. Its share of auto insurance premium is half that of Allstate and a third of State Farm. The Company has among the industry's highest levels of consumer satisfaction in terms of overall experience, policy offerings, and claims handling. Uncharacteristic of a smaller player, this bucking bronco selected "price" and "massive advertising" ... normally the weapons of choice for the larger cowboys.

A strong positioning on pricing in insurance virtually guarantees self-selection and the accumulation of a portfolio of price-sensitive Consumers. Nevertheless, this "maverick" discovered the opportunity not to be all things to all people, but to create and dominate a new and ignored value space.

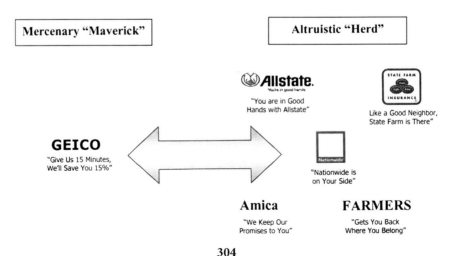

GEICO ratcheted its media investment to over $400 million annually, virtually forcing the altruistic herd of competitors to follow. Such levels of firepower enable the Brand to paint its presence virtually everywhere possible, from television to toll plazas, billboards to plane banners. Dramatic exposure can expose a Brand a substantial degree of irritation, unless the message is refreshing.

Here again, whether smart or just lucky, GEICO found the loveable lizard and namesake. This talking lizard creative would have been a very difficult sell to a tradition-bound insurance company. Soon he became the darling of the airwaves. Consumers became enthralled, but competitors were not so easily amused. Allstate's Chief Marketing Officer is quoted as saying, "I would like to squash it," referring to our Loveable Lizard.

Most good consultants... including ourselves... marketing gurus, advertising agencies, and most mother-in-laws will recommend that an advertiser speak with a single creative voice. No tenet is more ingrained. But not for this cowboy! In addition to the Loveable Lizard, GEICO added multiple intermingled, widely varying advertising campaigns such as "cavemen," and the juxtaposition of real customers with funky celebrities, like Little Richard and "Mrs. Butterworth" to help deliver the selling message.

Crafty like a desert fox! Of course with the luxury of $400 million in media, GEICO could afford to adequately support multiple campaigns simultaneously. And where most advertisers are lucky to have one great campaign, GEICO had multiple entries strong enough in their own right to coexist even with massive expenditures.

House of Ill Repute

GEICO's Marketing Innovations not only made the industry "fierce" but also made the consumer... "promiscuous."

Annual "shopping" for auto insurance, like health insurance, has become an ingrained consumer behavior, due to the cost or other sources of dissatisfaction. Fully 25% of Consumers changed auto insurance companies last year. The Consumer shifts "in" and "out" of the same companies with regularity is often based on a "savings promise."

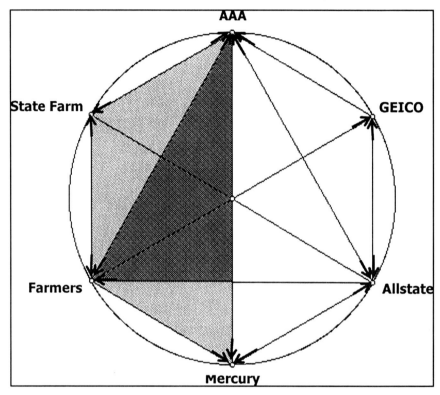

This dynamic is incredibly inefficient, costly, and destructive to the industry, but not necessarily so for GEICO, who has a highly efficient transactional business model.

The Consumer's rationale for both "shopping" and "selecting" is centered on cost savings, which many consider to be a commodity product. This is further inflamed by the shift of industry's advertising to focus on price.

The type of company or channel selected by the Consumer does not change the essential rank order of influencers or reasons for selecting their auto insurance... mainly price discounts and reputation. The actual product and coverage are rated relatively low as influencers, perhaps from lack of knowledge.

As a result, the Consumer "churn" is a problem for all companies, even as GEICO's competitors fought back with their own deep discount programs.

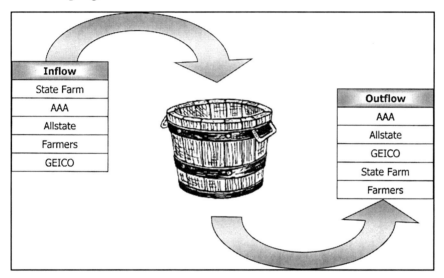

Inflow
State Farm
AAA
Allstate
Farmers
GEICO

Outflow
AAA
Allstate
GEICO
State Farm
Farmers

Collectively the industry, particularly the "price" Brands, has taught the Consumer to frequently shop for "price."

GEICO has accumulated a book of business with a high percentage of "price switchers" with 65% of the customers willing to switch for price. But this "maverick" makes it work, and makes it profitable.

"Mavericks" often intrude on other people's ranches and elicit a competitive reaction. This is particularly true when the idea is revolutionary.

Gunfight at the OK Corral

The Gunfight at the OK Corral, Cochise County, Arizona Territory in 1881 has come to epitomize the age-old battle between the rule of law and the bandits. The gunfight matched Wyatt Earp, his two brothers, and Doc Holiday against the McLaury and the Clantos brothers. But the argument was really more about differing business practices than the law.

In the vast desert of our healthcare system, "mavericks" have introduced the concept of retail healthcare clinics, which is bringing out the gunslingers.

There is a battle raging now, with physicians across the nation fighting every other stakeholder over the future of retail healthcare clinics. There is no question whether the retail clinic concept is catching fire, with an estimated jump from 150 or so at the start of 2007 to over 900 by year's end.

The AMA's *Marcus Welby, MD* and *Ozzie and Harriet* view of the world no longer exists. Many people do not have healthcare insurance, and those who do are bearing a much greater percentage of the costs. Families are time-constrained and have two or three jobs just to get by financially. So to be quite candid, after our pediatrician cancelled our son's camp exam six times, the concept of a convenient, any-time retail medical clinic has a great deal of appeal. Who wants to load up the kids in the horse and buggy and take the long ride into town to see the sawbones?

A "maverick" must be prepared for a voracious competitive attack and response to a game-changing idea. We tend to upset the status quo and be quite threatening to the entrenched traditionalists. Retail medical clinics, if sufficient traffic can be generated, have the potential to be a game-changer.

Town Crier

Much of today's discussion regarding "maverick" marketing gravitates to advertising and promotion due to the ready visibility. The creative component of advertising and promotional activities has remained relatively constant for some time. However, the major change in the Wild West of New Marketing has occurred in media and the ability to execute a promotional or CRM program more immediately and efficiently. Not so long ago, media was an after-thought to the creative product… but certainly no longer.

Dueling Banjos

The Net has become so powerful so quickly that its aura and buzz have yet to intersect with reality. As fact-based business people, we must also consider the issue that much of the data, information, opinion, anecdotes, case histories, and metrics originate with "sellers" … "sellers" with a vested interest in the Net. And that includes the Consumer and Trade press, who have to "sell" stories based on what is new and different. Hyperbole has crept into the coverage and stories concerning the Net versus so-called traditional media.

Even internally within companies like Kraft, Kinkos, or Kohl's, the people responsible for digital advertising are "selling" up, down, and sideways within the corporation. That is their responsibility, and the measure of "how" and "if" they can create their own fiefdom within the Company. They are proactive advocates of digital execution and are less than totally objective. The Net-Nowledgeables have a vested career interest in promoting their particular expertise over traditional media. That is acceptable, as long as Management understands the filtering of information and varying points of view.

In terms of metrics, ComScore Networks is one of a few global leaders in providing key syndicated research on the metrics of the digital community. It owns a massive panel of 2 million Consumers, who have "opted-in" to permit capture of their Net use and transactions. In contrast, ACNielsen utilizes a sample of 10,000 to deliver television ratings on which all video broadcast is planned and purchased.

A monthly report of currently 250 properties is measured providing the key macro score of unique visitors, through which all digital programs are designed. Unique visitors to the Net on a specific website roughly translates to maximum reach, in traditional media terminology. The number of hits or logins represents frequency.

However, consideration of the underlying metrics is equally important.

- Less than 60% of the entire U.S. population logged onto any website in an entire month

- Unique visitors vary in age from 5 to 105

- Visit duration can be an hour or nanosecond

- A "visit" implies no interest in or actual engagement in any commercial messaging

- Unique visitors are highly concentrated in the Big Five wholesalers... Yahoo!, AOL Time Warner, Microsoft, Google, and eBay.

The traffic to all other sites drops off faster than did stock prices in the dotcom bubble burst. As in any comprehensive analysis, it is absolutely essential to consider Net traffic in context and relations to other pathways to the Consumer.

	NBC's Sunday Night Football	Google	Wal-Mart Retail Stores
Average Number of "Unique Visitors" Per Week	22.4 Million	25.7 Million	111 Million

In other words, four times as many people get in their car or board a bus and shop and buy at a Wal-Mart retail store than even click on Google... ditto, Microsoft sites... every week. And compare the Wal-Mart store's weekly traffic of 111 million retail shoppers to walmart.com's unique visitors of 6.6 million. Roughly the same number visit Sunday Night Football's website in a three-hour period, as go to Google sites all week.

Reflective of the more integrated approach to marketing is the action by major advertisers such as Procter and J&J to forge the function of strategic planning, creative and media together into single-account dedicated teams. This reduces the spurious "either traditional or digital" debate, which is highly counter productive. The medium is, in fact, the message. The greatest impact of digital media may be to enhance and enforce a more holistic commercial messaging. Ignore the hyperbolic discussions and the froth and drumbeat of digital media's superiority. The true and dominant issue is not the battle of the "Nets," Internet versus Network television.

Dead Man's Hand

In 1876, "Wild Bill" Hickock, who earned his nickname both as an army scout and lawman, was shot and killed during a raucous poker game. His cards, two aces and two eights, became known as the Dead Man's Hand and harbinger of disaster.

Has traditional media been dealt a Dead Man's Hand? Many think so.

For newspapers, the loss of ad revenue has become an avalanche of monumental proportions, with double-digit declines. Even the most prestigious newspapers in the largest markets have not been immune. More threatening is the fact that declines in ad revenue greatly exceeded the losses in actual circulation.

Advertisers have found the "maverick" digital alternatives to be newer and sexier. Newspapers, as a group, have failed to "youthenize." The industry responses to salvage the bottom-line have included layoffs, firings, reduced circulations, smaller formats, and any action that would save a silver dollar.

The totality of the landscape of media expenditure is relatively fixed, with only minor gains each year. Some of the ranches, primarily "maverick" media, are expanding their acreage while others are contracting. Alternative or non-traditional media such as online, video games, word-of-mouth, mobile, and interactive is growing roughly at a rate of 20%. These media have the common characteristic of being more oblique and less shotgun-in-your-face than traditional means. Television and newspapers are suffering most from the digital outlaws.

However, there are some storm warnings in that measurement of investment in alternative and digital media remains is elusive as a timber wolf. The 2007 spending estimates in online advertising by four industry-accepted experts, Interactive Advertising Bureau,

International Data, TNS Media Intelligence, and PQ Media, vary by as much as 100%. It is like attempting to count prairie dogs.

And the first quarter 2008 investment in online advertising declined from the previous quarter for the first time in more than three years.

Scalped

However, there are ominous concrete signs that newspapers, in particular, have been scalped by the digital alternatives that have not only diverted readership, but also wounded vital organs and revenue streams such as classified advertising. All of the major newspaper groups... Gannett, New York Times, The Tribune Company... have reduced staffing, reduced circulation guarantees, changed their editorial model, and written down the value of their properties. Similarly, *Newsweek*, *U.S. News*, and *Time* have experienced double-digit declines in advertising revenue.

Chicken Wire Saloons

The Western saloons were bawdy and brawly. The mixture of alcohol, women, and six-guns often proved to be explosive. Even the entertainers were not safe from the ribald ruffians. To protect the banjo players and salacious singers from groping hands and thrown bottles and chairs, many saloon owners installed a handy barrier of chicken-wire.

There is another "bar fight" underway in Media, which is a manifestation of the outer and more visible layer of the New World of Marketing. It is a fight not necessarily between "good" and "evil" but rather the newer, less well-measured channels, versus the more traditional.

The initial shock and tendency to ignore digital Media has worn off. Traditional media has sobered up and is fighting back with techniques to enliven and make their product more relevant and interactive. Consider some of the "maverick" actions being unveiled by magazines,

... lickable ads (lime-flavored mojitos)

... embedded musical tunes

... three-dimensional pop-ups

and... photo-friendly ad links to websites

The various television networks have set up designated planning and sales groups to proactively market integrating Brands into their programming. This goes beyond mere added value, to creating a specific reason why advertisers should invest in and commit to new programming much earlier in the process. This is a powerful tool that is often multi-media.

Traditional media has joined the enemy and the digital age with substantial investments and activity. *People* is now both a traditional magazine and a highly promoted digital magazine. CBS is investing in online properties. Newspapers own the top local websites in 22 of the top 25 markets, and generate fifteen percent of their revenue online.

It is a duel, but do not fall into the mental trap of considering the issue as being "either-or." New media and traditional media work best in a complementary role.

In defining their business corral, the television networks may have found the best defense against online alternatives — join them. Both ABC and CBS are offering their prime grade Angus Beef in online broadcasts, through their own broadband channel. Similarly, magazines are rapidly expanding into video content. Once again, the traditional media organizations have been slow but deliberate in their embracing, co-opting, and absorbing of "new" media. This further blurs and melds different mediums into a single entity. The single-dimension, pure-play, media company will end up like the buffalo — wounded and staggering across The Great Plains.

Grandest Rodeo

The marketing game has been forever altered, but traditional media will be the lead horse for decades, driving people to a deeper level of communication and transaction on the Net.

The best example of the inter-relationship of traditional and digital media is the grandest marketing rodeo of all time, the Super Bowl. This is the "Big Enchilada," representing both the confluence of media as well a test market of techniques to come with a price tag of $100,000 per second to match.

The Super Bowl is no longer a television event… it is an omni-media event. After the last Super Bowl, over nine million people viewed the commercials online, and almost 29 million visited the websites of sponsors. Future advertisers will garner added value of appearance on myspace.com, with links to their own website. This is the future in the Wild West of New Marketing.

Procter & Gamble, to simulate internal creativity, awards the selected brand group and agency a commercial appearance in the Super Bowl. This year much was made in the marketing press that the Tide-to-Go stain remover commercial in the Super Bowl achieved 32,000 unique visitors to the Brand's website… that day! Not to confuse marketers or the press with the facts, but that is about … one person for every outlet where you can buy Tide-to-Go.

Pissin' In The Mississippi

Bill Walton, the President of Holiday Inn, was one of my Clients when he was opening an inn every three days. Once, he interrupted my presentation at a particularly important juncture with a statement,

"Tom, we caught you down at the Mississippi pissin' into it." In marketing terminology, translated from "Southern," that means what I was saying was largely "irrelevant."

I think we have caught Marketers and the press "down at the Mississippi, pissin' into it." Over 30,000 hits to the website can only contribute to a mass product — not drive it. In the euphoria of digital media, marketers can mistakenly ignore the 93 million Super Bowl TV viewers that drove the 30,000 website visitors.

And if we are headed toward the total integration or a future of combination of media, how can we establish the metrics of each component's contribution?

Fred Huser, prior head of Novartis Consumer Healthcare and current Partner at NECG, warns:

> "The toughest task we, as Marketers, face is finding the right combination of marketing variables to use to support and grow the business. But whatever combination one selects, the overarching principle for selection has got to be effectiveness first and efficiency second. No matter how efficient something is, if no one notices, it is not worth doing."

I'll drink to that.

Lone Cowboy

The scene with the "lone cowboy" silhouetted against the shimmering vastness of The Great Plains without another human being in sight is representative of current media consumption.

Back in the day, Marshall McLuhan described television as an "electronic hearth." BTV or "before television," people read magazines and newspapers or listened to radio by themselves. Television became the medium that brought people together for social consumption. A single enormous Magnavox home entertainment system dominated the living room, as well as family habits, from Levittown to Palo Alto.

Fast-forward to the present, where the number of TV sets in the average home is three. Everyone can have their own personal TV. This has been further compounded by the digital revolution and its magnified number of TV screens: CD players, gaming console, computers, and even cell phones.

Today, media consumption is personal... and alone.

Camouflage

Being deceptive and hidden was an act of survival in the Wild West. Being unseen provides a great deal of flexibility in dealing with competitors and a hostile environment.

The same could be said of the Wild West of New Marketing. Many large advertisers and advocates with a vested interest in promoting digital media are clouding the issue. These pundits have made much of Johnson & Johnson's double-digit decline in annual, traditional media advertising, while increasing its investment online by 38%. Cause and effect, right? Wrong! The real news is that J&J decreased its total advertising by 20% and the Internet receives less than 3% of the total budget.

Camouflage is a useful tool. And the Net is a superior rationalization when the real intent is to reduce the overall advertising budget without corporate embarrassment.

Fort Sam Houston

Wrong Sam... Sam Adams!

"Maverick" marketers in a particular category may be forced to take a different pathway to growth. They are likely to be the smaller yearlings in a herd of gnarled, open range longhorns. Acting as the "maverick" is its only chance of survival or success. The traditional methodologies of Marketing are often dominated by deep-pocketed giants.

One of our Clients in the beer industry, Samuel Adams, is an instructive analog. Having survived the explosion, and then the subsequent implosion of the handcrafted microbreweries, Sam Adams had to make some very tough decisions regarding the future development of the Company and how to compete with the Anheuser Busch, Miller, and Coors juggernauts on one flank and the micro-breweries on the other.

Given that brewing heritage, it is not surprising that Jim Koch focused on finding a pasture where only a true "maverick" could roam more freely. Two proven areas of leverage were targeted while avoiding the big guns of the industry... product and distribution.

In the expansion of distribution, it was key to maintain an aura of specialness and exclusivity but yet, an exploding a geographic footprint beyond that of a Northeast microbrewery. Samuel, rather Sam Adams embarked on a visibility distribution strategy, with actual physical retail locations in high traffic airports. This achieved instant distribution, while at the same time functioning both as advertising and as a sampling venue. These multi-locations made the Company and the Brand appear larger and more important than the geographic reality.

Jim, the consummate brewmeister, focused heavily on the product itself, with an intensity difficult to achieve by non-founders. The first step was the development of a "light" beer, which was only released after a totally new flavor-level was achieved... meaning one that would satisfy Jim and his astute brewery team.

Secondly, Jim led the charge into a unique and unoccupied space, very high-end, beer-based beverages somewhere, between beer and spirits. At a $100 per bottle and an alcoholic content ranging from 17–25%, he did not have to fight the Clydesdales. A sequence of exotic launches, Triple Bock Reserve, Millennium, and Utopia, each with a unique taste, raised the awareness and perception of the Samuel Adams brand as superlative and different beer company.

Koch was so focused on a unique positioning and specialness that Sam Adams joined the prestigious National Association for the Specialty Food Trade. It was the only beer company among the exclusive Brands of pate, champagne, sauces, and other fine foods. As the "maverick," Sam Adams pilgrimaged where Miller would not and could not go.

Mama Grizzly

As indicated by our consideration of companies like Wal-Mart and Procter & Gamble, the size of the organization is not necessarily a fatal and determinant factor of being a "maverick." We have found, in working with the Fortune 500 to the small private equity-funded start ups, that corporate culture and attitude are much more important than corporate size or complexity in governing a Company's "maverick" or renegade tendencies.

The sheer size of an organization can be an inhibiting environmental factor … but, as true with every aspect of "maverick" marketing, there are exceptions. PepsiCo is just that deviation from the norm. Its "degree of maverickness" is best defined relative to its peer competitor and nemesis, Coca-Cola. The latter company is less aggressive, more predictable, and historically more traditional in its marketing activities.

PepsiCo is a rule-breaker of the highest order and tends to embrace and enjoy going against traditional wisdom, just like a rebellious teenager… The Pepsi Generation. As an example, Pepsi-Cola altered its soda can graphics every few weeks, as a means of engaging and responding to the Consumers' craving for change. Normally, the packaging is always to remain the constant in the presentation to the Consumer. Pepsi sagely refused to accept the standard diction.

We classify companies or organizations into three basic groups along the "maverick" continuum. First are the one hundred percent "mavericks," whose companies are run based on a "Do something different," mantra. These companies tend to be smaller and are not fully mature or developed. The most distinguishing characteristic is the presence of a bull-headed founder… who themselves are personally a "maverick."

Most typical are the hybrid organizations, which have a blend of traditional and "maverick" attitudes. These companies are larger and more complex in their operations and are more likely to be NYSE than NASDAQ.

Is Procter & Gamble, as a company, a "maverick" marketing company? Absolutely not! Are some of their divisions more innovative than others? Definitely. Are some of their personnel "renegade" in their marketing approach? Absolutely and sometimes, "way off the reservation."

The traditional marketers are often in industries, where due to the cost structure or operational issues, marketing is theoretically less important to the organization. The product or service categories are older and more mature. A key factor is that the category and corporate culture which tend to be staid and mechanical. Marketers rarely occupy the C-level suite in these companies. Examples would include companies that are quite innovative in technological aspects but traditional in their overall approach to marketing… DuPont, 3M, and IBM as evidenced by their flow of patents.

Several categories where many traditional marketers reside are insurance, healthcare, financial services, and subsets of the pharmaceutical industry. It is from these industries that the New England Consulting Group often gets requests to assist them in moving from "manufacturing" to "marketing," as a business model. These organizations tend to think "inside-out."

Wyatt Earp

Should your Company strongly police the overall operation to have your entire herd of Brands and business sectors following exactly the same rules and pathways? That is a key decision, which bears considerable discussion and soul-searching, because this can have a long-range and profound impact on the ultimate success of your organization.

In complex organizations with multiple categories, divisions, and numerous brands, there is the logic of rather refined corporate policies and procedures. Management has to be able to deal in common formats and with standardized metrics. Certain processes are employed that are the result of management and corporate learning.

On the other hand, many marketing decisions have become bureaucratized and evolved higher and higher within the organization. Fewer and fewer Marketers are making real decisions, leaving companies with less diverse and totally new thinking. Today, marketing decisions are made much slower by a chain-link series of the sheer number of people involved. All of us develop "poker tendencies" and often play in the same manner with the same risk assessment, hand after hand. The fates of today's Companies are being placed in the hands of fewer and fewer "players."

We attribute at least some of the dismal failure rate of new products in CPG, Food, Beverage, OTC, and other categories, to be the result of over-centralized and standardized approaches. The very skills and insights that lead to new product "homeruns" can be killed by the corporate sheriffs and their dictates of process and bureaucracies.

Many of us at the New England Consulting Group have seen and experienced the tremendous and positive impact that a few individual "mavericks" can have on a Company, even at a large and entrenched one. We recommend that Management utilize the industry's best practices in a corporate or divisional role. However, it is vital to encourage, nurture, and foster a "maverick" marketing attitude within the Company. This is an ideal opportunity to force responsibility "downward" and to open up more sites of exploration. The younger, better Marketers within your organizations are restless and eager to implement some of their own ideas, even if the gray-haired management teams regard them as divergent from established procedure. "Doing" is the best form of management training.

Creating more internal "test markets" within the Company raises the energy level and excitement in the organization. Sponsoring "new thinking" and regarding learning-from-mistakes as valuable, can pay compounding dividends for the future of your Company.

Highly complex and globally directed organizations like the Ford Motor Company, with 8 vehicle brands, 55 sub brands, 3 automotive service brands, and over 15,000 dealers in 130 markets worldwide have severe management issues. Management control, consistency, and alignment are absolutely imperative. The troops and the brigades must follow the same order and direction. Or else, chaos takes over and all efficiencies and economies of scale are lost.

However, for the very same reasons, a company like Ford must not only allow but also proactively promote a certain tolerance of "maverickness." A bureaucracy can smother a company cutting off its oxygen and catalyst for growth.

A company like Ford needs its "Mustangs."

Guerilla Raids

In the initial stages of confrontation, the Indian tribes had an inherent set of advantages over the flood of settlers cascading across The Great Plains. The Arapahoe, Comanche, Sioux, and Apache were highly mobile and could select their point of attack, at will and do so with no warning.

Similarly in business, the "maverick" marketers have significant opportunities for competitive advantage… only the opportunity and not necessarily the advantage itself that must be earned.

"Maverick" marketers are more flexible and can address an issue from any direction.

A "maverick" company has a competitive advantage over a traditional company… a "maverick" division or business sector has an advantage over traditional division within a traditional company. A "maverick" individual, even within a traditional corporation, possesses substantial advantages of staging-lighting guerrilla raids rather than large-pitched battles.

The legendary football coach of Florida A&M, Jake Gaither, a true "maverick" himself, described what he wanted his players to be, "Agile, mobile, and hostile."

Tom Hayes

In today's Wild West, the prevailing wind is "guerilla" rather than "gorilla" marketing… the stealthily puma rather than the blatant lion.

Puma

According to Wikipedia, the puma or cougar has the greatest range of any wild terrestrial mammal in the Western Hemisphere. The puma's frightening screams awakened many settlers, with its piercing nighttime cry. This ferocious cat has superlative agility in the harsh and demanding environment of the Western mountains and deserts.

Agility is one of the key factors that separate a "maverick" from the herd. He or she possesses the quality of legerity, or being mentally or physically quick. When confronted with an obstacle or impediment, the "maverick" can and will change directions more quickly than the traditionalist person or organization. Remember all of the ultimate successes in new product from the developments of initial failures such as Viagra being initially tested as a cardiovascular drug. The "maverick" in this case was a large and rather rigid company who turned quickly to seize a golden opportunity.

Organizational and objective agility are other characteristics, in that a "maverick" tends to operate more independently of many corporate constrictions... even within a hidebound company that is fixated on the process rather than the product of that process.

Philosophically, "mavericks" tend to be highly mobile foraging across more terrain and searching for new ideas, new approaches, and new technologies. Not being confined to the corporate corral is a distinct advantage, in that adjacent opportunities can be more readily explored. He or she can find new, unoccupied white space void of directly competitive ideas.

Totems

Totems or symbols of animals from the Spirit World are a major component of the culture of many Indian tribes. Each animal, not unlike Zodiac signs, represents a certain set of characteristics or strengths.

In these tumultuous times of declining program rating points and print readership, proactive avoidance of advertising, and a complete fragmentation of commercial messaging, some "maverick" marketers have elected to go against the flow of the digital "future" and back toward the "past" and their totems or icons. When traditional commercial messaging is imploding, it is ironic that one of the most valuable brand equities is the symbolic personality that previously represented the Brand. Brand icons, harnessed for decades, have become even more valuable fortresses of Brand equity today.

Icons grow with years of use. They survive only if, as the embodiment of the Brand, some degree of engagement with the Consumer is achieved. In today's "fast forward" messaging world and with a general

ADD attitude toward media, these strange "blasts from the past" creatures cut through the clutter and cacophony of advertising.

Icons are concentrated microbursts of communication... and well-suited for "maverick" marketing.

Brand icons are often referred to as "Leo Burnett critters." This is a well-deserved compliment to the infamous Leo Burnett advertising agency, which invented and nurtured so many powerful marketing characters that you know so well.

   ...   Keebler's Elves

   ...   Jolly Green Giant

   ...   The Marlboro Man

   ...   Pillsbury Doughboy

and   ...   many others

Leo, himself a "maverick", infused his very successful agency to develop a visual imagery for their clients' Brands. He called these icons, "brand pictures engraved on the Consumer's mind." Even when we just verbalize a part of the name, you can fill in the blank and conjure up a commercial message image... Tony the _____... Morris the _____ and Charlie the _____.

Reload!

In these perilous times of difficult communication, marketers are "reloading" and dusting off their Brand icons with "maverick" techniques, enabled by digital media. The Consumer is being engaged and involved as a key component of evolving successful brand icons. Contests, polls, and surveys are utilized to tweak these icons such as Mr. Peanut or The Michelin Man and include the Consumer in the actual developmental process... and subsequently reinforcing their relationship to the Brand.

Some "mavericks" are making the "reloading" of their icons the focal point of their advertising and promotional campaigns. It is a celebratory event. All such makeovers and revitalizations have an objective to generate press coverage and buzz.

With the digital empowerment of the Net, the "mavericks" are wringing even more value out of their long-term positioning slogans. They are involving Consumers by having them vote on whether or not to change or alter a slogan. This alone brings attention to and consideration of the Brand and its positioning.

Very close and converging on Brand icon status are great marketing propositions, summed up in an advertising slogan, which includes Maxwell House ("Good to the Last Drop"), California Milk Board ("Got Milk") and Texas ("Don't Mess with Texas"). They are the verbalization of the Brand and its essence.

A Brand-defining marketing slogan can catapult a small, "maverick" marketer into a major player. In the thirty-two years BMW has been using, "The Ultimate Driving Machine" positioning, its sales have increased by fifteen times. Its rank in the U.S. among European car manufacturers has gone from "non-existent" to Number One. Coincidence? Correlated?

Blurring

While traditionalist companies tend to segregate marketing and customer relationships into mutually exclusive silos, "maverick" marketers tend to view these functions along the same continuum. "Mavericks" consider any conversation or communication with a customer as an opportunity to sell. Your best customer may very well be the one who has a complaint and can be repatriated. They are the zealous converts. When dealing with customers, complaints and, specifically, vehement complaints are perhaps the very best source of information for a change in direction... or attitude... in dealing with customers.

Tame a Mustang?

Perhaps this is the wrong question. With enough technique and deprivation, one can almost assuredly do so.

But should a manager or company break the spirit out of a "maverick?"

As a manager, we can teach our people marketing or manufacturing techniques, but we cannot teach them to be intelligent. Similarly, it is easier to break a "maverick" than to create one. True "mavericks" are a rare and valued asset. In order to maximize their value to the corporation, we should be asking how do we

- tolerate

- stimulate

- reward

- incentivize

- protect

- leverage

"maverick" within a traditional organization? How do you assist in creating more new "mavericks?"

As a final comment and warning, "mavericks" must be aware of and address the corporate misoneism... or the strong fear of and resistance to change and Innovation... that permeates many organizations.

Smoke Signals

When considered within the context of the time frame, there are a number of similarities between the Net and the "smoke signals" utilized by the pioneers and the Indians for communication across The Great Plains. Both operate on binary code and communicate over long distances at a rapid pace.

Yet, you are never quite sure of the exact identity of who is sending the message. And until the advent of a better communication technology in the heliograph, "smoke signals" were state-of-the-art.

In keeping with the tone and philosophy of the book, I am making a dramatic "maverick" move and enlist, you, the reader to contribute to *Maverick Marketing*. We are going to make this an interactive, living breathing component of the book, by soliciting your input to be incorporated into updated printings on a periodic basis.

Our unique means of publishing with Amazon's BookSurge and its printing-on-demand model for each individual printing order, even for a single book, enables the book to be potentially altered each time. Periodically, we will change and update the book with your own "smoke signal" inputs, the readers... with attribution.

Just go to (www.maverickmarketingbook.com) and sound off! Your comments, observations, musings, point-of-view, additions to the glossary, or any input are welcomed. You will have to provide explicit persuasion for us to quote you. When there is sufficient content or merit, we will include the reader-generated material in subsequent printings.

If you input your email address, you will be notified when the next edition, containing your "smoke signal," is available.

In the words of Roy Rogers and Dale Evans, "Happy trails to you."

Tom Hayes

CHAPTER NINE

THE GOOD BOOK

Above The Fold (New Media) – The web page section that is seen upon downloading without having to scroll down the page.

Above The Fold (Traditional Media) – The top half of the newspaper page that is first seen, when the paper is folded over.

Acquisition – The acquiring of a client when a media channel fulfills its role. Most commonly marked by a sale, but can also include subscriptions or services.

Ad Blocking – The blocking of web advertisements that are typically (but not limited to) pop-up advertisements on web pages.

Ad Creep – The gradual process of advertising slowly expanding into non-traditional marketing places, such as walls, floors, bathrooms, and plates.

Ad Network – The sharing of content and revenue by disparate websites to generate a larger audience.

Adevasion – Intentional consumer's actions designed at purposely avoiding commercial messaging.

Adlets – Five-second radio commercials which are offered.

Adultescent – An adult whose activities and interests are typically associated with youth culture.

Advercation – A hybrid form of advertising, created by the fusion of commercial messaging and information. Also known as advermation.

Advergaming – Product placement and commercial messaging written into the plot or background of a video game.

Advertainment – Advertising subtly implanted in short entertainment films, designed to capture audiences through entertainment.

Advertecture – The use of architectural structures to display forms of advertisements with banners, painting, or signs.

Advertorial – An advertisement in the form an editorial, to gain credibility.

Affiliate Fraud – Phony activity spawned by an affiliate in order to generate illegitimate, unearned revenue from Net traffic.

Affiliate Marketing – Advertisers/merchants and publishers/salespeople sharing revenue, where compensation is based on performance measures. Metrics for this arrangement are typically in the form of registrations, clicks, or sales.

Affiliate Merchant – The advertiser in an affiliate marketing relationship.

Alternative Reality Game – Online multi-media games that present consumers with a virtual world where consumers can represent themselves through virtual characters.

Animated GIF – A graphical image format that creates an animation effect, by rotating through a series of motionless images.

Apologement (Mark Cuban, The Dallas Mavericks) – An event designed to create issues, which force the marketer into a pre-planned public apology. How appropriate!

Assvertising – Advertising brand names or messages on the derriere of a human body, as a means of producing a shock effect.

Astroturfing – A public relations campaign that is coordinated to seem spontaneous and grass roots. event or movement.

Avatar – Derivative from Hindu mythology. Now, a digital image that represents the embodiment of a person.

Banner Ad – A graphical advertisement on web pages. The standard banner typically is displayed 468 pixels wide and 60 pixels tall.

Banner Blindness – Consumers having the tendency of generally ignoring banner ads, even though the banners displayed may contain information the consumers are actively seeking.

Banner Exchange – A network of marketers who display banner ads on websites in exchange for credits that can be converted into ads that are shown on other sites.

Barketing (NECG term) – One-to-one marketing in social venues such as bars and clubs.

Beyond the Banner – Slang term referring to online advertising that utilizeses non-traditional, digital ads.

Bid Capping – The act of setting of a limit for a maximum bid on online auctions, by the use of a bid-listing monitoring service.

Bill Advertising – Advertising by a third-party on the bill or invoice of another company, sometimes in a cash-free swap.

Blinks – Commercials in television or radio that are only one to five seconds in duration and provide a simple and concise message.

Blog – A frequent, chronological publication of personal thoughts, links, and other content/media.

Boomer – In my opinion... one of the most dangerous and fraudulent terms used to describe an age cohort as homogenous, when it is most certainly not.

Bots – A program search engines use to read the content and body of qualifying website, in order to determine its contents and relevancy.

Brandalism (NECG Term) – Counterculture and often illegal activities designed to promote a brand, such as the act of placing unwanted advertisements and brand logos on property without proper permission.

Brand Infringement – Non-ethically using another company's Brand by pretending to be that certain company — making false claims, or having a role in the company's activities.

Brand-Aid (NECG term) – A quick fix used to address a Brand's decline, but that does not help to solve the real problem.

Brand Bait – Having select individuals use products in order to spread trends and create a viral effect on remaining consumers.

Branded Communities – Online social networks, sponsored by and directed at a certain brand.

Brandscape – The scope and reach of a brand within a distinct culture or market.

Brandwagon – Using branding techniques to create a distinct market identity to consumers through marketing.

Brandwidth – The reach of a brand to a given consumer base.

BTH (NECG term) – Costco's retail strategy and business model, called a Branded Treasure Hunt.

Button Ad – A graphical advertising unit that is smaller than a banner and often an external link.

Button Exchange – A network of marketers who display button ads on websites in exchange for credits that can be converted into ads that are shown on other sites.

Buzzword – A trendy word or phrase that is used to grab the attention of a consumer rather than to explain details to the consumer.

CGC – Consumer generated content, regularly in written or video format, that can be shared with other consumers.

CGI (NECG term) – Consumer generated ideas, proactively solicited by a company.

Chatterbarking – The utilization of Consumer "chatter" sites for research and proactive purposes.

Cinemads – Commercial mini-dramas, representing the life experiences of consumers.

Click-Through – The process of clicking through an online advertisement to the advertiser's destination.

Click-Through Rate (CTR) – Average number of click-throughs per hundred ad impressions.

Co-Branded Entertainment – A chic synonym for product placement.

Competitor Clicks – Clicks by competitors to clear out the position.

Contagious Behavior – Behavior which copies or mimics the action of others.

Cost-Per-Action (CPA) – Advertising payment model in which payment is based exclusively on the actions of consumers, such as sales, subscriptions or registrations.

Cost-Per-Click (CPC) – The cost or cost-equivalent paid per click-through.

CPM – Cost per thousand impressions.

Cross-Channel – Deliberate and specific use of multiple media in a co-coordinated manner.

Customer Acquisition Cost – The cost associated with acquiring a new customer.

Cybercrud – Slang term referring to the digital equivalent of bureaucratese.

Drip marketing – The act of presenting promotional pieces to a number of potential consumers in order to generate a steady flow of consumer interest to a product line.

Egg-vertising –The utilization of venue promotion which features Commercial messaging lasered on to eggs.

E-Commerce – The process of selling merchandise online through a website.

EDLP – Wal-Mart's marketing mantra of Everyday Low Prices.

Email Marketing – The promotion of products or services via email.

Emergency Alerts – An alert through SMS, email, or phone when a monitored event is occurring, such as a flight, concert, or bid.

Evangelistic Marketing (NECG term) – Capitalizing and encouraging committed users to want to share your praises.

Ezine – An electronic magazine distributed through a web site or email newsletter.

Ezine Directory – Directory of electronic magazines, most commonly in the form of email newsletters.

Feature Shock – A user's confusion when confronted with a package that has too many features and poor tech writing.

Fingerprinting – Digital system used by YouTube to identify uploaded, copyrighted content.

FFA – Free-For-All links list where there are no qualifications for adding a link.

Forum – An online community where visitors may read and post topics of common interest.

Flog (Traditional) – To promote or sell aggressively (derisive term).

Flog (2.0) – Narrow line between fake and real blog postings.

Genericide – When a product or brand becomes the common reference for an entire category of products. i.e. Sea-Doo, Coke, Band-aid.

Geoarching – Harnessing GPS as a marketing tool.

Group Photo – Creating affinity groups to send announcements, targeted ads, etc on Facebook or other social networking sites.

Half Clicks – Clicks that do not fully load to the browser.

Hit – Request of a file from a web server, or the physical act of accessing a size.

Headvertising – Advertising brand names, logos, or messages on the head of a human body, typically done with hair styles or tattoos (real or fake).

Hobson's Choice – Accepting an offer when there is no acceptable, alternative option.

Hormonal Marketing (NECG Term) – Increased targeting and hyper-marketing based on pure sex (e.g. Miller Beer "Real Men" Campaign).

Hybrid – Ads integrally linked and blurred with show content.

In-Call Media – Advertising placed in wait-time telephone call space.

Impression (New media) – A single instance of an online advertisement being displayed.

Impression (Traditional Media) – Single exposure to a commercial message.

Infector Commercials – Commercials posted on key websites, designed to induce the consumer to produce and post parody versions.

Influencer Marketing – Targeting small segments selected for their prosperity to communicate and lead others to your product.

Informational Clicks – Just searching for more information.

Inserted Consumer-Generated Media (ICGM) – Inducement of consumer-generated media with financial and/or other incentives by marketers.

Invisible Web – The portion of the Web not accessible through Web search engines. Estimated to be several multiples of the Web normally searched.

Invitation-Only Social Networks – Niche online groups only available through invitation or pre-selection to deliver a focused network. These groups are often utilized for research and customer relationship management to monitor thoughts and behavior.

International Clicks – Clicks from Tibet, Thailand, and Timbuktu.

iPod-jacking – Rampant and specific crime of robbery of iPod robbery.

Irritainment – A form of advertising and marketing that irritates a consumer to the point that they are compelled to pay attention.

Jujitsu Marketing (NECG Term) – Utilization of a competitor's strength and action against them (ex. Caribou Coffee agreeing to accept Starbuck's coupons.)

Key Phrases – Combinations of keywords used in search engines to provide better-directed search results.

Keyword Density – Keywords as a percentage of indexed words.

Keyword Search – A search made by typing a keyword, or combination of words, into a search box on a search engine

Link Farm – Web pages deliberately created to increase the number of links between sites, and therefore link popularity for search results. Link farms are often viewed as problematic by search engines, due to their ability to disrupt/fool search algorithms.

Link Love – The propensity of other sites to link to another site. Very similar to "Link Popularity" below.

Link Popularity – A method used by search engines to determine the importance of a listed site, based on the idea that sites which are frequently referenced are more credible than those which are not.

Magalogue – A catalogue designed to imitate a magazine.

Marketroid – A common worker in the marketing department who often makes false promises of grandeur, with upgrades and features of new products.

Message Planting – Depositing false or contrary messaging to the original intent or philosophy of a blog in order to redirect a blog's path of conversation.

Metadata – Data about data.

Microsite – A smaller subset of a website which is promoted separately.

Misoneism – Strong fear of and resistance to change.

Mocketing – Utilizing humor at the expense of the Brand, as a means of garnering Consumer engagement.

Mouse Marketing (NECG Term) – Marketing plans formulated and designed around the "click" mechanism.

Mousetrapping – The use of browser tricks in an effort to keep a visitor captive at a site, often by disabling the "Back" button or generating repeated pop-up windows.

Murketing – A Rob Walker, *Buying In* term, to describe the marketing process of deliberately blurring or obfuscating the traditional selling message.

NECG – Acronym for the New England Consulting Group.

Neophilla – The trait of being excited and pleased by novelty.

Netiquette – Short for "network etiquette," the code of conduct regarding acceptable online behavior.

Netralized (NECG Term) – Equalization of people, companies, and other forces powered by the Net.

Newsletter Marketing – The process of building relationships with existing customers and gaining new ones, by publishing and mass distributing an email containing features and articles of interest to them.

Nuisance Clicks – Just get it off my screen.

Oldsmobile Factor – Marketing stigma of a Brand being used by one's parents. Epitomized by the "not your father's Oldsmobile" campaign.

On-hold Advertising – Advertising messages that a consumer encounters while being placed on hold, during a phone call.

Open Rate (New Media) – Percentage of people opening or opting-in to an email. Can be greater than 100% due to re-opening and pass along.

Open Rate (Traditional) - Publicly published media cost, which represents the undiscounted high end.

Opinion Skews – Intentional praise in opinion rating sites to boost one's product or service.

Opt-In Email – Email that is explicitly requested by the recipient.

Pagejacking – The publication of an identical or nearly identical web page stolen from an original site and placed on a different site.

Paid Clicks – Fraudulent clicks made by paid experts to inflate revenue. Also, fraudulent clicks to inflate traffic.

Paid Linking – The function of paying for another site to link to your own.

Parodymercials (NECG Term) – Creation of a base commercial that is deliberately silly or provocative to encourage parody by media sources and bloggers.

Pass-Along Rate – The percentage of people who pass along a message or file to another viewer.

Passion Branding – Making a brand connect to an individual's sense of emotional connection.

Pay Per Post – Paying Consumers to post favorable reviews on blogs. Also a website payperpoint.com.

Pay Per Click (PPC) – Online advertising payment model, in which payment is based solely on qualifying click-throughs.

Pay Per Click Search Engine – Search engine where results are ranked according to a bid amount, and advertisers are charged when a searcher clicks on the search listing.

Pay Per Lead – Online advertising payment model, in which payment is solely based on qualifying leads.

Pay Per Sale – Online advertising payment model, in which payment is solely based on qualifying sales.

Permission Based Email – Email marketing that must first receive the permission of the recipient, and then carries out an ethical, permission-based campaign.

Permission Marketing – Marketing campaigns centered around obtaining customer consent to receive information from a company.

Pissin' into the Mississippi – A Southern consulting term for lack of relevance or importance.

Podcasting – Automatic downloads of audio information or entertainment in sequence, by subscription. First coined by Apple, inc.

Pop–Under Ad – An ad that displays in a new browser window behind the current browser window.

Pop–Up Ad – An ad that displays in a new browser window on top of the current browser window.

Porcelain Messaging – Utilization of the bathroom as a commercial messaging venue.

Post-Rolls – Commercial messaging at the end of web videos.

Postie – Pay per post label for its bloggers paid for supportive postings.

Pre-Rolls – Commercials of varying lengths within online videos.

Pre-Net Perspective (NECG Term and Expertise) – A professional understanding that the Net is a mere component and not the entire world of Media.

Price Point Marketing (NECG Term) – Working backward from a specific retail price as the driving force in marketing and manufacturing.

Prosumers – Amateur Consumers with the technical knowledge and equipment comparable to a professional.

Promotainment – Promotional ads presented as forms of entertainment to consumers.

Random Clicks – Oops... didn't mean to do that.

Rank – The position of relevance for a search on search engines, directories and searchable portals.

Result Baiting – Subversively planting false or negative messages about competition, through grass roots channels, to kill their promotion.

Rich Media – New media that offers an enhanced experience relative to the older, mainstream formats.

RSS (Really Simple Syndication) – A technology utilized for receiving/distributing blogs, news, and press releases directly, without having to visit the original source, on an ongoing and real-time basis.

Search Spy - Real-time views of actual Web searches, shown on a refreshing page.

Scraping – Gathering of bits of public information on a website to form insights.

Self-Serve Advertising – Advertising that can be purchased without the assistance of a sales representative.

SEO (Search Engine Optimization) – The process of capitalizing on search properly driving traffic to a site by analytical means.

Shopping Cart – Software used to make a site's product catalogue available for online ordering, whereby visitors may select, view, add/delete, and purchase merchandise.

Short Code SMS – Designated 5 to 6 digit number to which one can send a text message. Often used as shortcuts for addresses in contests, voting, or searching. As example, sending questions to Google's digital address is GOOGL or 46645.

Showmercial – Series of subtly branded commercials, resembling program material, that tells an entertaining story.

Site Stickiness – The amount of time spent at a site over a given time period.

Skip Generation Syndrome (NECG term) – Propensity for people to attitudinally and behaviorally resemble their grandparents, to a greater degree than their parents.

Skins – Graphic ad surrounding the window playing a video.

SKU – Stock keeping unit, one item.

Slotting Fee – Payment to a retailer for stocking a product, most normally a new product.

Snakernet – The transfer of electronic information by physically carrying tape, disks, or some other media from one machine to another. Used often in the context of jest with older systems.

Spam/Spammed – General term relating to practices or information not approved or wanted by a consumer, and sent without their consent.

Splash Page – A branding page before the home page of a Website.

Stacking – Consumer timing coupon redemption late in the expiration period in conjunction with other overlapping sales or promotional offers.

Surround Session – Advertising agreement where websites display only ads from a single company throughout the duration of each consumer's visit on the website.

Tachypsychia – Mental distortion of the perception of time… a danger for many Marketing organizations.

Text Tags – Summary of key words providing an indication of video or audio content.

Thread Jacking – Intervention into blogs of negative opinions to insert and bend the discussion.

Top 10 – The top ten search engine results for a particular search term.

Trail Marketers – Guideposts from which one can learn from those who have gone before.

Tribal Marketing – Marketing techniques that link a consumer to a community or network of other consumers through the use of a product or service.

Trick Banner – A banner ad that attempts to trick people into clicking by imitating an operating system message.

Trust Media – The Edelman Public Relations firm's term for Consumer-Generated Media.

Twitters – A social blog for short "status" updates from cell phones or text messaging.

Ultramercial – An interactive, disclosed advertisement, whereby an individual knowingly opts-in to view the message and provide some interaction in exchange for promotional value.

Unique Visitors – The number of consumers who have visited a website at least once in a fixed time frame. Usually used as an indication of a website's growth of users.

V-Cam – Consumer-generated commercial messaging for a specific marketer.

Vertical Banner – A banner ad measuring 120 pixels wide and 240 pixels tall.

Video Snacking (NECG term) – Compression of video content to reflect electronic viewing patterns. This includes smaller screens, shorter messages, and quicker cuts.

Viral Marketing – A form of marketing that is self-sustaining and self-promoting. Usually, the core idea is so appealing that the public takes on the role of "spreading the message" themselves. Control and even "ownership" of the campaign is relinquished.

VOD (Video-on-Demand) - The ability of a consumer to search and select videos and commercials based on topics of their choice.

Widget – Any code embedded in a web page that adds content without further compilation.

Wikitizing – Adding favorable views or descriptions to a new listing in Wikipedia.

XML Trusted Feed Campaign Management – An alternative of relying on search engine robots to create an index of your website. XML feeds let website hosts submit a feed of their site content to participating search engines. XML is particularly useful with websites whose content rapidly changes or cannot be accessed with conventional robot technology.

Youthenize (NECG term) – Opposite of brand euthanasia. Engendering your brand with younger age cohorts.

By the time this book is printed, the above excerpts from "The Good Book" will be out-of-date. Feel free to add your own input to emerging terms at www.maverickmarketingbook.com.

Sherriff In Town

This is to give companies their well-earned due for Brand equity, proprietary rights, and ownership of logos, trademarks, and selling lines. The respective logos, designs, and selling lines are the registered trademarks of the noted company.

AARP — American Association of Retired Persons

Allstate. "You are in Good Hands with Allstate" — Allstate Insurance Company

"We Keep Our Promises to You" — Amica

BEST BUY — Best BuyCo., Inc.

BURT'S BEES — Burt's Bees, Inc.

CLIF — Clif Bar & Co.

facebook — FaceBook, Inc.

"Gets You Back Where You Belong" — Farmers

Folgers — The Procter & Gamble Company

friendster — Friendster, Inc.

"Give Us 15 Minutes, We'll Save You 15%" — GEICO

THE HOME DEPOT — Homer TLC, Inc.

★**macy's** — Macy's, Inc.

myspace.com a place for friends — MySpace, Inc.

"Nationwide is on Your Side" — Nationwide Mutual Insurance Company

SAM'S CLUB — Wal-Mart Stores, Inc.

STATE FARM INSURANCE Like a Good Neighbor, State Farm is There" — State Farm Mutual Automobile Insurance Company

TARGET — Target Brands, Inc.

WAL★MART — Wal-Mart Stores, Inc.

TOM HAYES

Aspen, 2008

Tom is Managing Partner and Principal at the New England Consulting Group, leading and participating in the company's Marketing Due Diligence, Healthcare, Consumer Packaged Goods, Insurance, Business Intelligence, and other practice teams.

With over twenty-five years of action in some of the most competitive marketing battles in the annals of business today, Tom brings to bear an extensive and eclectic body of successful experience and learning for his clients.

Tom's successful assignments span an immense array of categories (condoms to cookies), companies (Allied Capital to Procter & Gamble), and brands (Abbott to Hershey). His creativity of bi-association has greatly assisted his Clients in creating growth and value.

Immediately prior to joining New England, Tom was Executive Vice President and Director of Publicis Healthcare. Tom was also a long-time senior executive with several major advertising agencies (JWT, Esty, Wells Rich Greene), specializing in managing their most demanding and intense marketing Clients, including Procter & Gamble, Nabisco, Pfizer and Chesebrough-Ponds.

His approach to his Clients is highly action-oriented and based on a fiduciary responsibility to solve the problem... and drive the business. Some of Tom's particular core competencies include maximizing growth situations and highly competitive battles as well as new product development. Tom is a balanced "left-brain" thinker (Thesis: Mathematical Prediction of the Formability of Metals) and "right brain" thinker (created and wrote a successful world-wide television series for M&M Mars). This confluence has proven to be highly successful for his clients, from Assurant to Ventus Medical... from AARP to MedPointe.

Tom has published numerous articles in various business and industry publications. He is often called by the press and quoted for his Consumer and Customer insights on an array of strategic business and marketing issues. Tom is a frequent speaker at industry conferences and corporate events.

Tom has a BS degree in Metallurgical Engineering from North Carolina State, an MBA from Wharton Graduate School, and an LLB. He served three combat tours in Vietnam and is in the Guinness Book of World Records as the first person ever to ski on all Seven Continents.

Tom can be reached at tom.hayes@necg.net.

TRAVIS BOYER

As a Project Manager at the New England Consulting Group, Travis actively participates in the company's Consumer Packaged Goods, Pharmaceutical, and Private Equity teams.

Immediately prior to joining New England, Travis was the Head Engineer of Materials Development for Eviation Jets Do Brazil, a company using innovative materials to develop experimental business jets. Travis also formerly worked designing military ballistic equipment with the Cubedot Company. Travis has a BS degree in Material Science and Materials Engineering from Rice University and a Masters of Science in Materials Engineering from the University of Pennsylvania. He holds a specialty in nanotechnology and a focus in entrepreneurship.